T0281316

Lecture Notes in Computer Science 13707

Founding Editors

Gerhard Goos
Karlsruhe Institute of Technology, Karlsruhe, Germany

Juris Hartmanis
Cornell University, Ithaca, NY, USA

Editorial Board Members

Elisa Bertino
Purdue University, West Lafayette, IN, USA

Wen Gao
Peking University, Beijing, China

Bernhard Steffen
TU Dortmund University, Dortmund, Germany

Moti Yung
Columbia University, New York, NY, USA

More information about this series at https://link.springer.com/bookseries/558

Thomas Erlebach · Michael Segal (Eds.)

Algorithmics of Wireless Networks

18th International Symposium on Algorithmics of Wireless Networks, ALGOSENSORS 2022
Potsdam, Germany, September 8–9, 2022
Proceedings

 Springer

Editors
Thomas Erlebach 🆔
Durham University
Durham, UK

Michael Segal 🆔
Ben-Gurion University of the Negev
Beer-Sheva, Israel

ISSN 0302-9743　　　　　　ISSN 1611-3349　(electronic)
Lecture Notes in Computer Science
ISBN 978-3-031-22049-4　　　ISBN 978-3-031-22050-0　(eBook)
https://doi.org/10.1007/978-3-031-22050-0

© The Editor(s) (if applicable) and The Author(s), under exclusive license
to Springer Nature Switzerland AG 2022
This work is subject to copyright. All rights are reserved by the Publisher, whether the whole or part of the material is concerned, specifically the rights of translation, reprinting, reuse of illustrations, recitation, broadcasting, reproduction on microfilms or in any other physical way, and transmission or information storage and retrieval, electronic adaptation, computer software, or by similar or dissimilar methodology now known or hereafter developed.
The use of general descriptive names, registered names, trademarks, service marks, etc. in this publication does not imply, even in the absence of a specific statement, that such names are exempt from the relevant protective laws and regulations and therefore free for general use.
The publisher, the authors, and the editors are safe to assume that the advice and information in this book are believed to be true and accurate at the date of publication. Neither the publisher nor the authors or the editors give a warranty, expressed or implied, with respect to the material contained herein or for any errors or omissions that may have been made. The publisher remains neutral with regard to jurisdictional claims in published maps and institutional affiliations.

This Springer imprint is published by the registered company Springer Nature Switzerland AG
The registered company address is: Gewerbestrasse 11, 6330 Cham, Switzerland

Preface

This volume contains the papers presented at ALGOSENSORS 2022: the 18th International Symposium on Algorithmics of Wireless Networks, held during September 8–9, 2022, at the Hasso Plattner Institute in Potsdam, Germany, as part of ALGO 2022.

ALGOSENSORS is an international symposium dedicated to algorithmic aspects of wireless networks. Founded in 2004, it originally focused on sensor networks, but ALGOSENSORS now covers algorithmic issues arising in wireless networks of all types of computational entities, static or mobile, including sensor networks, sensor-actuator networks, and systems of autonomous robots. The focus is on the design and analysis of algorithms, models of computation, and experimental analysis. The new title of the conference, the International Symposium on Algorithmics of Wireless Networks, reflects this broader scope.

In response to the Call for Papers, 21 submissions were received. Each submission was reviewed (using single-blind reviewing) by at least three Program Committee members and some trusted external reviewers, and evaluated on its quality, originality, and relevance to the symposium. The committee decided to accept 10 papers for presentation at ALGOSENSORS 2022 and inclusion in these proceedings. The program of ALGOSENSORS 2022 also included an invited talk by Roger Wattenhofer (ETH Zürich) entitled "Wireless Network Algorithmics: Looking Back & Moving Forward".

The Program Committee selected the following contribution for the Best Paper Award and the Best Student Paper Award, both kindly sponsored by Springer:

Davide Bilò, Gianlorenzo D'Angelo, Luciano Gualà, Stefano Leucci,
and Mirko Rossi: Blackout-Tolerant Temporal Spanners

We would like to thank the Steering Committee, chaired by Sotiris Nikoletseas, for giving us the opportunity to serve as Program Chairs of ALGOSENSORS 2022. Furthermore, we would like to thank all the authors who responded to the Call for Papers, the invited speaker for enriching the program of the event, and the Program Committee members and external reviewers for their fundamental contributions to the paper selection process, resulting in a strong program. We would also like to warmly thank the ALGO 2022 organizing committee, chaired by Tobias Friedrich, for enabling us to hold ALGOSENSORS as part of the ALGO symposium and taking care of all organizational matters. We would like to thank Springer for publishing the proceedings of ALGOSENSORS 2022 in the LNCS series and for their support and sponsorship.

Finally, we would like to acknowledge the use of the EasyChair system for handling the submission of papers, managing the review process, and preparing these proceedings.

October 2022   Thomas Erlebach
                                                                                                          Michael Segal

Organization

Steering Committee

Josep Diaz	Universitat Politècnica de Catalunya, Spain
Magnus M. Halldorsson	Reykjavik University, Iceland
Bhaskar Krishnamachari	University of Southern California, Los Angeles, USA
P.R. Kumar	Texas A&M University, USA
Sotiris Nikoletseas (Chair)	University of Patras and CTI, Greece
José Rolim	University of Geneva, Switzerland
Paul Spirakis	University of Liverpool, UK, and University of Patras, Greece
Adam Wolisz	TU Berlin, Germany

Program Committee

Tiziana Calamoneri	Sapienza University of Rome, Italy
Mihaela Cardei	Florida Atlantic University, USA
Federico Corò	Missouri University of Science and Technology, USA
Peter Davies	University of Surrey, UK
Michael Dinitz	Johns Hopkins University, USA
Thomas Erlebach (Co-chair)	Durham University, UK
Sándor Fekete	TU Braunschweig, Germany
Klaus-Tycho Foerster	TU Dortmund, Germany
Jie Gao	Rutgers University, USA
Olga Goussevskaia	Federal University of Minas Gerais, Brazil
Mohammad Taghi Hajiaghayi	University of Maryland, USA
Tomasz Jurdzinski	University of Wroclaw, Poland
Ralf Klasing	CNRS and University of Bordeaux, France
Dariusz Kowalski	Augusta University, USA
Evangelos Kranakis	Carleton University, Canada
Othon Michail	University of Liverpool, UK
William K. Moses Jr.	University of Houston, USA
Cristina M. Pinotti	Università degli Studi di Perugia, Italy
Rik Sarkar	University of Edinburgh, UK
Christian Schindelhauer	University of Freiburg, Germany
Michael Segal (Co-chair)	Ben-Gurion University of the Negev, Israel

Wanqing Tu   Durham University, UK
Yong Zhang   Shenzhen Institute of Advanced Technology,
                                        China

External Reviewers

Almalki, Nada   Keldenich, Phillip
Althoff, Stephanie   Olkowski, Jan
Connor, Matthew   Opatrny, Jaroslav
Di Stefano, Gabriele   Rossi, Mirko
Gasieniec, Leszek
Goudarzi, Samira   Schoeters, Jason
Jabbarzade, Peyman   Yang, Hao-Tsung

Contents

On Geometric Shape Construction via Growth Operations 1
Nada Almalki and Othon Michail

Optimal and Heuristic Algorithms for Data Collection by Using an Energy-
and Storage-Constrained Drone 18
*Francesco Betti Sorbelli, Alfredo Navarra, Lorenzo Palazzetti,
Cristina M. Pinotti, and Giuseppe Prencipe*

Blackout-Tolerant Temporal Spanners 31
*Davide Bilò, Gianlorenzo D'Angelo, Luciano Gualà, Stefano Leucci,
and Mirko Rossi*

Molecular Robots with Chirality on Grids 45
*Serafino Cicerone, Alessia Di Fonso, Gabriele Di Stefano,
and Alfredo Navarra*

Centralised Connectivity-Preserving Transformations by Rotation: 3
Musketeers for All Orthogonal Convex Shapes 60
Matthew Connor and Othon Michail

Triangle Evacuation of 2 Agents in the Wireless Model (Extended Abstract) ... 77
Konstantinos Georgiou and Woojin Jang

Resource Time-Sharing for IoT Applications with Deadlines 91
George Karakostas and Stavros G. Kolliopoulos

Fault-Tolerant Graph Realizations in the Congested Clique 108
Manish Kumar, Anisur Rahaman Molla, and Sumathi Sivasubramaniam

The Complexity of Growing a Graph 123
*George B. Mertzios, Othon Michail, George Skretas, Paul G. Spirakis,
and Michail Theofilatos*

Dispersing Facilities on Planar Segment and Circle Amidst Repulsion 138
Vishwanath R. Singireddy and Manjanna Basappa

Author Index 153

On Geometric Shape Construction
via Growth Operations

Nada Almalki$^{(\boxtimes)}$ and Othon Michail◉

Department of Computer Science, University of Liverpool, Liverpool, UK
{N.Almalki,Othon.Michail}@liverpool.ac.uk

Abstract. In this work, we investigate novel algorithmic *growth processes*. Our system runs on a 2-dimensional grid and operates in discrete time steps. The growth process begins with an initial shape of nodes $S_I = S_0$ and, in every time step $t \geq 1$, by applying (in parallel) one or more *growth operations* of a specific type to the current shape-instance S_{t-1}, generates the next instance S_t, always satisfying $|S_t| > |S_{t-1}|$. Our goal is to characterize the classes of shapes that can be constructed in $O(\log n)$ or polylog n time steps, n being the size of the final shape S_F, and determine whether a shape S_F can be constructed from an initial shape S_I using a finite sequence of *growth operations* of a given type, called a *constructor of S_F*.

In particular, we propose three *growth operations*, *full doubling*, *row and column doubling*, which we call *RC doubling*, and *doubling*, and explore the algorithmic and structural properties of their resulting processes under a geometric setting. For *full doubling*, in which, in every time step, every node generates a new node in a given direction, we completely characterize the structure of the class of shapes that can be constructed from a given initial shape. For *RC doubling*, in which complete columns or rows double, our main contribution is a linear-time centralized algorithm that for any pair of shapes S_I, S_F decides if S_F can be constructed from S_I and, if the answer is yes, returns an $O(\log n)$-time step constructor of S_F from S_I. For the most general *doubling* operation, where a subset of individual nodes can double, we show that some shapes cannot be constructed in sublinear time steps and give two universal constructors of any S_F from a singleton S_I, which are efficient (i.e., up to polylogarithmic time steps) for large classes of shapes. Both constructors can be computed by polynomial-time centralized algorithms for any shape S_F.

Keywords: Centralized algorithm · Geometric growth operations · Programmable matter · Constructor

1 Introduction

The realization that many natural processes are essentially algorithmic, has fueled a growing recent interest in formalizing their algorithmic principles and in developing new algorithmic approaches and technologies inspired by them. Examples of algorithmic frameworks inspired by biological and chemical systems are population protocols [5,6,24], ant colony optimization [9,14], DNA

© The Author(s), under exclusive license to Springer Nature Switzerland AG 2022
T. Erlebach and M. Segal (Eds.): ALGOSENSORS 2022, LNCS 13707, pp. 1–17, 2022.
https://doi.org/10.1007/978-3-031-22050-0_1

self-assembly [14,25,26,28], and the algorithmic theory of programmable matter [1,3,22].

Motivated by these advancements and by principles of biological development which are apparently algorithmic, we introduce a set of geometric *growth processes* and study their algorithmic and structural properties. These processes start from an initial shape of nodes S_I, possibly a singleton, and by applying a sequence of *growth operations* eventually develop into well-defined global geometric structures. The considered *growth operations* involve at most one new node being generated by any existing node in a given direction and the resulting reconfiguration of the shape as a consequence of a set of nodes being generated within it. This node-generation primitive is also inspired by the self-replicating capabilities of biological systems, such as cellular division, their higher-level processes such as embryogenesis [7], and by the potential of the future development of self-replicating robotic systems.

In a recent study, Mertzios *et al.* [20] investigated a network-growth process at an abstract graph-theoretic level, free from geometric constraints. Our goal here is to study similar *growth processes* under a geometric setting and show how these can be fine-tuned to construct interesting geometric shapes efficiently, i.e., in polylogarithmic time steps. Aiming to focus exclusively on the effect of *growth operations*, we do not allow any other form of shape reconfigurations apart from local growth. Preliminary such *growth processes*, mostly for rectangular shapes, were developed by Woods *et al.* [27]. Their approach was to first grow such shapes in polylogarithmic time steps and then to transform them into arbitrary geometric shapes and patterns through additional reconfiguration operations, the latter essentially capturing properties of molecular self-assembly systems. Like them, we study the problem of constructing a desired final shape S_F starting from an initial shape S_I via a sequence of shape-modification operations. However, in this work the considered operations are restricted to local *growth operations*. To the best of our knowledge, the structural characterization and the underlying algorithmic complexity of constructing geometric shapes by *growth operations*, have not been previously considered as problems of independent interest.

1.1   Our Approach and Contribution

In this work, our main objective is to study *growth operations* in a centralized geometric setting. Applying a sequence of such operations in a centralized way, yields a centralized geometric growth process. Our model can be viewed as an applied, geometric version of the abstract network-growth model of Mertzios *et al.* [20]. The considered model is discrete and operates on a 2D square grid. Connectivity preservation is an essential aspect of both biological and of the so-inspired robotic and programmable matters, because it allows the system to maintain its strength and coherence and enables sharing of resources between devices in the system [8,22]. In light of this, all the shapes discussed in this work are assumed to be connected and the considered *growth operations* cannot break the shape's connectivity.

For all types of considered operations, the study revolves around the following main questions: (i) *What is the class of shapes that can be constructed efficiently from a given initial shape via a sequence of growth operations?* (ii) *Is there a polynomial-time centralized algorithm that can decide if a given target shape S_F can be constructed from a given initial shape S_I and, whenever the answer is positive, return an efficient constructor of S_F from S_I?*

The *growth operations* considered in this paper are characterized by the following additional properties:

- In general, more than one *growth operation* can be applied at the same time step (parallel version). To simplify the exposition of some of our results and without losing generality, we shall sometimes restrict attention to a single operation per time step (sequential version).
- To avoid having to deal with colliding operations, we restrict attention to single-direction *growth operations*. That is, for each time step t, a direction $d \in \{$north, east, south, west$\}$ is fixed and any operation at t must be in direction d. For clarity of presentation of the results in this work, we shall focus mostly on the *east* and *north* directions of the considered operations. Due to the nature of these operations, generalizing to all four directions is immediate.

We study three *growth operations, full doubling, RC doubling,* and *doubling,* where full doubling is the most restricted and doubling the most general one. In *full doubling*, in every time step, every node generates a new node in a given direction, in *RC doubling,* complete columns or rows double, and in *doubling* up to individual nodes can double.

For *full doubling*, we completely characterize the structure of the class of shapes that are reachable from any given initial shape. For *RC doubling*, our main contribution is a linear-time centralized algorithm that for any pair of shapes S_I, S_F decides if S_F can be constructed from S_I and, if the answer is yes, returns an $O(\log n)$-time step constructor of S_F from S_I. For *doubling*, we show that some shapes cannot be constructed in sublinear time steps and give two universal constructors of any S_F from a singleton S_I, which are efficient (i.e., up to polylogarithmic time steps). for large classes of shapes. Both constructors can be computed by polynomial-time centralized algorithms for any shape S_F.[1]

In Sect. 1.2, we discuss the related literature. Section 2 presents all definitions that are used throughout the paper. Sections 3, 4, and 5 present our results for *full doubling, RC doubling,* and *doubling,* respectively.

---

[1] Note that there are two distinct notions of time used in this paper. One represents the time steps of a growth process, while the other represents the running time of a centralized algorithm deciding reachability between shapes and returning constructors for them. We shall always distinguish between the two by calling the former *time steps* and the latter *time*.

1.2 Related Work

Recent work has focused on studying the algorithmic principles of reconfiguration, with the potential of developing artificial systems that will be able to modify their physical properties, such as reconfigurable robotic ensembles and self-assembly systems. For example, the area of algorithmic self-assembly of DNA aims to understand how to train molecules to modify themselves while also controlling their own growth [14]. Several theoretical models of programmable matter have been developed, including DNA self-assembly and other passively dynamic models [14,21] as well as models enriched with active molecular components [27].

One example of a geometric programmable matter model, which is presented in [12], is known as the *Amoebot* and is inspired by amoeba behavior. In particular, programmable matter is modeled as a swarm of distributed autonomous self-organizing entities that operate on a triangular grid. Research on the Amoebot model has made progress on understanding its computational power and on developing algorithms for basic reconfiguration tasks such as coating [11] and shape formation [10,13]. Other authors have investigated cycle-shaped programmable matter modules that can rotate or slide a device over neighboring devices through an empty space [8,15,16,22], with the goal of capturing the global reconfiguration capabilities of local mechanisms that are feasible to be implemented with existing technology. The authors in [22] proved that the decision problem of transformation between two shapes is in **P**. In addition, another recent research work [3] investigated a linear-strength mechanism through which a node can push a line of one or more nodes by one position in a single time step. Other linear-strength mechanisms are the one by Woods *et al.* [27], where a node can rotate a whole line of connected nodes, simulating arm rotation, or the one by Aloupis *et al.* [4] on crystalline robots, equipped with powerful lifting capabilities.

A recent study in the field of highly dynamic networks, which is presented in [20], is partially inspired by the abstract-network approach followed in [23]. The authors completely disregard geometry and develop a network-level abstraction of programmable matter systems. Their model starts with a single node and grows the target network G to its full size by applying local operations of node replication. Local edges are only activated upon a node's generation and can be deleted at any time but contribute negatively to the edge-complexity of the construction. The authors develop centralized algorithms that generate basic graphs such as paths, stars, trees, and planar graphs and prove strong hardness results. We similarly focus on centralized structural and algorithmic characterizations as a first step that will promote our understanding of such novel models and will facilitate the future development of more applied constructions, like fully distributed ones.

2 Model and Preliminaries

The programmable matter systems considered in this paper operate on a 2-dimensional square grid. Each grid position (cross point) is identified by its x and y coordinates, $x \geq 0$ representing the row and $y \geq 0$ the column. Systems of this type consist of n nodes that form a connected shape S. Each node u of shape S is represented by a circle occupying a position on the grid. Time consists of discrete time steps and in every time step $t \geq 1$, zero or more *growth operations* can occur depending on the type of operation considered. At any given time step t, each node $u \in S$ is determined by its coordinates (u_x, u_y) and no two nodes can occupy the same position at the same time step. Two distinct nodes $u = (u_x, u_y)$ and $v = (v_x, v_y)$ are *neighbors* if $u_x \in \{v_x - 1, v_x + 1\}$ and $u_y = v_y$ or $u_y \in \{v_y - 1, v_y + 1\}$ and $u_x = v_x$, that is, if they are at orthogonal distance one from each other. In that case, we are assuming that, unless explicitly removed, a connection (or edge) uv exists between u and v.

Definition 1 (Row and Column of a Shape). *A row (respectively column) of a shape S is the set of all nodes of S with the same fixed y-coordinate (respectively x-coordinate).*

By $S_{.,i}$ we denote the row of S consisting of all nodes whose y-coordinate is i, i.e., $S_{.,i} = \{(x, i) \mid (x, i) \in S\}$. Similarly, column j of S, denoted as $S_{j,.}$, is the set of all nodes of S whose x-coordinate is j, i.e., $S_{j,.} = \{(j, y) \mid (j, y) \in S\}$. When the shape S is clear from context, we will refer to $S_{.,i}$ as R_i and to $S_{j,.}$ as C_j.

Definition 2 (Translation Operation). *Given a set of integer points Q, the north (south) k-translation of Q is defined as $\uparrow_k Q = \{(x, y + k) \mid (x, y) \in Q\}$ ($\downarrow_k Q$, similarly defined). The east (west) l-translation of Q is defined as $\xrightarrow{l} Q = \{(x + l, y) \mid (x, y) \in Q\}$ ($\xleftarrow{l} Q$, similarly defined).*

Definition 3 (Rigid Connection). *A connection uv between two nodes u and v of a shape S is rigid if and only if a 1-translation of one node in any direction d implies a 1-translation of the other in the same direction, unless uv is first removed.*

Throughout, all connections are assumed to be rigid.

The basic concept of *growth operation* is that a node $u \in S_t$ generates a new node $u' \in S_{t+1}$. In particular, we are exploring three specific *growth operations* a *full doubling*, *row and column doubling* and *doubling*. In most cases, every node $u \in S_t$ is colored black while its generations are colored gray at the next time step $t + 1$ after any type of *growth operations*. Furthermore, any type of *growth operation* o is equipped with a *linear-strength* mechanism, which is the ability of a generated node u' to translate its connected component on a growing direction in a single time step.

Throughout this paper, l, k will represent the total number of horizontal and vertical *growth operations* performed (respectively). By horizontal, the direction d is either *east* or *west*, while the vertical d is either *north* or *south*.

Definition 4 (Growth Operation). *A growth operation o is an operation that when applied on a shape instance S_t, for all time steps $t \geq 1$, yields a new shape instance $S_{t+1} = o(S_t)$, such that $|S_t| > |S_{t-1}|$.*

In this work, we consider three specific types of *growth operations* moving from the most special to the most general: *full doubling, RC doubling* and *doubling* operation. For the sake of clarity, we will provide a high-level overview of these three operations, with the more technical versions appearing in their respective Sects. 3, 4 and 5. First, a *full doubling* operation is a growth operation in which every node $u \in S_t$ generates a new node $u' \in S_{t+1}$, that is, $|S_{t+1}| = 2|S_t|$. Then, *row and column doubling* denoted by *RC doubling*, is a growth operation where in each time step t, a subset of columns (rows) is selected and these are fully doubled. Finally, the most general version of these operations is a *doubling* operation, in which, in each time step t, any subset of the nodes can double in a given direction. The differences between these three operations are highlighted in Fig. 1.

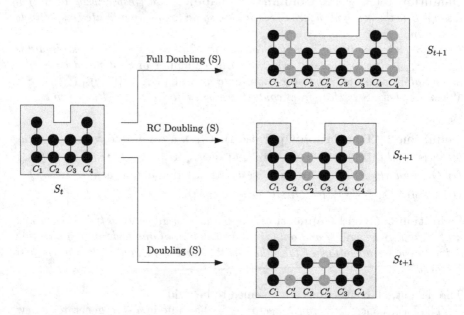

Fig. 1. Illustration of the results S_{t+1} when applying different growth operations on the same shape S_t where the direction of growing is east.

Definition 5 (Reachability Relation). *Given a growth operation of a given type, we define a reachability relation $\rightsquigarrow$ on pairs of shapes S, S' as follows. $S \rightsquigarrow S'$ iff there is a finite sequence $\sigma = o_1, o_2, \ldots, o_{t_{last}}$ of operations of a given type for which $S = S_0, o_1, S_1, o_2, S_2 \ldots, S_{(t_{last}-1)}, o_{t_{last}}, S_{t_{last}} = S'$, where $S_i = o(S_{i-1})$ for all $1 \leq i \leq t_{last}$. Whenever we want to emphasize a particular such sequence σ, we write $S \overset{\sigma}{\rightsquigarrow} S'$ and say that σ constructs shape S' from S.*

Definition 6 (Constructor). *A constructor $\sigma = (o_1, o_2, \ldots, o_{t_{last}})$ is a finite sequence of doubling operations of a given type, $1 \leq i \leq t_{last}$.*

Remark 1. Note that in Definition 6 the directions of different o_i's do not need to be the same.

2.1 Problem Definitions

We now formally define the problems to be considered in this paper.

Class Characterization. Identify the family of shapes S_F that can be obtained from a given initial connected shape S_I via a sequence of *growth operations* of a given type.

SHAPECONSTRUCTION. Given a pair of shapes (S_I, S_F) decide if $S_I \rightsquigarrow S_F$. If yes, compute a sequence σ that constructs S_F from S_I. In the special case of this problem in which S_I is by assumption a singleton, we shall assume that the input is just S_F.

3 Full Doubling

In this section, after providing a formal definition of the full doubling operation, we investigate the class characterization problem under this operation. Note that when the initial shape consists of a single node, i.e., $|S_I| = 1$, the characterization is straightforward. Section 3.1 discusses the more general case where $|S_I| \geq 1$.

Definition 7 (Full Doubling). *After applying a* full doubling operation *on S a new shape S' is obtained, depending only on the direction d of the operation:*

1. *If the direction d of a full doubling operation is an east, then for every column $S_{j,\cdot}$ of S a new column is generated to the east of $S_{j,\cdot}$. The effect of applying this to all columns is that every column $S_{j,\cdot}$ of S is translated to the east by $j - 1$, such that $S'_{2j-1,\cdot} = \overset{j-1}{\longrightarrow} S_{j,\cdot}$, and generates the new column $S'_{2j,\cdot} = \overset{j}{\longrightarrow} S_{j,\cdot}$. Therefore, the new shape S' of this doubling operation is $S' = \bigcup_j (S'_{2j-1,\cdot} \cup S'_{2j,\cdot})$.*

2. *If the direction d of a full doubling operation is a north, then for every row $S_{\cdot,i}$ of S a new row is generated to the north of $S_{\cdot,i}$. The effect of applying this to all rows is that every row $S_{\cdot,i}$ of S is translated to the north by $i - 1$, such that $S'_{\cdot,2i-1} = \uparrow_{i-1} S_{\cdot,i}$, and generates the new row $S'_{\cdot,2i} = \uparrow_i S_{\cdot,i}$. Therefore, the new shape S' of this doubling operation is $S' = \bigcup_i (S'_{\cdot,2i-1} \cup S'_{\cdot,2i})$.*

In other words, if a full doubling operation is performed on S in the east direction, then a set of columns equal to the original is generated. Every original column is translated by the number of original columns to its west and its own copy is generated to the east of its final position. Similarly for rows.

3.1   An Arbitrary Connected Initial Shape $|S_I| \geq 1$

In this section we characterize shapes that can be obtained by a sequence of full doubling operations from an arbitrary connected initial shape S_I, where $|S_I| \geq 1$.

Definition 8 $(w(C_j, u))$. *Let $w(C_j, u)$ denote the number of columns to the left (west) of a node u in a column j, that is, $w(C_j, u) = u_x - C_l$, where C_l is the leftmost column.*

Definition 9 $(s(R_i, u))$. *Let $s(R_i, u)$ denote the number of rows below (south) of a node u in a row i, that is, $s(R_i, u) = u_y - R_b$, where R_b is the bottom-most row.*

Definition 10 (Reconfiguration Function). *Given two integers $l, k > 0$, we define a reconfiguration function $F_{l,k}$ that maps a shape to another shape as follows:*

1. *First, the coordinates of $|S|$ points of $F_{l,k}(S)$ are determined as a function of the coordinates of the points of S. For each $u \in S$ the coordinates of $u' \in F_{l,k}(S)$ are given by $(u_x + (2^l - 1)w(C_j, u), u_y + (2^k - 1)s(R_i, u))$.*
2. *Generate the Cartesian product around u' such that, $Rec(u', 2^l, 2^k) = \{u'_x + 1, \ldots, u'_x + (2^l - 1)\} \times \{u'_y + 1, \ldots, u'_y + (2^k - 1)\}$ originating at u'. Adding all points of these rectangles to $F_{l,k}(S)$ completes the definition of $F_{l,k}(S)$.*

The output of the reconfiguration function after these two phases is a shape S, such that $F_{l,k}(S) = \bigcup_{u \in S} Rec(u', 2^l, 2^k)$, as presented in Fig. 2 (note that u' is a function of u in the union).

Lemma 1 (Additivity of Reconfiguration Function). *For all shapes S and all $l, k, l', k' \geq 0$ it holds that $F_{l',k'}(F_{l,k}(S)) = F_{l'+l,k'+k}(S)$.*

Theorem 1. *Given any initial shape S_I and any sequence of l east and k north full doubling operations, the obtained shape is $S_F = F_{l,k}(S_I)$.*

4   RC Doubling

After a formal definition of the *RC doubling* operation, in this section, we study both the class characterization and the SHAPECONSTRUCTION problems. In particular, we develop a linear-time centralized algorithm to decide the feasibility of constructing S_F from S_I and to return a constructor of S_F from S_I if one exists, both within $O(\log n)$-time steps.

Definition 11 (RC Doubling). *A row and column doubling is a growth operation where a direction $d \in \{east, west\}$ ($d \in \{north, south\}$) is fixed and all nodes of a subset of the columns (rows, respectively) of shape S generates a new node in d direction.*

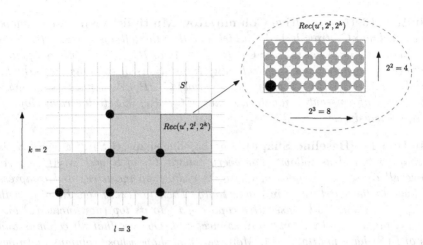

Fig. 2. An example of the output shape S' after applying the *reconfiguration function* $F_{l,k}(S)$.

We define an RC doubling operation *for columns in the east direction and the other cases can be similarly defined. The operation is applied to a shape S and will yield a new shape S'. Let J be the set of indices (ordered from west to east) of all columns of S and D its subset of indices of the columns to be doubled by the operation. For any $j \in J$, let $w(D, j) = |\{j' \in D \mid j' < j\}|$, i.e. $w(D, j)$ denotes the number of doubled columns to the west of column j. Then the new shape S' is defined as:*

$$S' = (\bigcup_{j \in J} \overset{w(C_j)}{\to} C_j) \cup (\bigcup_{j \in D} \overset{w(C_j)+1}{\to} C_j)$$

That is, every doubled column C_j, for $j \in D$, generates a copy of itself to the east. The result is that every column C_j, for $j \in J$, is translated east by $w(C_j)$ and additionally the final position of the copy of C_j, for $j \in D$, is an east $(w(C_j)+1)$ translation of C_j.

Definition 12 (Single RC Doubling Operation). *Let $d \in J$ be the index of the single doubled column. Define $S_{\leq C_d}$ $(S_{\geq C_d})$ to be the set of columns to the west (east, resp.) of column C_d, inclusive. That is, $S_{\leq C_d} = \bigcup_{j \in J, j \leq d} C_j$ $(S_{\geq C_d} = \bigcup_{j \in J, j \geq d} C_j$, resp.). Then,*

$$S' = S_{\leq C_d} \cup (\overset{1}{\to} S_{\geq C_d}).$$

Proposition 1 (Serializability of Parallel Doubling). *A shape S_F can be generated from a shape S_I through a sequence of RC (parallel) doubling operations iff it can be generated through a sequence of single row/column doubling operations.*

Definition 13 (Consecutive Column/Row Multiplicities). *Given a shape S and a column C_j (row R_i) of S which is either the leftmost column (bottommost row) (i.e., $j = 1$) or $C_{j-1} \neq C_j$ ((i.e., $i = 1$) or $R_{i-1} \neq R_i$) (where equality is defined up to horizontal (vertical) only translations of columns (rows)), the multiplicity $M_S(C_j)$ $(M_S(R_i))$ of column (row) C_j (R_i), is defined as the maximal number of consecutive identical copies of C_j (R_i) in S to the right (top) of C_j (R_i) (inclusive).*

Definition 14 (Baseline Shape). *The baseline shape $B(S)$ of a shape S, is the shape obtained as follows. For every column C_j of S with $M_S(C_j) > 1$, remove all consecutive copies of C_j to its right (non-inclusive) and compress the shape to the left to restore connectivity. Then for every row R_i of S with $M_S(R_i) > 1$, remove all consecutive copies of R_i to its top (non-inclusive) and compress the shape down to restore connectivity. Observe that all columns and rows of $B(S)$ have multiplicity 1. Moreover, any shape whose columns and rows all have multiplicity 1 is called a baseline shape.*

4.1 $S_I \rightsquigarrow S_F$ Constructor

Theorem 2. *A shape S_I can generate a shape S_F through a sequence of RC doubling operations iff $B(S_I) = B(S_F) = B$ and for every column C and row R of B it holds that $M_{S_F}(C) \geq M_{S_I}(C)$ and $M_{S_F}(R) \geq M_{S_I}(R)$.*

Proof. To prove that the condition is sufficient, we can w.l.o.g. restrict attention to single RC doubling operations (as these are special cases of RC doubling operations). Then, for every column C of B for which $M_{S_F}(C) > M_{S_I}(C)$ holds, we double the west-most copy of column C in S_I, $M_{S_F}(C) - M_{S_I}(C)$ times to the east. Similarly, for rows. It is not hard to see that any sequence of these operations applied to S_I, yields S_F.

For the necessity of the condition, we need to show that if S_I can generate S_F through a sequence of RC doubling operations, then $B(S_I) = B(S_F) = B$ and the multiplicities are as described in the statement. We first observe that, by Proposition 1, S_I can also generate S_F through a sequence of single RC doubling operations. So, it is sufficient to show that violation of any of the conditions would not allow for a valid sequence of single RC doubling operations.

Let us first assume that $B(S_I) = B(S_F) = B$ holds, but $M_{S_F}(C) \geq M_{S_I}(C)$ does not, that is, $M_{S_F}(C) < M_{S_I}(C)$ for some column C of B. Then, there is no way of obtaining S_F from S_I as this would require deleting $M_{S_I}(C) - M_{S_F}(C)$ copies of C. Similarly, if $M_{S_F}(R) \geq M_{S_I}(R)$ is violated.

Finally, assume that $B(S_I) \neq B(S_F)$ and that $S_I \rightsquigarrow S_F$ still holds. By definition of baseline shapes, $B(S_I) \rightsquigarrow S_I$ and $B(S_F) \rightsquigarrow S_F$ hold, thus, we have $B(S_I) \rightsquigarrow S_I \rightsquigarrow S_F$ and $B(S_F) \rightsquigarrow S_F$. That is, there is a sequence of single column/row operations starting from $B(S_I)$ and another starting from $B(S_F)$ that eventually make the two shapes equal (starting originally from two unequal baseline shapes). So, there must be a pair σ and σ' of such sequences minimizing the maximum length $\max_{\sigma,\sigma'}(|\sigma|, |\sigma'|)$ until the two shapes first become equal.

Call S_t and $S'_{t'}$ the dynamically updated shapes by σ_t and $\sigma'_{t'}$, respectively. In what follows we omit the time step subscripts. Let us assume w.l.o.g. that it is the last step t_{min} of σ that first satisfies $S = S'$ and that this step is a doubling of a column C. Thus, after step t_{min}, both S and S' contain an equal number of at least two consecutive copies of C. But the only way a shape can first obtain two consecutive copies of a column is by doubling one of its columns, thus, there must be a previous single column doubling operation in σ' that doubled column C (note that, at that point, C could have been a subset of the final version of the column). Deleting that operation from σ' and the last operation at t_{min} from σ, yields a new pair of sequences that satisfy $S = S'$ at some $t \leq t_{min} - 1$, thus, contradicting minimality of the (σ, σ') pair. We must, therefore, conclude that $S_I \rightsquigarrow S_F$ cannot hold in this case. $\qquad\square$

Lemma 2. *For any S_I, S_F satisfying the conditions of Theorem 2, there is a constructor from S_I to S_F using at most $2 \log n$ time steps, where n is the total number of nodes in S_F.*

Proof. Since there is a constructor from S_I to S_F, then, by Theorem 2, $B(S_I) = B(S_F) = B$ and for every column C and row R of B it holds that $M_{S_F}(C) \geq M_{S_I}(C)$ and $M_{S_F}(R) \geq M_{S_I}(R)$. By Definition 5 (in Sect. 2) $S_I \rightsquigarrow S_F$, S_F can be obtained by applying on every column C and row R of S_I as many RC *doubling operations* as required to make its multiplicity equal to S_F. W.l.o.g. we only show this process applied to columns.

Let C be a column of B. Starting from $M_{S_I}(C)$ copies of C in S_I we want to construct the $M_{S_F}(C)$ copies of C in S_F. Note that neither $M_{S_F}(C)$ nor $M_{S_F}(C) - M_{S_I}(C)$ are necessarily powers of 2. Then, let 2^k be the greatest power of 2, such that $M_{S_I}(C)2^k < M_{S_F}(C)$, i.e., $M_{S_I}(C)2^k < M_{S_F}(C) < M_{S_I}(C)2^{k+1}$. Then, from the second inequality, it holds that $M_{S_F}(C) - M_{S_I}(C)2^k < M_{S_I}(C)2^{k+1} - M_{S_I}(C)2^k$ and this leads to $M_{S_F}(C) - M_{S_I}(C)2^k < M_{S_I}(C)2^k$, which means that if we construct $M_{S_I}(C)2^k$ columns then columns remaining to be constructed to reach $M_{S_F}(C)$ will be less than the constructed ones.

So, we construct $M_{S_I}(C)2^k$ columns (including the original column) by always doubling, within $k \leq \log(M_{S_F}(C))$ steps. Once we have those, we double in one additional time step $M_{S_F}(C) - M_{S_I}(C)2^k$ of those to get a total of $M_{S_F}(C)$ columns within $k + 1 \leq \log(M_{S_F}(C))$ steps. If we set $M_{S_F}(C)$ to be the maximum multiplicity of S_F, then for every column $C' \neq C$, its multiplicity $M_{S_F}(C') \leq M_{S_F}(C)$ can be constructed in parallel to the multiplicity of C, thus, within these $\log(M_{S_F}(C))$ steps. And similarly for rows. As $M_{S_F}(C) \leq n$ and $M_{S_F}(R) \leq n$, where n is the number of nodes of S_F, it holds that all column and row multiplicities can be constructed within at most $2 \log n$ time steps. $\quad\square$

We now present an informal description of a linear-time algorithm for SHAPECONSTRUCTION. The algorithm decides whether a shape S_F can be constructed from a shape S_I and, if the answer is positive, it returns an $O(\log n)$-time step constructor.
Given a pair of shapes (S_I, S_F), do the following:

Step 1 Determine the *baseline shapes* $B(S_I)$ and $B(S_F)$ of S_I and S_F, respectively. Then compare $B(S_I)$ with $B(S_F)$ and, if they are equal, proceed to Step 2, otherwise return *No* and terminate.

Step 2 Since we have $B = B(S_I) = B(S_F)$, if for all columns C (rows R) of B it holds that $M_{S_I}(C) \leq M_{S_F}(C)$ and $M_{S_I}(R) \leq M_{S_F}(R)$ then proceed to Step 3, else return *No* and terminate.

Step 3 Output the constructor defined by Lemma 2.

Finally, together Proposition 1, Theorem 2, and Lemma 2 imply that:

Theorem 3. *The above algorithm is a linear-time algorithm for* SHAPECONSTRUCTION *under RC doubling operations. In particular, given any pair of shapes* (S_I, S_F), *when* $(S_I \rightsquigarrow S_F)$ *the algorithm returns a constructor* σ *of* S_F *from* S_I *of* $O(\log n)$-*time steps.*

5   Doubling

This section studies *doubling* operations in their most general form, where a subset of individual nodes can be involved in a growth operation. We start with a formal definition of two sub-types of general doubling operations and then investigate both the class characterization and SHAPECONSTRUCTION problems. By focusing on the special case of a singleton S_I, we give a universal linear-time step (i.e., slow) constructor and, on the negative side, prove that some shapes cannot be constructed in sublinear time steps. Our main results are then two universal constructors that are efficient (i.e., polylogarithmic time steps) for large classes of shapes. Both constructors can be computed by polynomial-time centralized algorithms for any input S_F.

5.1   Rigidity in Doubling Operations

Given a shape S and two neighboring nodes $u, v \in S$, let $S(u)$ and $S(v)$ be the maximal connected sub-shapes of S containing u but not v and v but not u, respectively. When u is doubling in the direction of v, call that direction d, rigidity of connections (see Definition 3) implies that any $w \in S(u) \setminus S(v)$ must remain in its position while any $z \in S(v) \setminus S(u)$ must translate by 1 in direction d. For any node in $S(u) \cap S(v)$ these two actions would contradict each other. Such nodes belong to a $u, v, \dots, u$ cycle, and any such cycle must break or grow in at least one of its connections, in addition to the connection uv which will by assumption grow. In this paper, we focus on the case where all these cycles break (or grow) at the (C_j, C_{j+1}) cut. Depending on how we choose to treat such cycles, we shall define two sub-types of general *doubling operations*: *rigidity-preserving doubling* and *rigidity-breaking doubling*. Intuitively, in the former for all affected edges e in the (C_j, C_{j+1}) cut a node is generated over e, while in the latter any subset of those edges can simply break.

We start with a special case of the rigidity-breaking doubling operation in which, in every time step, a single node doubles. This special case is particularly convenient for the class characterization problem, as it can provide a (slower but simple) way to simulate both types of doubling operations. It also serves as an easier starting point towards the definition of the more general operations.

Definition 15 (Single-Node Doubling). *A single-node doubling operation is a growth operation in which at any given time step t, a direction $d \in \{north, east, south, west\}$ is fixed and a single node u of shape S doubles in direction d.*

Consider w.l.o.g. an east doubling operation applied on $u = (u_x, u_y) \in C_j$ of S. If u has no east neighbor in S, then, u generates a new node $u' = (u_x+1, u_y) \in C_{j+1}$ and the obtained shape is $S \cup \{u'\}$. Otherwise, u has a neighbor $v \in C_{j+1}$ of S which will need to translate by 1 in the east direction together with some sub-shape of $S(v)$. We identify the maximal connected sub-shape $S'(u) \subseteq S(u)$ that contains no node from columns C_m, for all $m \geq j + 1$, and the maximal connected sub-shape $S'(v) \subseteq S(v) \setminus S'(u)$. That is, $S'(u)$ contains all nodes on u's side that must stay put, while, from the remaining nodes, $S'(v)$ contains all nodes that must translate by 1. Any bicolor edge (one whose one endpoint is in $S'(v)$ and the other endpoint in $S'(u)$; we call these the bicolor edges associated with uv) must be an edge of the (C_j, C_{j+1}) cut. We remove all bicolor edges in order to perform the operation.

Definition 16 (Rigidity-Preserving Doubling Operation). *A rigidity-preserving doubling operation is a generalization of a single-node doubling operation. In every time step a direction d is fixed and, for any node u that doubles towards a neighbor v in direction d and for all bicolor edges e associated with uv, a node is generated over e (see Fig. 3).*

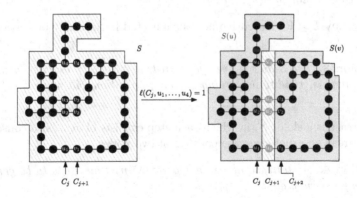

Fig. 3. An illustration of Definition 16, in which all nodes of (C_j) must double and the sub-shape $S(v)$ must be shifted to the east by one.

Definition 17 (Rigidity-Breaking Doubling Operation). *A rigidity-breaking doubling operation is a generalization of a single-node doubling operation.*

In every time step a direction d is fixed and, for any node u that doubles towards a neighbor v in direction d and for all bicolor edges e associated with uv, either a node is generated over e or e is removed (see Fig. 4).

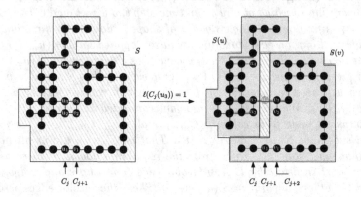

Fig. 4. An illustration of Definition 17, where there is one node $u_3 \in C_j$ doubles to the east and shifts the connected component in the same direction, while other edges in C_j are removed.

5.2 Universal Constructors of S_F

Proposition 2. *For any shapes S_I and S_F, where $S_I \subseteq S_F$, there is a linear-time step constructor of S_F from S_I.*

We call any $L \geq 1$ consecutive nodes connected horizontally or vertically an L-line.

Proposition 3. *If a 3-line is ever generated, it must be preserved in the final shape S_F, that is, rigidity-preserving doubling operation will never break the 3-line.*

A staircase is a shape S, in which each step consists of at least 3 consecutive nodes, whereas an exact-staircase consists of two nodes.

Proposition 4. *A staircase of size n requires $\Omega(n)$ time steps to be generated by rigidity-preserving doubling operations.*

Proposition 5. *A rigidity-preserving or rigidity-breaking doubling operation cannot build an exact staircase shape S within a sublinear time.*

Next, by putting together the universal linear-time steps constructor of Proposition 2 for doubling and the logarithmic-time steps constructor of Theorem 2 for RC doubling, we get the following general and faster constructor for doubling.

Theorem 4. *Given any connected target shape S_F, there is an $[O(|B(S_F)|) + O(\log|S_F|)]$-time step constructor of S_F from $S_I = \{u_0\}$ through doubling operations. Moreover, there is a polynomial-time algorithm computing such a constructor on every input S_F.*

The constructor of Theorem 4 is fast as a function of $n = |S_F|$, when $|S_F| - |B(S_F)|$ is large. For example, for all S_F for which $|B(S_F)| = O(\log|S_F|)$ holds, it gives a logarithmic-time steps constructor of S_F. It is also a fast constructor for all shapes S_F that have a relatively small (geometrically) *similar* shape S_I under *uniform scaling*. Note that shape similarity can be decided in linear time [2,19]. In such cases, S_I can again be constructed in linear time steps from a singleton, followed by a fast construction of S_F from S_I via full doubling in all directions in a round-robin way.

Finally, we give an alternative constructor, based on a partitioning of an orthogonal shape into the minimum number of rectangles. Note that there are efficient algorithms for the problem, e.g., an $O(n^{3/2}\log n)$-time algorithm [17,18]. These algorithms, given an orthogonal polygon S, partition S into the minimum number h of rectangles $S_1, S_2, \ldots, S_h$, "partition" meaning a set of pairwise non-overlapping rectangles which are sub-polygons of S and whose union is S.

Theorem 5. *Given any connected target shape S_F, there is an $O(h\log|S_F|)$-time step constructor of S_F from $S_I = \{u_0\}$ through doubling operations, where h is the minimum number of rectangles in which S_F can be partitioned. Moreover, there is a polynomial-time algorithm computing such a constructor on every input S_F.*

Acknowledgements. The authors would like to thank Viktor Zamaraev for useful conversations during the various stages of developing this work.

References

1. Akitaya, H.A., et al.: Universal reconfiguration of facet-connected modular robots by pivots: the O(1) musketeers. Algorithmica **83**(5), 1316–1351 (2021)
2. Akl, S.G., Toussaint, G.T.: An improved algorithm to check for polygon similarity. Inf. Process. Lett. **7**(3), 127–128 (1978)
3. Almethen, A., Michail, O., Potapov, I.: Pushing lines helps: efficient universal centralised transformations for programmable matter. Theoret. Comput. Sci. **830**, 43–59 (2020)
4. Aloupis, G., Collette, S., Demaine, E.D., Langerman, S., Sacristán, V., Wuhrer, S.: Reconfiguration of cube-style modular robots using $O(\log n)$ parallel moves. In: Hong, S.-H., Nagamochi, H., Fukunaga, T. (eds.) ISAAC 2008. LNCS, vol. 5369, pp. 342–353. Springer, Heidelberg (2008). https://doi.org/10.1007/978-3-540-92182-0_32
5. Angluin, D., Aspnes, J., Diamadi, Z., Fischer, M.J., Peralta, R.: Computation in networks of passively mobile finite-state sensors. Distrib. Comput. **18**(4), 235–253 (2006)

6. Angluin, D., Aspnes, J., Eisenstat, D., Ruppert, E.: The computational power of population protocols. Distrib. Comput. **20**(4), 279–304 (2007)
7. Chan, M.M., et al.: Molecular recording of mammalian embryogenesis. Nature **570**(7759), 77–82 (2019)
8. Connor, M., Michail, O., Potapov, I.: Centralised connectivity-preserving transformations for programmable matter: a minimal seed approach. Theoret. Comput. Sci. (2022)
9. Cornejo, A., Dornhaus, A., Lynch, N., Nagpal, R.: Task allocation in ant colonies. In: Kuhn, F. (ed.) DISC 2014. LNCS, vol. 8784, pp. 46–60. Springer, Heidelberg (2014). https://doi.org/10.1007/978-3-662-45174-8_4
10. Derakhshandeh, Z., Gmyr, R., Richa, A.W., Scheideler, C., Strothmann, T.: Universal shape formation for programmable matter. In: Proceedings of the 28th ACM Symposium on Parallelism in Algorithms and Architectures (SPAA), pp. 289–299 (2016)
11. Derakhshandeh, Z., Gmyr, R., Richa, W., Scheideler, C., Strothmann, T.: Universal coating for programmable matter. Theoret. Comput. Sci. **671**, 56–68 (2017)
12. Derakhshandeh, Z., Richa, A., Dolev, S., Scheideler, C., Gmyr, R., Strothmann, T.: Brief announcement: amoebot-a new model for programmable matter. In: Proceedings of the 26th ACM Symposium on Parallelism in Algorithms and Architectures (SPAA), pp. 220–222 (2014)
13. Di Luna, G.A., Flocchini, P., Santoro, N., Viglietta, G., Yamauchi, Y.: Shape formation by programmable particles. Distrib. Comput. **33**(1), 69–101 (2020)
14. Doty, D.: Theory of algorithmic self-assembly. Commun. ACM **55**(12), 78–88 (2012)
15. Dumitrescu, A., Pach, J.: Pushing squares around. In: Proceedings of the 20th Annual Symposium on Computational Geometry, pp. 116–123 (2004)
16. Dumitrescu, A., Suzuki, I., Yamashita, M.: Formations for fast locomotion of metamorphic robotic systems. Int. J. Robot. Res. **23**(6), 583–593 (2004)
17. Imai, H., Asano, T.: Efficient algorithms for geometric graph search problems. SIAM J. Comput. **15**(2), 478–494 (1986)
18. Keil, J.M.: Polygon decomposition. Handb. Comput. Geom. **2**, 491–518 (2000)
19. Manacher, G.K.: An application of pattern matching to a problem in geometrical complexity. Inf. Process. Lett. **5**(1), 6–7 (1976)
20. Mertzios, G.B., Michail, O., Skretas, G., Spirakis, P.G., Theofilatos, M.: The complexity of growing a graph. arXiv preprint arXiv:2107.14126 (2021)
21. Michail, O.: Terminating distributed construction of shapes and patterns in a fair solution of automata. Distrib. Comput. **31**(5), 343–365 (2018)
22. Michail, O., Skretas, G., Spirakis, P.G.: On the transformation capability of feasible mechanisms for programmable matter. J. Comput. Syst. Sci. **102**, 18–39 (2019)
23. Michail, O., Skretas, G., Spirakis, P.G.: Distributed computation and reconfiguration in actively dynamic networks. In: Proceedings of the 39th Symposium on Principles of Distributed Computing (PODC), pp. 448–457 (2020)
24. Michail, O., Spirakis, P.G.: Simple and efficient local codes for distributed stable network construction. Distrib. Comput. **29**(3), 207–237 (2016)
25. Rothemund, P.W.: Folding DNA to create nanoscale shapes and patterns. Nature **440**(7082), 297–302 (2006)
26. Rothemund, P.W., Winfree, E.: The program-size complexity of self-assembled squares. In: Proceedings of the 32nd Annual ACM Symposium on Theory of Computing (STOC), pp. 459–468 (2000)

27. Woods, D., Chen, H.L., Goodfriend, S., Dabby, N., Winfree, E., Yin, P.: Active self-assembly of algorithmic shapes and patterns in polylogarithmic time. In: Proceedings of the 4th Conference on Innovations in Theoretical Computer Science (ITCS), pp. 353–354 (2013)
28. Woods, D., et al.: Diverse and robust molecular algorithms using reprogrammable DNA self-assembly. Nature **567**(7748), 366–372 (2019)

Optimal and Heuristic Algorithms for Data Collection by Using an Energy- and Storage-Constrained Drone

Francesco Betti Sorbelli[1], Alfredo Navarra[1], Lorenzo Palazzetti[2(✉)],
Cristina M. Pinotti[1], and Giuseppe Prencipe[3]

[1] University of Perugia, Perugia, Italy
{francesco.bettisorbelli,alfredo.navarra,cristina.pinotti}@unipg.it
[2] University of Florence, Florence, Italy
lorenzo.palazzetti@unifi.it
[3] University of Pisa, Pisa, Italy
giuseppe.prencipe@unipi.it

Abstract. We consider Internet of Things (IoT) sensors deployed inside an area to be monitored. Not all the sensors are connected via single-hop to the depot that requires the data. Inversely, a multi-hop implementation can bring the network connectivity at risk because the sensors closer to the depot consume more energy when relaying the aggregated data. Therefore, a viable solution is to use a drone that collects the data from the sensors flying close to them. A drone moves faster than a ground robot, and it is not affected by eventual obstacles on the terrain, but it is constrained in both the energy (when flying and hovering), and the storage (when collecting data). Moreover, a drone cannot transmit the collected data to the cloud because the Internet connectivity can be absent. Therefore, the drone needs to select a subset of sensors whose data is the most relevant to be acquired. Such a relevance is modeled by assigning a reward to that data based on its freshness and suitability. We present an optimization problem called Single-drone Data-collection Maximization Problem (SDMP) whose objective is to plan a drone's mission aimed at maximizing the overall reward from the collected data, and such that the mission's energy cost and the total collected data are within the energy and storage limits. Since SDMP is NP-hard, we give an optimal Integer Linear Programming formulation, and also devise an approximation and two time-efficient heuristic algorithms. Finally, we test our algorithms on randomly generated synthetic data.

Keywords: Drones · Sensor networks · Approximation algorithms

This work was supported in part by the "GNCS – INdAM", by "HALY.ID" project funded by the European Union's Horizon 2020 under grant agreement ICT-AGRI-FOOD no. 862665, no. 862671, by MIPAAF, and by RB_DMI_2019.

© The Author(s), under exclusive license to Springer Nature Switzerland AG 2022
T. Erlebach and M. Segal (Eds.): ALGOSENSORS 2022, LNCS 13707, pp. 18–30, 2022.
https://doi.org/10.1007/978-3-031-22050-0_2

1   Introduction

With the recent advent of the Unmanned Aerial Vehicles (UAVs), such as drones, we have seen a rapid growth of civilian applications [1] like search and rescue [5], delivery of goods [11], or smart agriculture [3] just to mention a few. In this work, we consider a smart agriculture application in which a drone is in charge of collecting the data from a set of ground Internet of Things (IoT) sensors [16], randomly deployed on an area for sensing particular phenomena like the current temperature or air humidity, or for taking pictures or videos. Since these sensors have a limited radio communication range [4] and available storage [2], the sensed data need to be periodically offloaded into an external device for further analysis [19]. Since that the deployment area can be very large, sensors cannot directly transfer their perceived data to the main base station [10] (depot). Also, even relying on a multi-hop paradigm, there is the problem that the sensors closer to the depot consume more energy in the process of relaying data [9].

In our proposed architecture, a drone has to perform a mission (route) to/from the depot, with the objective to selectively collect the data from the sensors via single-hop close to the sensors. However, the drone itself is limited in terms of energy battery (when flying and hovering) and available storage (when collecting data). In principle, due to these limitations, the drone cannot collect the data from all the deployed sensors, but it has to plan a suitable route and parsimoniously use both its available energy and storage. The ground sensors generate data, and depending on their relevance, the farmer can require to give more priority to some sensors than others. Namely, in order to model the relevance and the consequent prioritization of some data to be collected, we assign a specific reward to each sensor. Therefore, the goal of the drone is to collect the most important data, i.e., maximizing the total reward, while ensuring that the mission energy cost does not exceed the battery budget, and the total collected data does not exceed the storage limit. An example is depicted in Fig. 1.

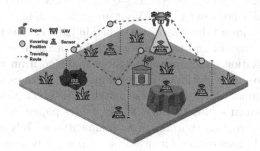

Fig. 1. The sketched representation of our application. The surface is not flat, and therefore the sensors have different heights with respect to the depot.

The contributions of this paper are summarized as follows.

- We define a novel optimization problem, called *Single-drone Data-collection Maximization Problem* (SDMP), and prove it to be *NP*-hard;

- We devise an Integer Linear Programming formulation for optimally solving SDMP, as well as an approximation plus two heuristic algorithms for obtaining sub-optimal solutions;
- We evaluate the performance of our algorithms on randomly generated synthetic data.

The rest of the paper is organized as follows. Section 2 reviews the related work. Section 3 formally defines the SDMP. Section 4 presents algorithms for solving SDMP. Section 5 evaluates the effectiveness of our algorithms, and Sect. 6 offers conclusions and future research directions.

2   Related Work

Many papers have been proposed in the realm of data collection in sensor networks with the help of drones.

In [7,8], the authors consider the problem of scheduling the flight of a drone in charge to maximize the utility due to the data collected in a sensor network composed by homogeneous sensors deployed on a flat surface. The drone has the ability to simultaneously collect data from multiple sensors, and its hovering time depends on the size of data to be collected. The authors discretize the possible hovering points for the drone in order to bound the amount of them. Differently from the above works, in our paper we deal with heterogeneous sensors at different heights, we consider the energy required also for flying, and we take into account the drone's storage constraint. Moreover, we do not allow for a simultaneous data collection from multiple sensors since the available bandwidth could saturated. In [21], the authors consider the problem of determining the minimum number of UAVs to be deployed to collect all the data from sensors on a flat area without exceeding a given budget time. Two algorithms are proposed to solve the problem. Once again, only the hovering time is a constraint for drones, while in our paper we consider both the energy and the storage.

The problem of scheduling the UAV's tour which minimizes the maximum energy consumption for all the sensors is studied in [20]. The authors jointly consider the sensors' wake-up and the UAV's path by formulating a mixed-integer non-convex optimization program, and a suboptimal algorithm which iteratively applies a successive convex optimization technique. The authors in [15] propose a clustering algorithm and meta-heuristics to address a similar problem where the sensors are deployed in a hilly terrain. All the above papers deal with homogeneous sensors which rely on continuous communications. Only computationally expensive exact solutions or meta-heuristic solutions are proposed, while in this paper we propose an approximation and two time-efficient heuristic solutions.

The problem of maximizing the *freshness* of the data collected by a UAV has been studied in [14]. In particular, two problems of Age-of-Information (AoI) data collection are formulated to minimize both the sensors' maximal and average AoI. In [13] the authors propose a framework for controlling the flight speed of the UAV to improve the *fairness* of data collection. They formalize the fairness as a metric which depends on the energy level of the sensor nodes, and on the amount of data to be sent to the UAV. Specifically, since only cluster heads have to transfer data collected via multi-hops from the other nodes to the UAV, their fairness is the least. Therefore, the authors develop a method which controls and adjusts the UAV's speed according to the density intra-cluster of sensors, and the distance from the UAV and each sensor. We tackle both the *freshness* and the *fairness* of the data by encoding them with a reward function. However, they do not take into account the energy of the drone, as we do.

3 Problem Definition

In this section, we introduce the system model, formally define our new drone-based problem for data collection in an IoT sensor network, and devise the optimal solution for it.

3.1 System Model

Let F be the *field*, whose center $O = (0,0,0)$ is the *depot*, to be monitored by a set $V = \{v_1, \ldots, v_n\}$ of n heterogeneous *ground sensors*. Each sensor $v_i \in V$ is randomly deployed in F, and its position is (x_i, y_i, z_i) with respect to O. The sensors collect data like the temperature, pressure, or even pictures or videos to be saved on their local storage of size W_i, assumed to be different for each sensor. In fact, tiny sensors that record text data would have a small storage, but camera sensors that have to store large videos, would need a much larger storage. Since W_i is limited, sensors have to periodically transfer the recorded data to an external device. Let $0 < w_i \le W_i$ be the *size* of the data that needs to be transferred by each v_i. As said before, the data is modeled by a *relevance*, and relevant data should be prioritized when ground sensors have to start the data transferring. This is modeled by associating a *reward* $r_i > 0$ to each sensor v_i. So, the more is the reward, the more relevant is to off-load the data to the external device.

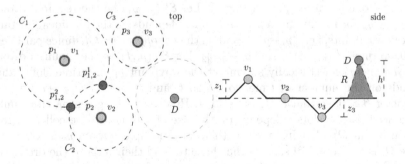

Fig. 2. Top and side representations of the field F.

The external device which collects the data from the sensors is a *drone* denoted as D (see Fig. 2). The *flight mission* of the drone starts and finishes at O. The drone flies at a fixed altitude h above the ground, and it has a *communication range* with a radius R. So, it can collect data from a sensor v_i if $\|D - v_i\|_2 \leq R$, i.e., if their relative *Euclidean distance* is within the communication range. In this work we neglect communication issues like shadowing, fading, or multipath propagation. Moreover, we assume that the drone and the sensors are always line of sight, and hence no obstacles are present. We also assume that the drone cannot collide with any sensor.

The drone is allowed to fly only at specific locations over F, called *waypoints*, represented by a set P of possible positions. Firstly, P contains all projected sensors' positions at height h, i.e., $\forall v_i = (x_i, y_i, z_i) \in V$ we have that $p_i = (x_i, y_i, h) \in P$. Moreover, P also contains other points as follows. For each sensor v_i, we define an admissible region in which the drone can actually communicate with it. Such a region is delimited by a circumference C_i of radius $\leq \sqrt{R^2 - (h - z_i)^2}$. Therefore, in order to bound the number of waypoints for the drone [6], for each pair of sensors v_i and v_j, we add in P all the possible intersection points $p_{i,j}^1$ and $p_{i,j}^2$ between C_i and C_j (see Fig. 2). Also the depot $O = p_0 \in P$. So, given the n sensors, the number of waypoints $m = |P| \leq n + n(n-1) + 1$.

The drone is constrained by the limited energy by its battery that consumes when it *moves* between locations, or when it *hovers* at a position. The sensors can start the data transferring procedure only when the drone hovers at waypoints. Hence, the sensors cannot transfer the data if the drone is currently moving even if their relative distance is within the communication range. We also assume that the drone cannot concurrently collect data from multiple sensors, but separately one at a time. So, if two sensors v_i and v_j are in range with the drone, only one can transfer the data (say v_i), while the other one has to wait (say v_j) until the first sensor finishes the procedure. Also, we do not allow for a partial transferring, so when a sensor starts to transfer data, the drone necessarily must hover at the waypoint until the data is completely collected.

Given a waypoint $p_i \in P$, let Q_i^C be the set of ground sensors in range with the drone, i.e., *covered* by the drone. So, each sensor $v_k \in Q_i^C$ can communicate with the drone because $\|p_i - v_k\|_2 \leq R$. Let $\mathcal{E}^F(p_i, p_j)$ be the required drone's *flying energy* for moving from p_i to p_j, which depends on the Euclidean distance between waypoints, i.e., $\|p_i - p_j\|_2$, and on the *energy per unit distance* parameter $\alpha > 0$, so that $\mathcal{E}^F(p_i, p_j) = \alpha \cdot \|p_i - p_j\|_2$. Let $\mathcal{E}^H(p_i, t)$ be the required drone's *hovering energy* for statically staying at the waypoint p_i for t time slots, which depends on the number of time slots, i.e., t, and on the *energy per time slot* parameter $\beta > 0$, so that $\mathcal{E}^H(p_i, t) = \beta \cdot t$. However, for a given p_i, the number of the needed time slots t depends on the size of the data to be collected from the sensors in Q_i^C. For instance, if there are multiple sensors $v_k \in Q_i \subseteq Q_i^C$ where Q_i is the subset of sensors that have to send their data to the drone, and $K_i = \sum_{v_k \in Q_i} w_k$ is the cumulative data to transfer from the sensors in Q_i at the waypoint p_i, the required time depends on the total quantity of data to be transferred, i.e., K_i, and on the *data-transfer rate* parameter $\gamma > 0$, so that we can finally redefine the hovering energy function as $\mathcal{E}^H(p_i, K_i) = \frac{\beta}{\gamma} \cdot K_i$.

Let M be the drone's *mission* formed by a sequence of distinct waypoints to be visited to/from the depot $O = p_0$, i.e., M is a sequence $p_0, \ldots, p_i, \ldots, p_0$. The drone can potentially reach all the sensors $Q^C = \bigcup_i Q_i^C, \forall p_i \in M$. However, the drone actually obtains the data from a subset $Q \subseteq Q^C$ of sensors due to its storage constraint. Finally, $\mathcal{C}_M = \mathcal{C}_M^F + \mathcal{C}_M^H$ is the *total mission cost* (in terms of energy) of M where $\mathcal{C}_M^F$ is the *flying cost*, and $\mathcal{C}_M^H$ is the *hovering cost*. So, given the sequence of consecutive waypoints $(p_i, p_j) \in M$, the flying and the hovering energy costs are $\mathcal{C}_M^F = \sum_{(p_i,p_j) \in M} \mathcal{E}^F(p_i, p_j)$ and $\mathcal{C}_M^H = \sum_{p_i \in M} \mathcal{E}^H(p_i, K_i)$, respectively. The other aspect to consider is the overall transferred data from the sensors to the drone. Namely, let $\mathcal{U}_M$ be the *total used storage* by the drone when doing the mission M, i.e., $\mathcal{U}_M = \sum_{p_i \in M} K_i$. To conclude, let $\mathcal{R}_Q$ be the *total obtained reward* by the drone after having transferred the whole data from the sensors belonging to Q. So, we have $\mathcal{R}_Q = \sum_{v_i \in Q} r_i$.

Concerning the drone's constraints, let E be the *available energy budget* on its battery for performing M. Moreover, let S be the *available storage budget* on its mass storage for collecting the sensors' data. So, it is required that $\mathcal{C}_M = \mathcal{C}_M^F + \mathcal{C}_M^H \leq E$ and $\mathcal{U}_M \leq S$.

In this paper, due to the fact that the sensors' deployment is not dense, we assume that any mission formed by *only a single waypoint* is both energy- and storage-feasible for the drone. Specifically, all the sensors in the neighborhood of such a waypoint can safely offload their data to the drone.

3.2   The *Single-Drone Data-Collection Maximization Problem*

In this paper, we present the *Single-drone Data-collection Maximization Problem* (SDMP) whose goal is *to find a route for the drone to/from the depot, and a selection of sensors, such that the reward is maximized, and both the energy and storage budgets are not exceeded*. Given the set of sensors V, and the drone's energy and storage budgets E and S, respectively, the objective is to determine the optimal mission M^* and the optimal selection of sensors Q^* such that

$$(M^*, Q^*) = \underset{M,Q}{\arg\max} \, \mathcal{R}_Q \; : \; \mathcal{C}_M \leq E, \, \mathcal{U}_M \leq S. \qquad (1)$$

Now, we are in the position to show that:

Theorem 1. *The* SDMP *is NP-hard.*

Proof. Omitted due to page limit constraints. The proof comes from the fact that the Orienteering Problem is a special case for this problem.

3.3   Optimal ILP Formulation

The SDMP can be optimally solved using an Integer Linear Programming (ILP) formulation. We enumerate the sensors as $\mathcal{V} = \{1, \ldots, n\}$, and the waypoints as $\mathcal{P} = \{0, \ldots, m\}$ (0 is the depot). Let $x_{ij} \in \{0, 1\}$ be a decision variable that is 1 if the sensor $i \in \mathcal{V}$ transfers its data to the drone at the waypoint $j \in \mathcal{P}$;

otherwise it is 0. Let $y_{lj} \in \{0,1\}$ be a decision variable that is 1 if the drone travels from the waypoint $l \in \mathcal{P}$ to the waypoint $j \in \mathcal{P}$; otherwise it is 0. Finally, let $1 \leq u_i \leq m$ by a dummy variable that indicates the temporal order of the visited waypoints, i.e., $u_l < u_j$ if waypoint l is visited before waypoint j [17]. So, the ILP formulation is:

$$\max \sum_{i=1}^{n} \sum_{j=0}^{m} r_i x_{ij} \qquad (2)$$

subject to:

$$\sum_{j=0}^{m} x_{ij} \leq 1, \qquad\qquad \forall i \in \mathcal{V} \qquad (3)$$

$$\sum_{j=1}^{m} y_{0j} = \sum_{l=1}^{m} y_{l0} = 1, \qquad\qquad \forall l, j \in \mathcal{M} \backslash \{0\} \qquad (4)$$

$$y_{jj} = 0, \qquad\qquad \forall j \in \mathcal{M} \qquad (5)$$

$$\sum_{l=1}^{m} y_{lk} = \sum_{j=1}^{m} y_{kj} = \max_{i \in \mathcal{V}} x_{ik}, \qquad\qquad \forall k \in \mathcal{M} \backslash \{0\} \qquad (6)$$

$$u_l - u_j + 1 \leq (m-1)(1 - y_{lj}), \qquad\qquad \forall l, j \in \mathcal{M} \backslash \{0\} \qquad (7)$$

$$1 \leq u_l \leq m, \qquad\qquad \forall l \in \mathcal{M} \backslash \{0\} \qquad (8)$$

$$\sum_{i=1}^{n} \sum_{j=0}^{m} w_i x_{ij} \leq S \qquad (9)$$

$$\sum_{j=0}^{m} \left(\sum_{i=1}^{n} h_i x_{ij} + \sum_{l=0}^{m} f_{lj} y_{lj} \right) \leq E \qquad (10)$$

Equation (2) maximizes the overall reward. About the constraints, Eq. (3) states that each sensor can transfer its data no more than one time; Eq. (4) forces that the drone's route begins and ends at the depot; Eq. (5) forbids self loops; Eq. (6) guarantees that the generated path is a simple cycle which contains the selected sensors; Eq. (7) ensures that no more than a single loop is allowed [17]; Eq. (8) indicates the temporal order of the visited waypoints, i.e., $u_l < u_j$ if l is visited before j [17]; Eq. (9) guarantees the storage constraint; Eq. (10) guarantees the energy constraint, where $h_i = \mathcal{E}^H(p_i, w_i) \geq 0$ is the drone's hovering cost for transferring the data from sensor i, and $f_{lj} = \mathcal{E}^F(p_l, p_j) \geq 0$ is the drone's flying cost for moving from waypoints l to j. We denote this formulation as OPT. Since OPT is only suitable for small-sized inputs, in the following we propose faster sub-optimal algorithms suitable for any input.

4   Proposed Algorithms

In this section, we propose an approximation algorithm, called *Reward-Storage-first Energy-then Optimization* (RSEO), and two greedy heuristic algorithms called *Max ratio Reward-Energy* (MRE), and *Max ratio Reward-Storage* (MRS), respectively, which are faster than OPT.

4.1   The RSEO Algorithm

We devise an approximation algorithm that sub-optimally solves SDMP, called *Reward-Storage-first Energy-then Optimization* (RSEO). It is split in two phases. In the first phase we select a subset of sensors such that the collected reward is maximized while ensuring that the storage requirement is met. Once the selection of sensors is done, we choose the minimum number of waypoints capable of covering all the selected sensors. On these waypoints, we compute the minimum energy cost traveling route to/from the depot. Notice that the resulting route might be energy-unfeasible. If it is so, in the second phase we reduce the main route into a smaller one by removing the most non-convenient waypoint, i.e., the one that reduces the most the energy, and reduces the least the lost reward. This strategy is repeatedly done until we reach an energy-feasible route. The pseudo-code of RSEO is given in Algorithm 1.

Algorithm 1: The RSEO Algorithm

---

1 $V' \leftarrow knapsack(V, S)$;
2 $P' \leftarrow min\text{-}set\text{-}cover(V', P)$;
3 $M \leftarrow traveling\text{-}salesman(P')$;
4 **while** $\mathcal{C}_M > E$ **do**
5 $\quad\lfloor\ p \leftarrow \arg\min_{p_i \in M} \mathcal{R}_{p_i}, M \leftarrow M \backslash p$;
6 **return** M

The algorithm RSEO works as follows. During the first phase, we initially determine a subset of sensors $V' \subseteq V$ such that the obtained reward is maximized, and the storage constraint S is satisfied, by invoking the *knapsack* procedure [18] (Line 1). Then, recalling that a sensor can be reached from multiple waypoints, we minimize the number of waypoints to visit in order to cover the entire set V' by invoking the *min-set-cover* procedure [18], determining so a subset of $P' \subseteq P$ of waypoints with cardinality $|P'| \leq |V'|$ (Line 2). Finally, since the drone has to perform a mission M to/from the depot visiting the waypoints P', we try to minimize the energy required by performing the *traveling-salesman* procedure [18] (Line 3). If the mission M is energy-feasible, then M is returned, otherwise we have to reduce M by removing a vertex (along with two edges) during the second phase. From all the waypoints that form M, we remove the one that minimizes the loss of reward associated to the that waypoint (Line 5). When we remove such a waypoint, we need to add an edge that ensures the existence of a closed path to/from the depot. This is repeatedly done until M is energy-feasible. Eventually, the solution M is returned.

Theorem 2. RSEO *solves* SDMP *with an approximation ratio of* $\frac{\psi}{\mu\phi}$ *where* $\mu\phi$ *is the number of waypoints returned by a ϕ-approximation algorithm for the min-set-cover whose optimal solution has μ elements, which cover the sensors selected by a ψ-approximation algorithm for the knapsack.*

Some considerations on the time complexity. We rely on the greedy strategy for the *fractional knapsack* which requires $\mathcal{O}(n \log n)$ time, and also guarantees a $\frac{1}{2}$-approximation [18]. Recall that, $|P'| \leq |V'| \leq n$. To implement *min-set-cover* we rely on a greedy strategy which takes $\mathcal{O}(m|V'|)$ (because m

is the cardinality of the subsets of sensors given by the waypoints) and guarantees a $(\log |V'|)$-approximation [18]. As regard to the *traveling-salesman*, we exploit the $\frac{3}{2}$-approximation algorithm [18] (although it does not affect our ratio) which takes $\mathcal{O}(|P'|^3)$. Finally, since M comprises of $\mathcal{O}(|P'|)$ edges, and considering that at each iteration we remove one vertex, the time required by the loop (Line 4) is $\mathcal{O}(|P'| \log |P'|)$. Thus, the overall time complexity of RSEO is $\mathcal{O}(n \log n + m|V'| + |P'|^3 + |P'| \log |P'|) = \mathcal{O}(|P'|^3)$, and our approximation bound is bounded from below by $\Omega(\frac{1}{\mu \log |V'|})$.

4.2 The MRE Algorithm

We devise an algorithm that sub-optimally solves SDMP, called *Max ratio Reward-Energy* (MRE). MRE greedily adds, to the current solution, the waypoint whose ratio between the overall obtainable reward from collecting the data from all the sensors covered by such a waypoint, and the additional energy cost with respect to the current drone's mission, is the largest. For decreasing the complexity, in MRE we only consider the waypoints perpendicularly on the top of the sensors, i.e., $p_0, p_1, \ldots, p_n$. When computing this ratio for any new waypoint, we have to consider also the energy for going back to the depot, since the drone cannot remain without energy. Obviously, the ratios do not consider the sensors' reward from previous collected data. Moreover, a waypoint can be selected only if the current drone's residual storage is enough. The pseudo-code of MRE is given in Algorithm 2.

Initially, the solution M is empty, and an auxiliary set of waypoints $\hat{P}$ perpendicular to the sensors is extracted from P (Algorithm 2, Line 1). Then, the main cycle starts (Line 2) evaluating all the possible waypoints. The most important procedure that MRE uses is *best-waypoint-ratio-reward-to-energy* (briefly, *best-waypoint*) (Line 3) which returns the waypoint p that has the largest ratio among the total obtainable reward collecting all the data from the sensors reachable from the waypoint, and the additional energy cost if adding the waypoint itself. This greedy selection is justified by the fact that we aim at maximizing the reward while trying to keep low the energy consumption. When determining the ratio we only consider data not already collected by the drone, otherwise we would sum the same reward multiple times. Then, we evaluate if p can be added to the current solution M without violating both the energy and storage constraints by evaluating *is-augmentable* (Line 4). In any case, p will not be considered anymore and removed from $\hat{P}$ (Line 6). Finally, the solution M is returned (Line 7).

Since the number of waypoints is $n+1$, the main loop is repeated $\mathcal{O}(n)$ times (Line 2). Since the *best-waypoint* procedure considers at most $\mathcal{O}(n)$ waypoints at each iteration, the overall time complexity of the MRE algorithm is $\mathcal{O}(n^2)$.

4.3 The MRS Algorithm

We propose an algorithm that sub-optimally solves SDMP, called *Max ratio Reward-Storage* (MRS). MRS, similar to MRE, relies on the largest ratio over-

---

Algorithm 2: The MRE Algorithm

1 $M \leftarrow \varnothing, \hat{P} \leftarrow \{p_0, p_1, \ldots, p_n\}$;

2 **while** $\hat{P} \neq \varnothing$ **do**

3 $\quad$ $p \leftarrow$ *best-waypoint-ratio-reward-to-energy*$(M, \hat{P})$;

4 $\quad$ **if** *is-augmentable*(M, p) **then**

5 $\quad\quad$ $M \leftarrow M \cup p$

6 $\quad$ $\hat{P} \leftarrow \hat{P} \backslash p$;

7 **return** M

---

all reward to storage (instead of overall reward to energy). The Line 3 in Algorithm 2 is replaced by $p \leftarrow$ *best-waypoint-ratio-reward-to-storage*$(M, \hat{P})$. Once the selection is done, MRS tries to add p to the solution by evaluating if the energy and storage constraints are satisfied or not. In either cases, p will not be considered anymore. Eventually, the solution is returned.

Since MRS works as MRE, its time complexity is $\mathcal{O}(n^2)$.

5 Performance Evaluation

In this section, we evaluate the performance, in terms of obtained reward, of the presented algorithms for solving SDMP, i.e., OPT, RSEO, MRE, and MRS.

5.1 Settings

The field F is a square of side 5 km. We uniformly generate $n = \{10, \ldots, 200\}$ sensors whose height is $-5\,\mathrm{m} \leq z_i \leq 5\,\mathrm{m}$. Each sensor has $100\,\mathrm{MB} \leq w_i \leq 1\,\mathrm{GB}$ data to transfer, and an associated reward $1 \leq r_i \leq 10$ which models the data relevance. Both w_i and r_i are generated according to the Uniform distribution. The drone flies at an altitude $h = \{20, 40\}\,\mathrm{m}$ and has a communication range of $R = 50\,\mathrm{m}$. Its storage is $S = \{16, 32\}\,\mathrm{GB}$ and its battery capacity is $E = \{5, 10\}\,\mathrm{MJ}$. We fix an average energy consumption for flying $\alpha = 200\,\mathrm{J/m}$ and for hovering $\beta = 700\,\mathrm{J/s}$ [12]. The data transfer rate is $\gamma = 9\,\mathrm{MB/s}$ (Wi-Fi 4 standard).

5.2 Results

In Fig. 3, we report the reward (y-axis) of our algorithms in an *ideal scenario* assuming no communication issues, while varying the number of sensors n (x-axis). We run OPT only for small instances: with $n = 25$ it returns a solution in 2 s, while often with $n = 30$ is still pending after 1 h.

For all the plots reported in Fig. 3, we fixed $\theta = 0.0$ for both w_i and r_i. Note that, when $\theta = 0.0$, the numbers are uniformly distributed inside their interval.

In the first row of Fig. 3, we fixed $h = 20\,\mathrm{m}$ and varied one single parameter for each plot. The leftmost plot assumes $h = 20\,\mathrm{m}$, $E = 5\,\mathrm{MJ}$, and $S = 16\,\mathrm{GB}$.

In this configuration, we can see that the best performing algorithms are MRE and RSEO followed by MRS. We obtain quite poor performance for RSEO because the instances under consideration were run with low energy budget with respect to the size of the field. In fact, the lower is the energy budget, the more is the probability that RSEO prunes the solution. However, in the rest of the scenarios RSEO performs really well, reaching at least the 93% of the optimal solution when $n \leq 25$ and outperforming the other algorithms in the other cases. This is justified by the fact that RSEO optimizes the selection of the sensors considering both the energy and storage constraints, while the other two heuristics consider one constraint (either energy or storage) at a time. In all the scenarios, the worst performing algorithm is MRS probably because the drone's selection ignores the energy, which is indeed the most stringent constraint when $E = 5\,\text{MJ}$. In the second plot, we doubled the size of the storage with respect to the first plot ($S = 32\,\text{GB}$): the performance of RSEO, MRE and MRS does not change. Probably, the energy budget does not allow to benefit of the largest storage budget. In the third plot, the battery capacity is doubled with respect to the first plot: in this case, instead, all the algorithms improve their performance and RSEO almost reaches the optimum. In the fourth plot, we doubled the size of both the energy and the storage with respect to the first plot ($E = 10\,\text{MJ}, S = 32\,\text{GB}$). In this case, the three algorithms collect almost the same reward obtained in the third plot ($E = 10\,\text{MJ}, S = 16\,\text{GB}$). We can observe that the energy and the storage budgets are probably oversized when the number of sensors is limited (≤ 25). Even this experiment seems to confirm that the storage constraint is less stringent than the energy constraint.

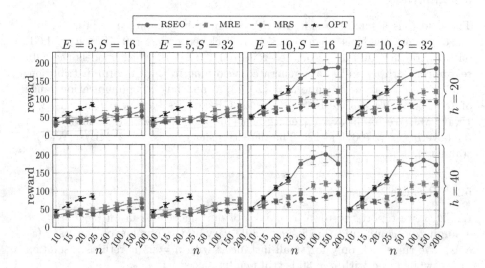

Fig. 3. Comparison between our proposed algorithms for solving SDMP.

In the second row of Fig. 3, we fixed $h = 40$ m and varied all other parameters, one at a time, as previously done. By increasing the height to $h = 40$ m, the distance between the drone and the sensors increases, and therefore the number of waypoints due to the intersections of the communication circumferences decreases accordingly. However, the performance of the algorithms remains almost the same, with slight differences with the previous analyzed row. In particular, we can observe that RSEO slightly improves its performance when both the energy budget and the number of sensors are low. This occurs since there are less intersections between communication circumferences, therefore the probability that a waypoint needs to be pruned after the selection is reduced. On the other hand, the RSEO performance slightly degrades when both the budget and the number of sensors increase, i.e., $E = 10$ MJ and $n = 200$. The reason behind this deterioration is again the reduction of the intersections between communication circumferences. In fact, we need to travel more distance to collect the same quantity of reward, concerning the reduction of the sensors covered by each waypoint.

6   Conclusion

In this paper, we investigated the problem of using a drone for collecting data from ground sensors deployed on a field to be monitored. As an example, in a smart agriculture scenario a drone is in charge of retrieving data from many sensors in order to detect the presence of bugs on orchards. The drone is constrained by both the available energy battery and the storage. The data that sensors have to be offload to the drone is characterized by a size and by a reward. The introduced problem is the SDMP, whose goal is to plan a suitable route for the drone such that the collected reward is maximized, and the energy and storage constraints are both satisfied. We showed that SDMP is *NP*-hard, and presented an optimal ILP formulation. Finally, we devised an approximation algorithm along with two time-efficient heuristics to solve the problem. As a future work, we plan to build a real test-bed with a single drone which aims to collect data from real sensors that store text and image information. Furthermore, we will also consider the multi-drone scenario, developing competitive approximation algorithms for it.

References

1. Abualigah, L., Diabat, A., Sumari, P., Gandomi, A.H.: Applications, deployments, and integration of internet of drones (IoD): a review. IEEE Sens. J. **21**(22), 25532–25546 (2021)
2. Aras, E., Ammar, M., Yang, F., Joosen, W., Hughes, D.: MicroVault: reliable storage unit for IoT devices. In: 2020 16th International Conference on Distributed Computing in Sensor Systems (DCOSS), pp. 132–140. IEEE (2020)
3. Betti Sorbelli, F., Corò, F., Das, S.K., Palazzetti, L., Pinotti, C.M.: Drone-based optimal and heuristic orienteering algorithms towards bug detection in orchards. In: 18th DCOSS. IEEE (2022)

4. Caillouet, C., Giroire, F., Razafindralambo, T.: Efficient data collection and tracking with flying drones. Ad Hoc Netw. **89**, 35–46 (2019)
5. Calamoneri, T., Corò, F., Mancini, S.: A realistic model to support rescue operations after an earthquake via UAVs. IEEE Access **10**, 6109–6125 (2022)
6. Chen, M., Liang, W., Das, S.K.: Data collection utility maximization in wireless sensor networks via efficient determination of UAV hovering locations. In: PerCom, pp. 1–10. IEEE (2021)
7. Chen, M., Liang, W., Li, J.: Energy-efficient data collection maximization for UAV-assisted wireless sensor networks. In: Wireless Communications and Networking Conference (WCNC), pp. 1–7. IEEE (2021)
8. Chen, M., Liang, W., Li, Y.: Data collection maximization for UAV-enabled wireless sensor networks. In: 29th International Conference on Computer Communications and Networks (ICCCN), pp. 1–9. IEEE (2020)
9. D'Angelo, G., Diodati, D., Navarra, A., Pinotti, C.M.: The minimum k-storage problem: complexity, approximation, and experimental analysis. IEEE Trans. Mob. Comput. **15**(7), 1797–1811 (2015)
10. He, X., Jin, R., Dai, H.: Multi-hop task offloading with on-the-fly computation for multi-UAV remote edge computing. IEEE Trans. Commun. **70**, 1332–1344 (2021)
11. Khanda, A., Corò, F., Betti Sorbelli, F., Pinotti, C.M., Das, S.K.: Efficient route selection for drone-based delivery under time-varying dynamics. In: 18th MASS, pp. 437–445. IEEE (2021)
12. Khochare, A., Simmhan, Y., Betti Sorbelli, F., Das, S.K.: Heuristic algorithms for co-scheduling of edge analytics and routes for UAV fleet missions. In: INFOCOM (2021)
13. Li, X., Tan, J., et al.: A novel UAV-enabled data collection scheme for intelligent transportation system through UAV speed control. IEEE Trans. Intell. Transp. Syst. **22**(4), 2100–2110 (2020)
14. Liu, J., Tong, P., Wang, X., Bai, B., Dai, H.: UAV-aided data collection for information freshness in wireless sensor networks. IEEE Trans. Wirel. Commun. **20**(4), 2368–2382 (2020)
15. Nazib, R.A., Moh, S.: Energy-efficient and fast data collection in UAV-aided wireless sensor networks for hilly terrains. IEEE Access **9**, 23168–23190 (2021)
16. Petkovic, S., Petkovic, D., Petkovic, A.: IoT devices vs. drones for data collection in agriculture. DAAAM Int. Sci. Book **16**, 63–80 (2017)
17. Vansteenwegen, P., et al.: The orienteering problem: a survey. Eur. J. Oper. Res. **209**(1), 1–10 (2011)
18. Vazirani, V.V.: Approximation Algorithms. Springer (2001). https://www.springer.com/computer/theoretical+computer+science/book/978-3-540-65367-7
19. Wang, H., Ke, H., Sun, W.: Unmanned-aerial-vehicle-assisted computation offloading for mobile edge computing based on deep reinforcement learning. IEEE Access **8**, 180784–180798 (2020)
20. Zhan, C., Zeng, Y., Zhang, R.: Energy-efficient data collection in UAV enabled wireless sensor network. IEEE Wirel. Commun. Lett. **7**(3), 328–331 (2017)
21. Zhang, J., et al.: Minimizing the number of deployed uavs for delay-bounded data collection of IoT devices. In: INFOCOM, pp. 1–10. IEEE (2021)

Blackout-Tolerant Temporal Spanners

Davide Bilò[1] , Gianlorenzo D'Angelo[2] , Luciano Gualà[3] ,
Stefano Leucci[1] , and Mirko Rossi[2]([✉])

[1] Department of Information Engineering, Computer Science and Mathematics,
University of L'Aquila, L'Aquila, Italy
{davide.bilo,stefano.leucci}@univaq.it
[2] Gran Sasso Science Institute, L'Aquila, Italy
{gianlorenzo.dangelo,mirko.rossi}@gssi.it
[3] Department of Enterprise Engineering, University of Rome "Tor Vergata",
Rome, Italy
guala@mat.uniroma2.it

Abstract. In this paper we introduce the notions of *blackout-tolerant* temporal α-spanner of a temporal graph G which is a subgraph of G that preserves the distances between pairs of vertices of interest in G up to a multiplicative factor of α, even when the graph edges at a single time-instant become unavailable. In particular, we consider the *single-source, single-pair*, and *all-pairs* cases and, for each case we look at three quality requirements: *exact* distances (i.e., $\alpha = 1$), *almost-exact* distances (i.e., $\alpha = 1 + \varepsilon$ for an arbitrarily small constant $\varepsilon > 0$), and *connectivity* (i.e., unbounded α). For each combination we provide tight bounds, up to polylogarithmic factors, on the *size*, which is measured as the number of edges, of the corresponding blackout-tolerant α-spanner for both *general* temporal graphs and for *temporal cliques*. Our result show that such spanners are either very sparse (i.e., they have $\tilde{O}(n)$ edges) or they must have size $\Omega(n^2)$ in the worst case, where n is the number of vertices of G. To complete the picture, we also investigate the case of multiple blackouts.

Keywords: Temporal graphs · Temporal spanners · Fault-tolerance

1 Introduction

In wireless and sensor networks the communication links among nodes frequently change over time due to the fact that hosts might move, be active at different times, or face interference. Recently, this dynamic behaviour has been modeled through so-called *temporal graphs*, which are graphs where the edge-set is allowed to change over time. There are multiple definitions of temporal graphs in the literature, with the simplest one being that of Kempe, Kleinberg, and Kumar [12] in which each edge of a graph $G = (V, E)$ has an assigned time-label $\lambda(e) \in \mathbb{N}^+$ representing the instant in which $e \in E$ can be used. A path from a vertex to another in G is said to be a *temporal path* if its traversed edges have non-decreasing time-labels. If there exists a temporal path from u to v, for every two vertices $u, v \in V$, then the graph is *temporally connected*.

© The Author(s), under exclusive license to Springer Nature Switzerland AG 2022
T. Erlebach and M. Segal (Eds.): ALGOSENSORS 2022, LNCS 13707, pp. 31–44, 2022.
https://doi.org/10.1007/978-3-031-22050-0_3

One of the main problems in network design is reducing the size (and hence the operational cost) of a network while preserving both its robustness to failures and its communication efficiency.

In static networks this problem has been extensively studied, and has been formalized using the notion of (*fault-tolerant*) *graph spanners* i.e., sparse subgraphs that approximately preserve distances between pairs of vertices of interest, possibly in the presence of edge/vertex failures. While the landscape in static networks is quite well-understood (see, e.g., [1] and the references therein), the problem is still under active investigation in temporal networks, where it is even more relevant. The problem of computing a sparse *temporal spanner*, i.e., a sparse temporally-connected subgraph of a given temporal graph, was first introduced in the seminal paper of Kempe, Kleinberg, and Kumar [12] in 2002, and has recently received considerable attention. In particular, [2] has shown that there are temporal graphs with $\Theta(n^2)$ edges that cannot be sparsified. This prompted [6] to focus on *temporal cliques*, i.e., complete temporal graphs. Here the situation drastically improves as any temporal clique admits a temporal spanner with $O(n \log n)$ edges, although the resulting *stretch factor*, i.e., the maximum ratio between the length[1] of the shortest temporal path in the spanner and the corresponding shortest temporal path in the original graph, can be $\Omega(n)$.

This motivated [3] to study temporal α-spanners, i.e., temporal spanners that also guarantee a stretch factor of at most α. In particular, the authors showed that temporal cliques always admit a temporal $(2k-1)$-spanner with $\widetilde{O}(kn^{1+\frac{1}{k}})$ edges,[2] where $k \geqslant 1$ is an integer parameter of choice. They also considered *single-source* temporal α-spanners, i.e., temporal α-spanners in which the upper bound of α on the stretch factor only needs to hold for distances from a given source, and showed that any general temporal graph admits a single-source temporal $(1+\varepsilon)$-spanner with $\widetilde{O}(n/\log(1+\varepsilon))$ edges, for any $0 < \varepsilon < n$.

In all the above results it is implicitly assumed that the temporal network remains *fault-free*, i.e., each edge e is available with certainty at the time instant specified by its time-label $\lambda(e)$. Real-world networks, however, are fault-prone and a link could fail to operate properly at the scheduled time (e.g., a connection fails to be established). Even worse, due to cascading failures or catastrophic events, the entire network might become unavailable for a limited amount of time.

In this paper we investigate the problem of computing sparse temporal spanners with low stretch in presence of a failure in all the edges with single unknown time-label τ. We name this kind of failure a *blackout* at time τ, and we say that the corresponding spanner is *blackout-tolerant* (BT). We also provide some complementary results for the case of *b-blackout tolerant* (*b*-BT) spanners, i.e., spanners in which up to b blackouts can occur.

Our results. Our focus is on the case of a single blackout and we consider different kinds of temporal spanners on both *general temporal graphs* and *tempo-*

---

[1] As in [3], the length of a temporal path is its number of edges.

[2] The notation $\widetilde{O}(f(n))$ is a shorthand for $O(f(n) \log^c f(n))$, for some constant $c > 0$.

ral cliques. We classify our temporal spanners along two dimensions. The first dimension pertains the pairs of vertices of interest: all our spanners provide some connectivity or distance guarantee from any vertex in some set $S \subseteq V$ to any vertex in some set $T \subseteq V$. We say that a temporal spanner is *all-pairs* if $S = T = V$; *single-source* if $S = \{s\}$, for some $s \in V$, and $T = V$; and *single-pair* if $S = \{s\}$ and $T = \{t\}$ for some $s, t \in V$. If not otherwise specified we refer to all-pairs spanners.

The second dimension concerns whether the temporal spanner is required to only preserve connectivity from the vertices in S to the vertices in T (in which case we simply talk about temporal spanners) or to guarantee α-approximate distances from the nodes in S to the nodes in T (i.e., it is a temporal α-spanner). The special $\alpha = 1$ corresponds to preserving exact distances and we refer to the corresponding temporal spanner as a *temporal preserver*.

From a high-level perspective our results show that, for each of the above combinations, the sparsest admissible blackout-tolerant temporal spanner is either very sparse, i.e., it contains $\widetilde{O}(n)$ edges, or it must have size $\Omega(n^2)$ for some worst-case family of temporal graphs with n vertices.(See footnote 2) This implies that all our upper and lower bounds are asymptotically optimal up to polylogarithmic factors.

In more detail, our main results are the following (see also the cells with the bold references in Fig. 1):

- Any temporal graph admits a BT single-pair temporal spanner of linear size. Such a temporal spanner can be computed in polynomial time.
- For any $0 < \varepsilon < n$, we can compute in polynomial time a BT single-pair temporal $(1 + \varepsilon)$-spanner of size $O\left(\frac{n \log^4 n}{\log(1+\varepsilon)}\right)$.
- There exists a temporal graph G such that any BT single-pair temporal preserver of G has size $\Omega(n^2)$.
- The above result can be extended to show that there exists a *temporal clique* G such that any BT single-source temporal spanner of G has size $\Omega(n^2)$.

For the case of multiple blackouts we adapt our lower bound of $\Omega(n^2)$ on the size of temporal spanners for the following cases: (i) 2-BT single-pair temporal spanners, (ii) 2-BT single-pair temporal preservers of temporal cliques, and (iii) 3-BT single-pair temporal spanners of temporal cliques.

Finally, we observe that, in the case of two blackouts, temporal cliques admit 2-BT single-pair temporal spanners and 2-BT single-pair temporal $(1+\varepsilon)$-spanners of size $O(n)$ and $O(n \log^4 n / \log(1 + \varepsilon))$, respectively.

Thanks to the above results and some additional observations that allow us to import known bounds from the literature, we can achieve a characterization of the landscape of blackout-tolerant temporal spanners along the considered dimensions that is tight up to polylogarithmic factors. We summarize the resulting upper and lower bounds in Fig. 1. All our bounds extend to the case in which each edge can have multiple time-labels (i.e., it can be used in multiple time-instants).

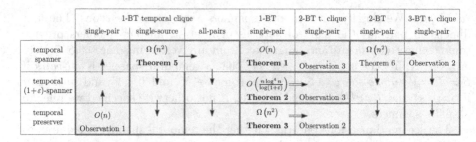

| | 1-BT temporal clique | | | 1-BT | 2-BT t. clique | 2-BT | 3-BT t. clique |
	single-pair	single-source	all-pairs	single-pair	single-pair	single-pair	single-pair
temporal spanner		$\Omega\left(n^2\right)$ Theorem 5		$O(n)$ Theorem 1	Observation 3	$\Omega\left(n^2\right)$ Theorem 6	Observation 2
temporal $(1+\varepsilon)$-spanner				$O\left(\frac{n\log^4 n}{\log(1+\varepsilon)}\right)$ Theorem 2	Observation 3		
temporal preserver	$O(n)$ Observation 1			$\Omega\left(n^2\right)$ Theorem 3	Observation 2		

Fig. 1. A summary of our results along the two considered dimensions. Each combination that admits a blackout-tolerant temporal spanner of size $\widetilde{O}(n)$ is shaded in blue, while those for which a strong lower bound of $\Omega(n^2)$ holds are shaded in red. The actual bounds are shown in the corresponding cells. A single-tailed arrow from a cell A to a neighboring cell B means that the upper/lower bound of A immediately implies the same result for B. A double-tailed arrow form A to B means that the result of A can be shown to also hold for B once it is paired with some additional minor observation. Missing columns (e.g., 1-BT single-source) only contain lower-bound results directly implied from an existing column (e.g., 1-BT single-source temporal-clique). (Color figure online)

Other Related Work. Besides the aforementioned papers, the problem of understanding the size of a temporal spanner for random temporal graphs has been considered in [7], where the authors study Erdős-Rényi graphs $G_{n,p}$ in which the time-label of an edge is its rank in a random permutation of the graph's edges, and provide sharp thresholds on the probability p for which the graph contains sparse single-pair, single-source, and (connectivity-preserving) temporal spanners.

For temporal graphs multiple distance measures are natural. In addition to the one considered in this work, i.e., the minimum number of edges of a temporal path, other common choices are the *earliest arrival time*, the *latest departure time*, *shortest time*, and *fastest time* (see, e.g., [5,13,15]). As far as temporal spanners are considered, [3] shows that these measures result in strong lower bounds on the size of any temporal subgraph preserving all-pair connectivity, even when the considered temporal graph is a clique.

The study of temporal-graph models and algorithms is a wide area of research, and we refer the interested reader to [14] for a survey and to [10] for a discussion on alternative models. Finally, other problems that aim to compute robust paths in temporal graphs that can be subject to disruptions have been studied in [8,9].

Paper Organization. Section 2 describes our model of temporal graphs and gives some preliminary definitions. Section 3 and Sect. 4 present our results for single-pair and single-source temporal spanners in the case of a single blackout, respectively. We discuss the case of multiple blackouts in Sect. 5.

2   Model and Preliminaries

Let $G = (V, E)$ be an undirected *temporal* graph with n vertices, and a labeling function $\lambda : E \to \mathbb{N}^+$ that assigns a *time-label* $\lambda(e)$ to each edge e. If G is complete we will say that it is a *temporal clique*. A temporal path π from vertex u to vertex v is a path in G from u to v such that the sequence $e_1, e_2, \ldots, e_k$ of edges traversed by π satisfies $\lambda(e_i) \leqslant \lambda(e_{i+1})$ for all $i = 1, \ldots, k - 1$. For a given (non-empty) temporal path π, the departure time of π and the arrival time of π are the time-labels of the first and last edge of π, respectively. For technical convenience we define the departure time of an empty path as $+\infty$ and the arrival time of an empty path as $-\infty$. A temporal path π_1 from u to v is *compatible* with a temporal path π_2 from v to z if the arrival time of π_1 does not exceed the departure time of π_2, and we denote by $\pi_1 \circ \pi_2$ the temporal path from u to z obtained by concatenating π_1 and π_2. If a simple temporal path π traverses the vertices u and v, in this order, then we denote by $\pi[u : v]$ the (temporal) subpath of π from u to v.

We say that a vertex u can *reach* a vertex v if there exists a temporal path from u to v in G. The *length* of a (not necessarily temporal) path π is the number of the edges in π and it is denoted by $|\pi|$. We define the *distance* $d_G(u, v)$ from u to v in G as the length of the shortest temporal path from u to v (in G). If u cannot reach v, then $d_G(u, v) = +\infty$.

We denote by $G^{\leqslant \tau}$, $G^{\geqslant \tau}$, and $G^{-\tau}$, the subgraphs of G that contain all vertices and exactly the edges with a time-label at most τ, at least τ, and different from τ, respectively. For the sake of readability we slightly abuse the notation for distances by moving the superscripts of the considered graph to the function d iteself, e.g., we may write $d_G^{\leqslant \tau}(u, v)$ to denote the distance from u to v in the graph $G^{\leqslant \tau}$. When the graph G is clear from context we may omit it altogether and write, e.g., $d^{\leqslant \tau}(u, v)$. The lifetime L of G is the maximum time-label assigned to an edge of G.

Given two sets of vertices $S, T \subseteq V$, a (S, T)-*temporal spanner* of G is a (temporal) subgraph H of G such that for every $u \in S$ and $v \in T$, u can reach v in H if and only if u can reach v in G. We call a (S, T)-*temporal spanner*: (i) *single-pair* temporal spanner if $S = \{s\}$ and $T = \{t\}$ for some vertices $s, t \in V$; (ii) *single-source* temporal spanner if S contains a single vertex $s \in V$ and $T = V$, (iii) temporal spanner if $S = T = V$.

We also define a different kind of *temporal spanner* called temporal α-spanner, where instead of preserving the reachability between two sets of vertices, we want to approximate their distances up to a factor $\alpha \geqslant 1$. More formally, for $\alpha \geqslant 1$ and two sets of vertices $S, T \subseteq V$, a (S, T)-temporal α-spanner of G is a (temporal) subgraph H of G such that $d_H(u, v) \leqslant \alpha \cdot d_G(u, v)$, for all $u \in S$ and $v \in T$. If $\alpha = 1$ we refer to a (S, T)-temporal 1-spanner as (S, T)-temporal preserver. The *size* of a temporal spanner (or α-spanner) is the number of its edges.

A *blackout* at time $\tau \in [1, L]$ is the failure of all the edges with time-label τ.

A (S, T)-temporal spanner (resp. (S, T)-temporal α-spanner) H of G is *blackout-tolerant* (BT) if for every $\tau \in [1, L]$, $H^{-\tau}$ is an (S, T)-temporal spanner (resp. (S, T)-temporal α-spanner) of $G^{-\tau}$.

3   Blackout-Tolerant Single-Pair Temporal Spanners

In this section we provide our upper and lower bounds on the size of single-pair temporal spanners and preservers in the case of a single blackout.

3.1   Upper Bounds on BT Single-Pair Temporal Spanners

Given a temporal graph G and two vertices $s, t \in V$, we provide a single-pair BT temporal spanner H of G with source s and target t. We define H as the union of two subgraphs A and D of G. In particular, A is a subgraph of G such that for every vertex v, A contains a temporal path from s to v with minimum arrival time. Symmetrically, D is a subgraph of G such that for every vertex v, D contains a temporal path from v to t with maximum departure time. From [11], we know that we can find such a temporal-subgraph A (resp. D) with size $O(n)$ in polynomial time.[3] We have:

Theorem 1. *A blackout-tolerant single-pair temporal spanner of G of size $O(n)$ can be computed in polynomial time.*

Proof. We only need to argue that H, as defined above, is a single-pair temporal spanner of G w.r.t. the two nodes s and t.

To this aim, fix a time-label $\tau \in [1, L]$ such that there exists a temporal path π_τ between s and t in $G^{-\tau}$. Let the vertices of π_τ be $s = v_0, v_1, \ldots, v_k = t$, as traversed from s to t and define d as the largest integer in $[1, k]$ such that $\lambda((v_{d-1}, v_d)) < \tau$. If no such integer exists, let $d = 0$.

As a consequence $\pi_\tau[s : v_d]$ (resp. $\pi_\tau[v_d : t]$) has an arrival time of at most $\tau - 1$ (resp. a departure time of at least $\tau + 1$). This shows that A (resp. D) must contain a temporal path π_A (resp. π_D) from s to v_d (resp. from v_d to t) with arrival time at most $\tau - 1$ (resp. departure time at least $\tau + 1$), i.e., π_A is in $A^{-\tau}$ (resp. π_D is in $D^{-\tau}$). Since π_A and π_D are compatible, their concatenation yields a temporal path from s to t that is entirely contained in $H^{-\tau}$.   □

We can modify the above construction to obtain, for any $\varepsilon > 0$ of choice, a blackout-tolerant single-pair temporal $(1 + \varepsilon)$-spanner H of G w.r.t. s and t. To this aim, we choose A and D as two temporal subgraphs of G having size $O\left(\frac{n \log^4 n}{\log(1+\varepsilon)}\right)$ and satisfying:

$$d_A^{\leqslant \tau}(s, v) \leqslant (1+\varepsilon) \cdot d_G^{\leqslant \tau}(s, v) \quad \text{and} \quad d_D^{\geqslant \tau}(v, t) \leqslant (1+\varepsilon) \cdot d_G^{\geqslant \tau}(v, t) \ \ \forall v \in V, \forall \tau \in [1, L].$$

These subgraphs can be found in polynomial time using the results in [3].(See footnote 3)[4] We can now show that the temporal graph H obtained as the union of A and D contains $(1 + \varepsilon)$-approximate blackout-tolerant temporal paths from s to t.

---

[3] This can be computed even for temporal graphs with multiple time-labels.

[4] A shortest path between x and y with departure time at least τ is a shortest path from y to x with arrival time $L - \tau + 1$ in the graph where each time-label $\lambda(e)$ is replaced with the time label $L - \lambda(e) + 1$, where L is the lifetime of G.

Theorem 2. *Let $0 < \varepsilon < n$. A blackout-tolerant single-pair temporal $(1 + \varepsilon)$-spanner of size $O\left(\frac{n \log^4 n}{\log(1+\varepsilon)}\right)$ can be computed in polynomial time.*

Proof. We only need to argue that H, with the updated definitions of A and D, is a single-pair temporal $(1 + \varepsilon)$-spanner of G w.r.t. s and t.

Fix a time label $\tau \in [1, L]$ such s can reach t in $G^{-\tau}$, and let π_τ be a *shortest* temporal path from s to t in $G^{-\tau}$. Let $s = v_0, v_1, \ldots, v_k = t$ be the vertices traversed by π_τ, in order, and d as in the proof of Theorem 1 so that the temporal path $|\pi_\tau[s : v_d]|$ has an arrival time of at most $\tau - 1$, while the temporal path $|\pi_\tau[v_d : t]|$ has a departure time of at least $\tau + 1$.

By our choice of A (resp. D), there must be a temporal path π_A in A (resp. π_D in D) such that the arrival time of π_A is at most $\tau - 1$ (resp. the departure time of π_D is at least $\tau + 1$) and $|\pi_A| \leqslant (1+\varepsilon) \cdot d_G^{\leqslant \tau - 1}(s, v_d) \leqslant (1+\varepsilon) \cdot |\pi_\tau[s : v_d]|$ (resp. $|\pi_D| \leqslant (1 + \varepsilon) \cdot d_G^{\geqslant \tau + 1}(v_d, t) \leqslant (1 + \varepsilon) \cdot |\pi_\tau[v_d : t]|$). Since π_A and π_D are compatible temporal paths and are both contained in H^{-t}, we have:

$$d_H^{-\tau}(s, t) \leqslant |\pi_A \circ \pi_D| = |\pi_A| + |\pi_D| \leqslant (1 + \varepsilon) \cdot |\pi_\tau[s : v_d]| + (1 + \varepsilon) \cdot |\pi_\tau[v_d : t]|$$
$$= (1 + \varepsilon) \cdot |\pi_\tau[s : v_d] \circ \pi_\tau[v_d : t]| = (1 + \varepsilon)|\pi_\tau| = (1 + \varepsilon)d_G^{-\tau}(s, t). \qquad \square$$

3.2 Lower Bounds on BT Single-Pair Temporal Preservers

In this section, we show that there exists a temporal graph G of $\Theta(n)$ vertices such that, any blackout-tolerant single-pair temporal preserver w.r.t. a fixed pair of vertices s and t of G has size $\Theta(n^2)$.

We will make use of a dense graph construction which we import from [3].[5]

Lemma 1 ([3]). *Given n, there exists a temporal graph G' with $\Theta(n)$ vertices and $\Omega(n^2)$ edges that satisfies the following properties:*

- *G' is the union of n edge-disjoint temporal paths $\pi_1, \ldots, \pi_n$;*
- *π_i is a path from a fixed source vertex σ to a distinct target vertex t_i.*
- *π_i uses only edges with time-label i;*
- *π_i is the unique shortest temporal path from σ to t_i;*
- *the largest time-label of an edge incident to vertex t_i is i;*
- *$|\pi_i| < |\pi_j| - (i - j)$ for all $j < i$;*
- *any single-source temporal preserver of G' with source σ has size $\Omega(n^2)$.*

Our lower-bound graph G contains the temporal graph G' as stated in Lemma 1, a temporal path P of $n + 1$ vertices $s_1, \ldots, s_{n+1}$ such that each edge (s_i, s_{i+1}) has time-label $n + i$, and an edge (t_i, s_{n-i+1}) with time-label i for each $i = 1, \ldots, n$. Finally, let $s = \sigma$ and $t = s_{n+1}$. See Fig. 2.

Lemma 2. *Let $1 \leqslant i < n$ and define $\tau = 2n - i$. The shortest temporal path from s to t in $G^{-\tau}$ is unique and is the concatenation of π_i, the edge (t_i, s_{n-i+1}), and the subpath from s_{n-i+1} to t in P.*

---

[5] For ease of presentation, we summarize the key properties of the construction in a single lemma. The details can be found in Sect. 4.3 of the full version [4] of [3].

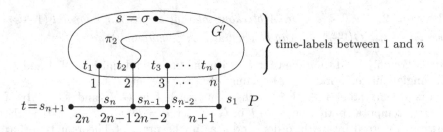

Fig. 2. Sketch of the construction of the graph G used to prove Theorem 3.

Proof. Notice that any vertex s_{n-j+1} with $j > i$ cannot reach t following a blackout at time $\tau = 2n - i$. Therefore, the shortest temporal path from s to t in $G^{-\tau}$ (this path exists since t is still reachable from s in $G^{-\tau}$) must go through an edge (t_j, s_{n-j+1}) with $j \leqslant i$ and then it must follow the subpath from s_{n-j+1} to t in P.

Observe that the shortest temporal path from s to t_j in G is π_j, and that the subpath from s_{n-j+1} to t in P has length j. For $j \leqslant i$, the concatenation of the above paths via the augmenting edge (t_j, s_{n-j+1}) is a temporal path π_j^* from s to t in $G^{-\tau}$ of length $|\pi_j| + j + 1$ and, in particular, it is the unique shortest temporal path from s to t in $G^{-\tau}$ among those passing through (t_j, s_{n-j+1}). Hence, to prove the claim we only need to show that the choice of $j \leqslant i$ that minimizes $|\pi_j^*|$ is $j = i$. This is true since, for any $j < i$, we can invoke Lemma 1 to obtain $|\pi_i^*| = |\pi_i| + i + 1 < |\pi_j| - (i - j) + i + 1 = |\pi_j| + j + 1 = |\pi_j^*|$. $\qquad\square$

We are now ready to state the following:

Theorem 3. *For any n, there exists a temporal graph G of $\Theta(n)$ vertices, such that any blackout-tolerant single-pair temporal preserver of G (w.r.t. a suitable pair of vertices) has size $\Omega(n^2)$.*

Proof. Consider the temporal graph G of this section and observe that any single-pair blackout-tolerant temporal preserver H of G w.r.t. s and t must contain all paths $\pi_1, \ldots, \pi_{n-1}$. Indeed, Lemma 2 ensures that, for any $i = 1, \ldots, n-1$, the unique shortest temporal path from s to t following a blackout at time $\tau = 2n - i$ contains π_i as a subpath. By Lemma 1, the union of the edges in all the temporal shortest paths $\pi_1, \ldots, \pi_n$ is exactly G', which has size $\Theta(n^2)$. Hence, since $|\pi_n| \leqslant n$, we can conclude that H must have size at least $\sum_{i=1}^{n-1} |\pi_i| = \Omega(n^2)$. The claim follows by noticing that G has $\Theta(n) + n + 1$ vertices (see Lemma 1). $\qquad\square$

3.3 Upper Bounds on BT Single-Pair Temporal Preservers on Cliques

Given a temporal clique G and two vertices s, t, with $s \neq t$, we have that the shortest temporal path between s and t coincides with the edge (s, t) for any blackout at time $\tau \neq \lambda(u, v)$. We can therefore build a blackout-tolerant single-pair temporal preserver of G w.r.t. s and t by selecting the edge (s, t) along with a shortest temporal path in $G^{-\lambda(u,v)}$.

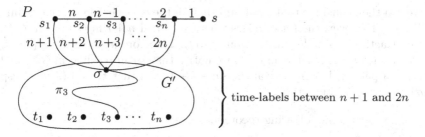

Fig. 3. Sketch of the construction of the graph G used to prove Theorem 4.

This is tight as it can be seen by considering the temporal clique in which there is a Hamiltonian path from s to t consisting of edges with time-label 2, and all other edges have time-label 1.

The above discussion is summarized by the following observation:

Observation 1. *For any temporal clique $G = (V, E)$ of n vertices and a pair of vertices $s, t \in V$, there exists a blackout-tolerant single-pair temporal preserver of G with source s and target t of size $O(n)$. This is tight.*

4   Lower Bounds on BT Single-Source Temporal Spanners

In this section we first show that there is a temporal graph G of $\Theta(n)$ vertices such that any blackout-tolerant single-source temporal spanner of G has size $\Omega(n^2)$. Then, we discuss how such a temporal graph G can be transformed into a clique for which the same lower bound holds.

Our temporal graph G is similar to the one used for the lower bound of the blackout-tolerant single-pair temporal preserver discussed in Sect. 3.2. We build G as the union of (i) a temporal path P of $n + 1$ vertices $s_1, \ldots, s_{n+1}$, such that for $i = 1, \ldots, n$, the time-label of the edge (s_i, s_{i+1}) is $n - i + 1$, (ii) a time-shifted copy of the temporal graph G' of Lemma 1 in which each time-label $\lambda(e)$ is replaced by $\lambda(e) + n$, and (iii) an *augmenting* edge (s_i, σ) with time-label $n + i$ for each $i = 1, \ldots, n$. Finally, we choose $s = s_{n+1}$ (see Fig. 3).

Lemma 3. *Let $2 \leqslant i \leqslant n$ and define $\tau = n - i + 2$. Vertex s can reach vertex t_i in $G^{-\tau}$. Moreover, all temporal paths from t to t_i in $G^{-\tau}$ contain π_i as a subpath.*

Proof. We first suppose that a temporal path π from t to t_i in $G^{-\tau}$ exists and we show that it must contain π_i as a subpath. Let (s_j, σ) be the first augmenting edge traversed by π (this edge exists since the augmenting edges form a s-t_i-cut in G). Since the time-label of (s_j, σ) is $n + j$ and π must have arrival time at most $n + i$ (see again Lemma 1), we must have $j \leqslant i$. At the same time, we notice that $\tau = n - i + 2$ is the time-label of the edge (s_{i-1}, s_i). Thus, after the blackout at time time τ, only the vertices s_j with $j \geqslant i$ can be reached by s without traversing an augmenting edge, hence we must have $j \geqslant i$.

We can then conclude that $j = i$ and that all the edges in $\pi[\sigma : t_i]$ have time-label $n + i$. However, the set of edges with time-label $n + i$ in G (and in $G^{-\tau}$) induces exactly the simple path π_i from σ to t_i. Therefore we have $\pi[\sigma : t_i] = \pi_i$.

To see that s can reach t_i in $G^{-\tau}$, we notice that s can reach s_i in $G^{-\tau}$ with a temporal path π_i' having arrival time $n - i + 1$, and that π_i' and (s_i, σ) (resp. (s_i, σ) and π_i) are compatible. $\qquad\square$

We can now prove the following theorem.

Theorem 4. *For any n, there exists a temporal graph G of $\Theta(n)$ vertices, such that any blackout-tolerant single-source temporal spanner of G (w.r.t. a suitable source vertex) has size $\Theta(n^2)$.*

Proof. Consider the temporal graph G of this section and notice that it has $\Theta(n)$ vertices. By Lemma 3, any blackout-tolerant single-source temporal spanner H of G w.r.t. s must contain all temporal paths π_i for $i = 2, \ldots, n$. By Lemma 1 these paths are edge disjoint and their overall number of edges is $\sum_{i=2}^{n} |\pi_i| = \Omega(n^2)$. Hence the size of H is $\Omega(n^2)$. $\qquad\square$

We now show how to strengthen Theorem 4 by transforming G into a temporal clique $\widetilde{G}$ for which the same asymptotic lower bound holds. The temporal clique $\widetilde{G}$ is obtained by starting from a time-shifted copy of G in which each time-label $\lambda(e)$ is replaced with $\lambda(e) + 2$ and augmenting such graph as follows (see Fig. 4):

- For every vertex t_i, create a new vertex z_i and add the edge (t_i, z_i) with time-label M, with $M = 2n + 3$;
- Add a new vertex $\widetilde{s}$ and an edge $(\widetilde{s}, z_i)$ with time-label $\tau_i = n - i + 2$ for each $i = 1, \ldots, n$. Add the edge $(\widetilde{s}, s)$ with time-label 2;
- Add all the remaining edges incident to $\widetilde{s}$, and set their time-labels to $M + 1$.
- Finally, add all remaining edges (between any pair of vertices in $\widetilde{G}$) and set their time-labels to 1.

Theorem 5. *For any n, there exists a temporal clique $\widetilde{G}$ of $\Theta(n)$ vertices, such that any blackout-tolerant single-source temporal spanner of $\widetilde{G}$ (w.r.t. a suitable source vertex) has size $\Theta(n^2)$.*

Proof. Consider the temporal graph $\widetilde{G}$ of this section. First of all, notice that all edges incident to $\widetilde{s}$ have time-label at least 2 and hence we can ignore all the edges with time-label 1, since they do not belong to any temporal path from $\widetilde{s}$.

Consider a vertex z_i with $i \geqslant 2$ and a blackout at time $\tau_i = n - i + 2$. We claim that any temporal path π from $\widetilde{s}$ to z_i must use $(\widetilde{s}, s)$ as its first edge and must enter in z_i with the edge (t_i, z_i). Indeed, the only edge incident to z_i in $\widetilde{G}^{-\tau_i}$ with a time-label different from 1 is (t_i, z_i). As consequence, no edge in π can have time-label $M + 1$. Moreover π cannot contain any vertex z_j with $j \neq i$, since then π would need to traverse (z_j, t_j) which has time-label M, but $\widetilde{G}^{-\tau_i}$ contains no path from z_j to t_i that only uses edges with time-label M.

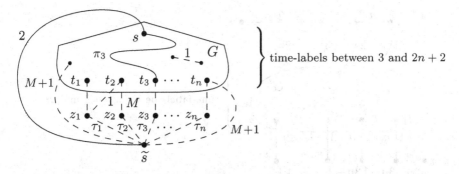

Fig. 4. Sketch of the construction of the graph $\widetilde{G}$ used to prove Theorem 5. Edges with time-label 1 or $M+1$ are dashed. All edges in (the time-shifted copy of) G have a time-label between 3 and $2n+2$, except for the additional edges with time-label 1.

Hence, we know that $\pi[s:t_i]$ is a path from s to t_i in $G^{-\tau_i}$ and, by Lemma 3, any such path includes π_i as a subpath. To show that at least one such π exists, notice that there is a temporal path π' from s to t_i in $G^{-\tau_i}$ and hence $(\widetilde{s}, s) \circ \pi' \circ (t_i, z_i)$ is a temporal path in $\widetilde{G}^{-\tau_i}$.

To conclude the proof we notice that $\widetilde{G}$ has $\Theta(n)$ vertices and that, by Lemma 1, $\sum_{i=2}^{n} |\pi_i| = \Omega(n^2)$. □

5   More Than One Blackout

In this section we consider b-blackout-tolerant temporal spanners, i.e., temporal spanners of temporal graphs that can withstand multiple blackouts. We start by formalizing this notion.

For a given temporal graph G with lifetime L and a subset F of $\{1, \ldots, L\}$, we denote by G^{-F} the temporal subgraph of G that contains all vertices and exactly the edges e with $\lambda(e) \notin F$. A b-blackout-tolerant (b-BT) temporal spanner (resp. α-spanner) of a temporal graph G with lifetime L is a temporal subgraph H of G such that H^{-F} is a temporal spanner (resp. α-spanner) of G^{-F} for all $F \subseteq \{1, \ldots, L\}$ with $|F| \leqslant b$.

We now provide a lower bound on the size of any 2-BT single-pair temporal spanner of a temporal graph. Our lower-bound graph G consists of a temporal path P' of $n+1$ vertices $s_1', \ldots, s_{n+1}'$, where $\lambda(s_i', s_{i+1}') = n-i+1$, a time-shifted copy of the graph G' of Lemma 1 in which each time-label $\lambda(e)$ is replaced with $\lambda(e) + n$, a temporal path P of $n+1$ vertices $s_1, \ldots, s_{n+1}$ where $\lambda(s_i, s_{i+1}) = 2n+i$, and the following additional edges:

- An edge (s_i', σ) with time-label $n+i$ for each $i = 1, \ldots, n$;
- An edge (t_i, s_{n-i+1}) with time label $n+i$ for each $i = 1, \ldots, n$.

Finally, we choose $s = s_{n+1}'$ and $t = s_{n+1}$. See Fig. 5.

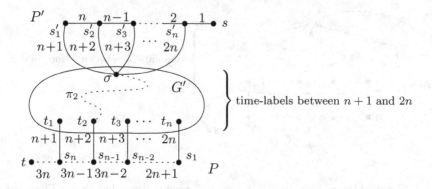

Fig. 5. Sketch of the construction of the graph G used to prove Theorem 6.

Theorem 6. *For any n, there exists a temporal graph G of $\Theta(n)$ vertices, such that any 2-blackout-tolerant single-pair temporal spanner of G (w.r.t. a suitable pair of vertices) has size $\Theta(n^2)$.*

Proof. Consider the temporal graph G of this section and notice that it has $\Theta(n)$ vertices. Pick any $i = 2, \ldots, n-1$ and let $\tau = n - i + 2$ and $\psi = 3n - i$.

Notice that any path from s to t in $G^{-\tau}$ must traverse an edge (s'_j, σ) with $j \geqslant i$ and, by definition of P', it has time-label $n + j \geqslant n + i$.

Symmetrically, by definition of P, any path from s to t in $G^{-\psi}$ must traverse an edge (t_j, s_{n-j+1}) with $j \leqslant i$, which has time-label $n + j \leqslant n + i$.

This implies that, if there is a path π from s to t in $G^{-\{\tau,\psi\}}$, π must contain a subpath between σ and s_i in the (time-shifted) graph G' that uses only edges with time-label $n + i$. By Lemma 1, the only such subpath is π_i.

To show that π exists, we notice that we can build a temporal path in $G^{-\{\tau,\psi\}}$ as a concatenation of (i) the unique simple path from s to s'_i in P', (ii) the edge (s'_i, σ), (iii) the path π_i in (the time-shifted version of) G', (iv) the edge (t_i, s_{n-i+1}), and (v) the subpath path from s_{n-i+1} to t in P.

Using the fact that the paths π_i are edge-disjoint (Lemma 1), we can conclude that any 2-blackout-tolerant single-pair temporal spanner of G with source s and target t has size at least $\sum_{i=2}^{n-1} |\pi_i| = \Omega(n^2)$.   □

We now show how to extend some of our upper and lower bound results to a larger number of blackouts by using the following observation: Let G be a temporal graph with lifetime L and $\tau \in \{1, \ldots, L\}$. Any b-BT spanner (resp. α-spanner) of G with $b \geqslant 1$ is a $(b-1)$-BT spanner (resp. α-spanner) of $G^{-\tau}$.

As a consequence, any lower bound on the size of a $(b-1)$-BT spanner (resp. α-spanner) on general (not necessarily complete) temporal graphs also applies to b-BT spanners (resp. α-spanner) on temporal cliques, since we can complete the lower-bound graph with edges having a new time-label τ.

Applying the above argument to our lower bounds of Theorem 3 and 6 on the size of all-pairs temporal-spanners on general graph, we have the following:[6]

Observation 2. *The following blackout-tolerant temporal spanners admit a lower bound of $\Omega(n^2)$ on their size:*

- *2-BT single-pair temporal preservers of temporal cliques;*
- *3-BT single-pair temporal spanners of temporal cliques.*

We conclude this section by arguing that our upper bounds for 1-BT single-pair temporal spanners on general graphs, extend to 2 blackouts on temporal cliques. Indeed, when the input graph is a temporal clique, the only blackout that affects the (single-edge) shortest path from s to t is the time-label τ of the edge (s,t). Thus, for a given temporal clique G and pair of vertices s and t, the subgraph H obtained by adding edge (s,t) to a 1-BT single-pair temporal spanner of $G^{-\tau}$ with source s and target t, is a 2-BT single-pair temporal spanner of G with source s and target t.

Applying the above argument to our upper bounds of Theorem 1 and Theorem 2, we have the following:

Observation 3. *Any temporal clique of n vertices admits:*

- *A 2-BT single-pair temporal spanner of size $O(n)$; and*
- *A 2-BT single-pair temporal $(1+\varepsilon)$-spanner of size $O(\frac{n \log^4 n}{\log(1+\varepsilon)})$, for any $0 < \varepsilon < n$.*

References

1. Ahmed, A.R., et al.: Graph spanners: a tutorial review. Comput. Sci. Rev. **37**, 100253 (2020). https://doi.org/10.1016/j.cosrev.2020.100253
2. Axiotis, K., Fotakis, D.: On the size and the approximability of minimum temporally connected subgraphs. In: Chatzigiannakis, I., Mitzenmacher, M., Rabani, Y., Sangiorgi, D. (eds.) 43rd International Colloquium on Automata, Languages, and Programming, ICALP 2016, 11–15 July 2016, Rome, Italy. LIPIcs, vol. 55, pp. 149:1–149:14. Schloss Dagstuhl - Leibniz-Zentrum für Informatik (2016). https://doi.org/10.4230/LIPIcs.ICALP.2016.149
3. Bilò, D., D'Angelo, G., Gualà, L., Leucci, S., Rossi, M.: Sparse temporal spanners with low stretch. In: Chechik, S., Navarro, G., Rotenberg, E., Herman, G. (eds.) 30th Annual European Symposium on Algorithms, ESA 2022, 5–9 September 2022, Berlin/Potsdam, Germany. LIPIcs, vol. 244, pp. 19:1–19:16. Schloss Dagstuhl - Leibniz-Zentrum für Informatik (2022). https://doi.org/10.4230/LIPIcs.ESA.2022.19
4. Bilò, D., D'Angelo, G., Gualà, L., Leucci, S., Rossi, M.: Sparse temporal spanners with low stretch. CoRR abs/2206.11113 (2022). https://doi.org/10.48550/arXiv.2206.11113

---

[6] This also provides an alternative way to show a lower bound of $\Omega(n^2)$ on the size of 1-BT temporal spanners on temporal cliques from the corresponding lower bound of [2] on temporal graphs.

5. Calamai, M., Crescenzi, P., Marino, A.: On computing the diameter of (weighted) link streams. In: Coudert, D., Natale, E. (eds.) 19th International Symposium on Experimental Algorithms, SEA 2021, 7–9 June 2021, Nice, France. LIPIcs, vol. 190, pp. 11:1–11:21. Schloss Dagstuhl - Leibniz-Zentrum für Informatik (2021). https://doi.org/10.4230/LIPIcs.SEA.2021.11

6. Casteigts, A., Peters, J.G., Schoeters, J.: Temporal cliques admit sparse spanners. J. Comput. Syst. Sci. **121**, 1–17 (2021). https://doi.org/10.1016/j.jcss.2021.04.004,https://doi.org/10.1016/j.jcss.2021.04.004

7. Casteigts, A., Raskin, M., Renken, M., Zamaraev, V.: Sharp thresholds in random simple temporal graphs. In: 62nd IEEE Annual Symposium on Foundations of Computer Science, FOCS 2021, Denver, CO, USA, 7–10 February 2022. pp. 319–326. IEEE (2021). https://doi.org/10.1109/FOCS52979.2021.00040

8. Füchsle, E., Molter, H., Niedermeier, R., Renken, M.: Delay-robust routes in temporal graphs. In: Berenbrink, P., Monmege, B. (eds.) 39th International Symposium on Theoretical Aspects of Computer Science, STACS 2022, 15–18 March 2022, Marseille, France (Virtual Conference). LIPIcs, vol. 219, pp. 30:1–30:15. Schloss Dagstuhl - Leibniz-Zentrum für Informatik (2022). https://doi.org/10.4230/LIPIcs.STACS.2022.30

9. Füchsle, E., Molter, H., Niedermeier, R., Renken, M.: Temporal connectivity: Coping with foreseen and unforeseen delays. In: Aspnes, J., Michail, O. (eds.) 1st Symposium on Algorithmic Foundations of Dynamic Networks, SAND 2022, 28–30 March 2022, Virtual Conference. LIPIcs, vol. 221, pp. 17:1–17:17. Schloss Dagstuhl - Leibniz-Zentrum für Informatik (2022). https://doi.org/10.4230/LIPIcs.SAND.2022.17

10. Holme, P.: Temporal networks. In: Alhajj, R., Rokne, J.G. (eds.) Encyclopedia of Social Network Analysis and Mining, 2nd edn. Springer, Cham (2018). https://doi.org/10.1007/978-1-4939-7131-2_42

11. Huang, S., Fu, A.W., Liu, R.: Minimum spanning trees in temporal graphs. In: Sellis, T.K., Davidson, S.B., Ives, Z.G. (eds.) Proceedings of the 2015 ACM SIGMOD International Conference on Management of Data, Melbourne, Victoria, Australia, 31 May - 4 June 2015, pp. 419–430. ACM (2015). https://doi.org/10.1145/2723372.2723717

12. Kempe, D., Kleinberg, J.M., Kumar, A.: Connectivity and inference problems for temporal networks. J. Comput. Syst. Sci. **64**(4), 820–842 (2002). https://doi.org/10.1006/jcss.2002.1829

13. Mertzios, G.B., Michail, O., Spirakis, P.G.: Temporal network optimization subject to connectivity constraints. Algorithmica **81**(4), 1416–1449 (2018). https://doi.org/10.1007/s00453-018-0478-6

14. Michail, O.: An introduction to temporal graphs: an algorithmic perspective. Internet Math. **12**(4), 239–280 (2016). https://doi.org/10.1080/15427951.2016.1177801

15. Wu, H., Cheng, J., Huang, S., Ke, Y., Lu, Y., Xu, Y.: Path problems in temporal graphs. In: Proceedings of the VLDB Endow, vol. 7, no. 9, pp. 721–732 (2014). https://doi.org/10.14778/2732939.2732945

Molecular Robots with Chirality on Grids

Serafino Cicerone[1], Alessia Di Fonso[1(✉)], Gabriele Di Stefano[1],
and Alfredo Navarra[2]

[1] Dipartimento di Ingegneria e Scienze dell'Informazione e Matematica,
Università degli Studi dell'Aquila, 67100 L'Aquila, Italy
{serafino.cicerone,gabriele.distefano}@univaq.it,
alessia.difonso@graduate.univaq.it
[2] Dipartimento di Matematica e Informatica, Università degli Studi di Perugia,
06123 Perugia, Italy
alfredo.navarra@unipg.it

Abstract. In the theoretical studies on distributed algorithms for swarm robotics, the complexity and capabilities of the robots are usually reduced to their minimum. Recently, the MOBLOT model has been introduced in order to deal with robots considered silent, anonymous, and oblivious but capable to aggregate into more complex structures, called *molecules*. We study the case where robots move along a regular square grid and we formally define the *Molecular Pattern Formation* (MPF) problem where a specific configuration of robots assembled into molecules must be reached. As general result, we provide a necessary condition for its solvability. Then, we actually show that dealing with molecules can resolve in some cases the symmetry breaking issue on grids where otherwise robots cannot. Finally, we introduce and resolve an interesting case study, where molecules are given by tetrominos (aka Tetris blocks).

1 Introduction

Swarm robotics concerns individual robots, usually mobile, with full autonomy (see, e.g., M-Blocks [17] or Kilobot [18]). The theoretical approach models such systems by reducing the complexity and capabilities of the robots to their minimum. On the one hand, this allows to investigate on the minimum circumstances that lead to solve specific problems. On the other hand, solutions that do not rely on strong assumptions are more robust also with respect to possible disruptions.

Interesting models considered in the literature are the Amoebot [10], and the recent Silbot [8] and Pairbot [15]. In general, these models can be approached by rigorous algorithmic analysis, thus allowing new theoretical insights for distributed computing, and helping to understand the practical capabilities of more realistic systems.

The work has been supported in part by the Italian National Group for Scientific Computation (GNCS-INdAM).

© The Author(s), under exclusive license to Springer Nature Switzerland AG 2022
T. Erlebach and M. Segal (Eds.): ALGOSENSORS 2022, LNCS 13707, pp. 45–59, 2022.
https://doi.org/10.1007/978-3-031-22050-0_4

Among others, the OBLOT model (see, e.g., [13]) is certainly one of the most investigated. It covers a large spectrum of settings. As minimal ones: robots are assumed to have no memory of past events, they are indistinguishable, without ids, without any centralized control, they all execute the same deterministic algorithm without any means of direct communication and each one operating with its own local coordinate system. In the OBLOT model, one of the most studied problems is certainly the *Gathering* [4,7,9,11], or the more general *Pattern Formation* (PF) [3,5,12,16,19]: given a team of robots and a geometric pattern in terms of specific vertices of the input graph with respect to an ideal coordinate system, the goal is to design a distributed algorithm so that eventually all robots together form the pattern, if possible.

In this work, we consider the recently introduced MOBLOT model [2] but for robots moving on a regular square grid. MOBLOT extends OBLOT to address a larger spectrum of problems. It stands for *Molecular OBLivious robOTs*, since the inspiration comes from nature: like atoms combine themselves to form molecules, in MOBLOT simple robots can move to form more complex computational entities (still called *molecules*), having an extent and different capabilities with respect to robots; like in nature molecules combine themselves to form the matter, the MOBLOT version of molecules can exploit their capabilities to arrange themselves to form any shape defined according to some compositional properties or specific patterns. This is what we later call the *Molecular Pattern Formation* (MPF) problem which is clearly well-related to PF.

As general result, we provide a necessary condition for the solvability of MPF which relies on two factors. The first is somehow inherited from the continuous case, that is the symmetricity. Informally, the symmetricity of a configuration measures the amount of symmetries of the robots' disposal. The second is instead specific of the discrete environment and concerns the type of center of the smallest enclosing box of the pattern. As we deal with regular square grids, such a center might be a vertex, the middle point of an edge, or the center of a square of the grid. We then show that dealing with molecules can resolve in some cases the symmetry breaking issue on grids where OBLOT cannot. Finally, we introduce an interesting case study, representative of the MPF problem, in which the set of potentially formable molecules is the set of the seven tetrominoes (aka Tetris blocks, see Fig. 1) For this case study, we provide a distributed algorithm for a set of robots that is able to form a molecular pattern whenever the necessary condition for the solvability of MPF is verified.

2   Molecular Oblivious Robots on Grids

In this section, we present the MOBLOT model for synchronous robots moving on a square grid. This is provided by revising most of the properties characterizing the MOBLOT model introduced in [2] for robots moving on the Euclidean plane, which in turn was an extension of the OBLOT model.

A MOBLOT system is composed by a set R of n robots, that live and operate in graphs. Robots are viewed as points (they are **dimensionless**), and more than one robot can occupy the same vertex, i.e., a **multiplicity** occurs.

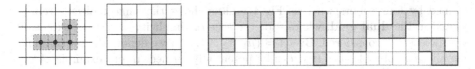

Fig. 1. (*left*) A molecule formed by four adjacent robots; (*middle*) The dual grid, where only the extent of the molecule is shown; (*right*) All possible tetrominos. According to their shape, they can be referred to as L, T, J, I, O, S, and Z, resp.

The robots are: **identical** (indistinguishable by their external appearance), **anonymous** (they do not have distinct ids), **autonomous** (they operate without a central control), **homogeneous** (they all execute the same algorithm), **silent** (they have no means of direct communication), and **disoriented** (each robot has its own local coordinate system - LCS) but they share a common handedness, i.e., *chirality* is assumed. A robot is capable of observing the positions (expressed in its LCS) of all the robots. We consider synchronous robots whose behavior follows three sequential phases:

- Look. The robot obtains a snapshot of the positions of all the other robots expressed in its own LCS.
- Compute. The robot performs a local computation according to a deterministic algorithm $\mathcal{A}$ (i.e., the robot executes $\mathcal{A}$), which is the same for all robots, and the output is a vertex among its neighbors or the one where it resides.
- Move. The robot performs a *nil* movement if the destination is its current location otherwise it instantaneously moves on the computed neighbor.

Such phases form a **computational cycle** of a robot. Robots are **oblivious**: they have no memory of past events, and the Compute phase is based only on the snapshot acquired in the current Look phase. A data structure containing all the information elaborated from the current snapshot represents what later is called the **view** of a robot. Since each robot refers to its own LCS, the view cannot exploit absolute orienteering but it is based on relative positions of robots. Hence, if symmetries occur, then symmetric robots have the same view. In turn, (i) the algorithm cannot distinguish between symmetric robots , and (ii) symmetric robots perform the same movements. As chirality is assumed, and we are considering a regular square grid as a field of movement, the only possible symmetries are rotations of 90 or 180°.

In MOBLOT the algorithmic task for robots is to form **molecules**. A molecule μ is specified by a **fixed pattern** defined with respect to the regular square grid. For instance, in what follows, for the ease of the discussion, we consider four robots to form a molecule if they are disposed as a possible **tetromino**. A tetromino is a geometric shape composed of four squares connected orthogonally (i.e., at the edges and not the corners, cf., Fig. 1) [14] Once a molecule is formed, it is assumed to have an extent $B(\mu)$ given by the union of four squares of the same dimensions of the squares of the grid, each one centered on one of the robots composing the molecule. Figure 1 left shows a molecule as formed by four robots whereas Fig. 1 middle shows the same molecule represented in the **dual grid**, where - for the sake of simplicity - only the extent of the molecule is considered. By $\mathcal{M} = \{\mu_1, \mu_2, \ldots, \mu_m\}$ we denote the set containing all kinds of molecules that can be potentially formed. In our example, $\mathcal{M}$ is composed by the 7 possible tetrominos, and each kind of tetromino is denoted by a single character among L, T, J, I, O, S, and Z, according to their shape, see Fig. 1 right). In order to make the model fair and as much general/weak as possible, we impose some constraints.

$\mathcal{C}_1$: in initial configurations, each pair of robots is at distance not less than 2, where the distance is the number of edges composing the shortest path connecting them.

A molecule μ is formed as soon as there are robots that form the pattern describing μ, however the following must hold:

$\mathcal{C}_2$: in $B(\mu)$, there are only the robots necessary to form μ suitably placed with respect to the pattern defining μ;

$\mathcal{C}_3$: for each μ' already formed or that could be formed at the same time of μ, $B(\mu) \cap B(\mu') = \emptyset$;

$\mathcal{C}_4$: as soon as a molecule μ is formed, each robot forming μ is no longer an independent entity (i.e., it stops executing its algorithm as a single robot and acts as a part of the molecule).

Once a molecule is formed, it constitutes a new computational entity with a physical dimension, i.e., it is solid. The basic properties of such new entities can still be modeled as in OBLOT systems (and its variants), with the main exception that a molecule not only can move by following an edge of the grid but it also may rotate of 90° with respect to one of the vertices occupied by the robots composing it. Being solid, any other entity in the system (robot or molecule) can touch the external surface of $B(\mu)$ – but cannot penetrate inside.

Each type of molecule in $\mathcal{M}$ is provided as input to the algorithm, and the algorithm is responsible to assemble all the molecules so that a more complex structure (i.e., the *matter*) is formed. Also the matter to be formed must be given as input to robots and it can be defined either as according to some adjacency properties or by providing a specific pattern made of molecules (cf., Fig 2.right). For the ease of the discussion, we refer to the latter case as the **Molecular Pattern Formation** (MPF) problem.

It is worth to remark that in MOBLOT, a robot r performing the Look phase is able to detect not only all the other robots but also any formed molecule μ. We denote by *Mol* the set of molecules detected at a given time by a robot r.

3   Necessary Condition on Feasibility

In this section, we first give all the necessary concepts and notation needed to formalize the MPF problem and then we state a necessary condition for its

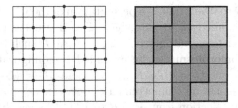

Fig. 2. (*left*) A configuration containing only robots with $\rho(C) = 4$. (*right*) A pattern F with $\rho(F) = 2$ on the dual grid (colors are used for better viewing only). (Color figure online)

feasibility. In the following, we use the term **entity** when we do not need to distinguish between robot and molecule.

CONFIGURATIONS AND MPF PROBLEM. A square tessellation of the Euclidean plane is the covering of the plane using squares of side length 1, called tiles, with no overlaps and in which the corners of squares are identically arranged. Let S be the infinite lattice formed by the vertices of the square tessellation. The graph G_S is called **grid graph**, its vertices are the points in S and its edges connect vertices that are distance 1 apart.

Let $R = \{r_1, r_2, \ldots, r_n\}$ be the set of robots.

The topology where robots are placed is the grid graph $G_S = (V, E)$. A function $\lambda : R \to V$ maps each robot to the vertex in G_S where the robot is placed. Assume that each robot knows the set of available molecules $\mathcal{M}$ and the set $\mathcal{F}$ of possible patterns describing the matter to form. As said above, during the Look phase, each robot detects in the local coordinate system both the robots' positions and the set Mol of already formed molecules. We call $C = (G_S, R, \lambda, Mol)$ a **configuration**. Notice that constraint $\mathcal{C}_1$ imposes $Mol = \emptyset$ in each initial configuration.

An **execution** of an algorithm $\mathcal{A}$ from an initial configuration C is a sequence of configurations $\mathbb{E} : C(t_0), C(t_1), \ldots$, where $C(t_0) = C$ and $C(t_{n+1})$ is obtained from $C(t_n)$ by moving some entities according to the result of the Compute phase as implemented by $\mathcal{A}$. With respect to the defined MOBLOT model, the **MPF problem** on the grid graph can be formalized as follows.

Definition 1. *Given an initial configuration $C = (G_S, R, \lambda, Mol = \emptyset)$, a set of molecules $\mathcal{M}$, and a set $\mathcal{F}$ of possible patterns describing the matter to form, the goal is to design a distributed algorithm $\mathcal{A}$ that works for each entity so that eventually they form some pattern in $\mathcal{F}$, if possible. Formally, $\mathcal{A}$ solves the MPF problem for C if, for each possible execution $\mathbb{E} : C = C(t_0), C(t_1), \ldots$ of $\mathcal{A}$, there exists a finite time instant $t_n > 0$ such that in $C(t_n)$ all robots have been assembled into molecules, the molecules form an element in $\mathcal{F}$, and no entity moves after t_n, i.e., $C(t_k) = C(t_n)$ for each $t_k \geq t_n$.*

SYMMETRICITY OF A CONFIGURATION. Two undirected graphs $G = (V, E)$ and $G' = (V', E')$ are *isomorphic* if there is a bijection φ from V to V' such that $\{u, v\} \in E$ if and only if $\{\varphi(u), \varphi(v)\} \in E'$. An automorphism on a graph G is an isomorphism from G to itself, that is a permutation of the vertices of G that maps edges to edges and non-edges to non-edges. Two distinct vertices $u, v \in V$ are equivalent if there exists an automorphism $\varphi \in \mathrm{Aut}(G)$ such that $\varphi(u) = v$. The concept of graph isomorphism can be extended to configurations in a natural way. Two configurations $C = (G_S, R, \lambda, Mol)$ and $C' = (G'_S, R', \lambda', Mol')$ are isomorphic if there exists an isomorphism φ between G_S and G'_S that can be extended to obtain a bijection from $V \cup R$ to $V' \cup R'$ such that:

- two robots can be associated by φ only if they reside on equivalent vertices: if $\varphi(r) = r'$ then $\varphi(\lambda(r)) = \lambda'(r')$;
- it preserves molecules: if $\mu = \{r_{i_1}, \ldots, r_{i_t}\} \in Mol$ then $\{\varphi(r_{i_1}), \ldots, \varphi(r_{i_t})\} = \mu' \in Mol'$ and $\mu' = \mu$.

In this way, analogously to graph automorphism, an automorphism of a configuration $C = (G_S, R, \lambda, Mol)$ is an isomorphism from C to itself, and the set of all automorphisms of C forms a group under the composition operation that we call automorphism group of C and denote as $\mathrm{Aut}(C)$. Moreover, if $|\mathrm{Aut}(C)| = 1$ we say that C is **asymmetric**, otherwise it is **symmetric**. Two distinct robots r and r' in a configuration C are **equivalent** if there exists $\varphi \in \mathrm{Aut}(C)$ such that $\varphi(r) = r'$. Note that, the notion of equivalence also applies to molecules.

Remark 1. Let $C = (G_S, R, \lambda, Mol)$ be a symmetric configuration, $\mathcal{A}$ be any algorithm acting on C, and E be any maximal subset of pairwise equivalent entities in C. Any move planned by $\mathcal{A}$ for an element of E applies to all set E.

As chirality is assumed, it is easy to see that any configuration C defined on G_S admits one type of automorphisms only: **rotations**. A rotation is an isometry defined by a center c and a minimum angle of rotation $\alpha \in \{90, 180, 360\}$ working as follows: if the configuration is rotated around c by an angle α, then a configuration coincident with itself is obtained. The **order** of a configuration is given by $360/\alpha$. A configuration is **rotational** if its order is 2 or 4. The **type of center** of a rotational configuration C is denoted by $tc(C)$ and is equal to:

- 1, when the center of rotation is on a vertex of G_S (see Fig. 2 right represented by the dual grid);
- 2, when the center of rotation is on a median point of an edge of G_S;
- 3, when the center of rotation is on the center of a square of the tessellation forming G_S (see Fig. 2 left).

The **symmetricity** of a configuration C, denoted as $\rho(C)$, is equal to its order unless its center is occupied by one entity, in which case $\rho(C) = 1$. It comes out that when the configuration is constrained on G_S, then $\rho(C) \in \{1, 2, 4\}$.

We defined $\rho()$ and $tc()$ for any configuration $C = (G_S, R, \lambda, Mol)$ regardless whether Mol is empty or not. Concerning notation, we use $\rho(F)$ and $tc(F)$ to refer to any configuration forming a pattern $F \in \mathcal{F}$. As a special case, we use $\rho(\mu)$ and $tc(\mu)$ to refer to robots within a single molecule μ only. Moreover, for a given pattern $F \in \mathcal{F}$, let $Mol(F)$ denote the set of molecules that form F; clearly, each molecule in $Mol(F)$ also appears in $\mathcal{M}$. Our general result can be then formally stated:

Theorem 1. *Let $C = (G_S, R, \lambda, Mol)$ be any configuration composed of synchronous robots and $(C, \mathcal{M}, \mathcal{F})$ be an instance of the MPF problem. If there exists an algorithm $\mathcal{A}$ able to form a pattern $F \in \mathcal{F}$ from C, then one of the following holds:*

1. $\rho(C)$ *divides* $\rho(F)$ *and* $(\rho(C) > 1 \Rightarrow tc(C) = tc(F))$;
2. $\exists\, \mu \in Mol(F)$: $\rho(C)$ *divides* $\rho(\mu)$ *and* $(\rho(C) > 1 \Rightarrow tc(C) = tc(\mu))$.

4 The Tetris-Like MPF Problem

In this section, we introduce **Tetris-Like MPF** (TL-MPF for short), a particular version of the MPF problem. TL-MPF will be used as a case study of the MOBLOT model in order to appreciate its facets in grids.

We recall that a tetromino is formed by 4 robots and that two tetrominos cannot overlap. We say that two tetrominos are **adjacent** when robots belonging to distinct tetrominos are adjacent in G_S. In TL-MPF, $\mathcal{M}$ contains all the seven tetrominos, $\mathcal{F} = \{F\}$ (where F is any set of four or more tetrominos), and accordingly to the definition of F, the set of **initial** configurations consists of configurations in G_S having a multiple of 4 and with at least 16 robots. According to constraint $\mathcal{C}_1$, robots are pairwise non-adjacent.

Note that, each initial configuration C with $\rho(C) = 1$ is necessarily asymmetric. This implies that, in each initial configuration C, the symmetricity induces a partition of all the entities in subsets having the following relevant properties: (1) each set has size equal to $\rho(C)$, and (2) in each set, the entities are pairwise equivalent. Each set in this partition is called an **orbit**.

In principle, given an initial configuration C and a pattern F to be formed, it is possible that no algorithm exists for solving TL-MPF. We now specialize Theorem 1 to provide the definition of **potentially-formable patterns** from C. According to $\rho(C)$, we have the following cases:

Corollary 1. *Given a configuration C and a pattern $F \in \mathcal{F}$, F is potentially-formable from C if one of the following conditions hold:*

1. $\rho(C) = 1$;
2. $\rho(C) = 2$ *and*
   (a) $tc(C) = tc(F)$ *and* $\rho(F) \in \{2, 4\}$, *or*
   (b) $tc(C) = 2$ *and* $\{\mathtt{S}, \mathtt{Z}, \mathtt{I}\} \cap Mol(F) \neq \emptyset$, *or*
   (c) $tc(C) = 3$ *and* $\mathtt{O} \in Mol(F)$;
3. $\rho(C) = 4$ *and*
   (a) $tc(C) = tc(F)$ *and* $\rho(F) = 4$, *or*
   (b) $tc(C) = 3$ *and* $\mathtt{O} \in Mol(F)$.

In the following, we describe algorithm $\mathcal{A}_{\mathsf{TL}}$ that solves TL-MPF for each pair (C, F), where C is an initial configuration and F is potentially-formable from C. This provides a complete characterization of the feasibility of TL-MPF.

Table 1. The decomposition of TL-MPF into tasks, with SB standing for subproblem symmetry breaking by means of the formation of one central molecule.

Problem	Sub-problems	Task	Transitions
TL-MPF	MS: Make working Space	T_1	T_2, T_3
	Forming $\rho(C)$ new Molecules	T_2	T_4
	SB: forming one central molecule	T_3	T_4
	AM: Adding Molecules to pattern	T_4	T_2, T_5
	Term: problem Termination	T_5	–

4.1   How the Algorithm is Designed and Organized

The algorithm $\mathcal{A}_{\mathsf{TL}}$ has been designed according to the methodology proposed in [6]. It is based on a preliminary decomposition approach: the problem is divided into a set of sub-problems so that each sub-problem is simple enough to be thought as a **task** to be performed by (a subset of) entities. Table 1 (that will be better explained later) shows the decomposition into tasks for TL-MPF. $\mathcal{A}_{\mathsf{TL}}$ is responsible for allowing entities to detect which task must be accomplished in any configuration observed during an execution. This is realized by assigning a **predicate** P_i to task T_i, for each i. The predicate is evaluated in the Compute phase on the basis of the view acquired during the Look phase. As soon as entities recognize that a task T_i must be accomplished, a move m_i – associated to that task, is performed by a subset of designed entities. Predicates P_i are designed to guarantee the following required properties:

- Prop$_1$: each P_i must be computable on the configuration perceived in each Look phase;
- Prop$_2$: $P_i \wedge P_j = \mathtt{false}$, for each $i \neq j$;
- Prop$_3$: for each possible perceived configuration there must exists a predicate P_i evaluated as true.

In order to make Prop$_2$ valid, P_i is defined as follows:

$$P_i = \mathtt{pre}_i \wedge \neg(\mathtt{pre}_{i+1} \vee \mathtt{pre}_{i+2} \vee \ldots \vee \mathtt{pre}_5), \tag{1}$$

where $\mathtt{pre}_i$ is the **precondition**[1] that characterizes T_i. To be sure that Prop$_3$ holds, in the Compute phase each entity evaluates – with respect to the perceived configuration and the provided input – the preconditions starting from $\mathtt{pre}_5$ and proceeding in the reverse order until a true precondition is found. In case all predicates $P_5, P_4, \ldots, P_2$ are evaluated false, then task T_1, whose precondition is simply $\mathtt{true}$, is performed. It follows that the provided algorithm $\mathcal{A}_{\mathsf{TL}}$ can be used by each entity in the Compute phase as follows:

- *if an entity executing the algorithm detects that predicate P_i holds, then it simply performs move m_i associated with T_i.*

---

[1] Specific conditions that must be verified in order to start a given task.

In the next section, we give a description of each task T_i, by including details about the corresponding move m_i and precondition pre_i. The reader will be able to observe that, from the definition of the preconditions, it follows that also $Prop_1$ holds.

4.2 Detailed Description of the Five Tasks

As shown in Table 1, the problem has been decomposed into five tasks. To describe $\mathcal{A}_{TL}$ in detail, some further definitions are required. Let $mbr(R)$ denote the **minimum bounding rectangle** of R, that is the smallest rectangle (with sides parallel to the edges of G_S) enclosing all robots. Note that $mbr(R)$ is unique. By $c(R)$ we denote the center of $mbr(R)$. Similarly, $mbr(F)$ is defined for the minimum bounding rectangle enclosing the molecules forming F. In the following, we use the term *partial-molecule* to refer to a pair of adjacent robots that can be later used to assemble a molecule. Note that, by Property $\mathcal{C}_1$, a partial-molecule cannot exist in initial configurations. We define *point-joined-robots*, the configuration in which two robots are aligned along the diagonal of a cell of the grid and their corresponding monominoes in the dual graph intersect in one point. *Mol* denotes the set of all the molecules formed so far; $F' \subseteq Mol$ is the set of formed molecules that are already assembled to form the matter, i.e., a sub-pattern of F.

THE VIEW OF THE ROBOTS. Robots encode the perceived configuration into a binary string denoted as $LSS(R)$ (Lexicographically Smallest String) and computed as follows (cf. [1]). They assign a string to each corner of $mbr(R)$: the grid enclosed by $mbr(R)$ is analyzed row by row or column by column - the direction is given by the smallest side of $mbr(R)$ - and 1 or 0 correspond to the presence or the absence, resp., of a robot for each encountered vertex. From the 4 corners they get up to 8 different strings, and the lexicographically smaller one is $LSS(R)$. Note that if two strings obtained from opposite corners along opposite directions are equal, then the configuration is rotational, otherwise it is asymmetric. The robot(s) with **minimum view** is the one with minimum position in $LSS(R)$. The same approach can be used for F but with strings formed by letters (i.e., if the analyzed vertex is occupied by a robot forming molecule Z, then Z is inserted in the string, otherwise, if the vertex is unoccupied, X is inserted).

TASKS T_1 - MAKE WORKING SPACE. The goal of this task is to increase the distance between robots. In fact, in an initial configuration, robots might be too close to each other (e.g., when robots occupy alternatively the vertices of the grid) and the movements might cause the formation of undesired partial-molecules. During T_1, according to Remark 1, robots move away from $c(R)$. At the end of the task, consecutive orbits of robots are at distance at least $\delta = 2$ from each other and there is also an empty space Q in the center of the configuration that contains at most the robots of the orbit closest to $c(R)$. The space Q is a square centered in $c(R)$ and its side is $side(Q) = 2S$, where $S = \max\{w(F), h(F)\}$ and $w(F)$ and $h(F)$ are the width and the height, resp.,

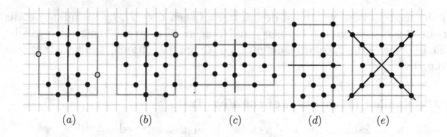

Fig. 3. Division of $mbr(R)$ into regions based on shape and $\rho(C)$. The $mbr(R)$ is shown in blue. Robots with the minimum view are shown in grey only when needed. (Color figure online)

of $mbr(F)$. The fixed distance δ guarantees that robots have enough space for moving and creating a molecule.

We now provide all details necessary to formalize the move m_1. The first necessary step is that of dividing $mbr(R)$ into **regions** according to $\rho(C)$, cf. Figure 3. If $\rho(C) = 4$ then $mbr(R)$ is a square and hence it is partitioned by using two diagonals. If $\rho(C) = 2$ and $mbr(R)$ is a square, it is partitioned into 2 equal regions by a line passing through $c(R)$ and parallel to the sides of $mbr(R)$ where the robots with minimal view reside.[2] If $\rho(C) = 1$ and $mbr(R)$ is a square, it is partitioned into 2 equal regions by a line passing through $c(R)$ and parallel to the side of $mbr(R)$ where the robot with minimum view resides. If $\rho(C) = 1, 2$ and $mbr(R)$ is a rectangle, it is partitioned into 2 equal regions by a line passing through $c(R)$ and parallel to the shorter sides.

Each robot belongs to one of the formed regions, unless it is on a half-line of the lines used for partitioning $mbr(R)$; in this case, the robot belongs to the region to the right of the half-line. Each side ℓ of $mbr(R)$ entirely contained in a region is said to be "associated with" that region.

When $\rho(C) = 2, 4$, robots in each region are numbered as follows. Let ℓ be the side of $mbr(R)$ associated with the region, and v be the leftmost vertex of ℓ. Robots are numbered starting from v, proceeding along ℓ, then continuing in order with all the lines parallel to ℓ. By assuming that the region contains t robots, the first met robot is numbered as r^t and the remaining, in order, as $r^{t-1}, \ldots, r^1$. It is clear that the robots in a region all belong to different orbits and therefore the numbering of robots can be understood as a numbering for the orbits. Hence, orbits are denoted as $O^t, O^{t-1}, \ldots, O^1$.

When $\rho(C) = 1$, the two defined regions may have a different number of robots inside, say t_1 and t_2. Robots are numbered as in the previous cases in both the regions, but they are denoted as $\dot{r}^{t_1}, \ldots, \dot{r}^1$ in the region containing the robot with minimum view, and as $\ddot{r}^{t_2}, \ldots, \ddot{r}^1$ in the other region. Hence, orbits are denoted as $\dot{O}^{t_1}, \dot{O}^{t_1-1}, \ldots, \dot{O}^1$, and $\ddot{O}^{t_2}, \ddot{O}^{t_2-1}, \ldots, \ddot{O}^1$. Let $O^t, \ldots, O^1$,

---

[2] If the robot with minimum view is on a corner, it is assumed to reside on the clockwise side of $mbr(R)$.

with $t = t_1 + t_2$, such that $O^t = \dot{O}^{t_1}, O^{t-1} = \ddot{O}^{t_2}$ and the remaining orbits $O^{t-2}, \ldots, O^1$ are defined by keeping orbits from the two regions in an alternating fashion as long as possible. Let r be a robot in a region associated with a side ℓ, and assume $r \in O^i$: $cd_Q(O^i)$ represents the "current distance" of O^i from Q (that is the distance between r and the side of Q parallel to ℓ), it is negative if r is inside Q; $fd_Q(O^i)$ represents the "final distance" of O^i from Q, that is the distance that robots on O^i must have when the orbit is correctly positioned. These functions are formally defined as follows. When $\rho(C) = 2, 4$:

- $fd_Q(O^1) = \max\{S + 1, cd_Q(O^1)\}$
- $fd_Q(O^i) = \max\{fd_Q(O^{i-1}) + \delta, cd_Q(O^{i-1})\}, \forall i > 1$

When $\rho(C) = 1$:

- $fd_Q(O^1) = \max\{S + 1, cd_Q(O^1)\}$
- $fd_Q(O^i) = \max\{fd_Q(O^{i-1}) + \delta, cd_Q(O^{i-1})\}, \forall i > 1, i < t - 1$
- $fd_Q(O^t) = fd_Q(O^{t-1}) = \max\{fd_Q(O^{t-2}) + \delta, cd_Q(O^{t-2})\}$

Move m_1 works as follows: *each robot in O^j, for each $j > 1$, moves perpendicularly to the side ℓ of $mbr(R)$ which it is associated to, increasing its distance from $c(R)$, until $cd_Q(O^j) = fd_Q(O^j)$*. Note that the task makes all robots moving concurrently. By defining the two Boolean variables

- $P(k) = $ *each orbit O^i , $i > k$, is correctly positioned with respect to $fd_Q()$*;
- $Q = $ *square Q is formed with at most one orbit inside*,

it can be observed that task T_1 ends when both $P(1)$ and Q hold.

TASK T_2 - MOLECULES FORMATION. The goal of this task is to create $\rho(C)$ new molecules to be added to the matter F' formed so far. Let B' be a Boolean variable that is true when one among the conditions 1, 2.a, and 3.a of Corollary 1 hold. Notice that in all such cases $\rho(F)$ is a multiple of $\rho(C)$, and when $\rho(C) > 1$ then C and F have the same type of center.

In order to be executed, T_2 requires that B' holds and T_1 is completed (i.e., $P(1)$ and Q hold). If *ParMol* denotes the number of partial molecules formed, then the precondition of T_2 is the following:

$$\mathbf{pre}_2 = B' \wedge |Mol \setminus F'| = 0 \wedge ((P(1) \wedge Q) \vee ParMol = \rho(C)).$$

In this task, a relevant issue is that robots have to agree on which molecule μ in F must be formed (in $\rho(C)$ copies).

Definition 2 (Disassembling sequence). *Let F be a pattern and ℓ be a side of $mbr(F)$ encoded with the minimal string within $LSS(F)$. Perform the following iterative process: (1) mark all molecules in F and create an empty ordered list $S(F)$, (2) with respect to the marked molecules only, compute the set E of all the molecules that can be "extracted" from F through ℓ;[3] (3) insert in $S(F)$ the molecule $\mu \in E$ with minimum view, (4) unmark all the molecules belonging to the same orbit of μ, (5) iterate from (2) until marked orbits exist. The order of the elements belonging $S(F)$ constitutes a disassembling sequence for F.*

---

[3] I.e., when the molecule's projection on ℓ is not obstructed by any other molecule.

For instance, $\mathcal{S}(F) = (\mathtt{J}, \mathtt{0}, \mathtt{Z})$ for the pattern F shown in Fig. 2 (where ℓ coincides with the left and right sides). The algorithm selects the molecule μ to build by comparing the formed sub-pattern F' with F. According to this comparison, the algorithm searches for molecules μ' and μ'' in F' having minimum and maximum positions in $\mathcal{S}(F)$, resp.; if μ'' is not the last element in $\mathcal{S}(F)$, then μ is the next to μ'' in $\mathcal{S}(F)$, otherwise it precedes μ' in $\mathcal{S}(F)$. In this way, the disassembling sequence in $\mathcal{S}(F)$ is used to correctly compose the pattern.

Let $O_1^*, O_2^*, O_3^*, O_4^*$ be the consecutive orbits closest to $c(R)$ and containing robots not involved in any molecule. Move m_2 works as follows:

- If no partial-molecule is formed, then each robot in O_1^* moves toward the robot in O_2^* belonging to the same region,
- else, each robot closest to $c(R)$, excluding those forming the partial-molecule, moves toward the partial-molecule within the same region toward a position adjacent to the partial-molecule and according to molecule μ to be formed.

The configuration obtained after task T_2 contains $\rho(C)$ **new molecules**.

TASKS T_3 - CENTRAL MOLECULE FORMATION. This task processes the configurations of robots fulfilling one among the conditions 2.b, 2.c, and 3.b from Corollary 1 defining the patterns F that are potentially-formable from C.

This task is alternative to T_2 as it builds a single molecule μ in the center of C, usually when it is required to break the symmetry by means of a molecule. Let B be a Boolean variable that it is true if one among the conditions 2.b, 2.c, and 3.b from Corollary 1 holds. Note that T_3 activates only when the square Q is formed. Let PJR be a boolean variable that is true if there exist two point-joined-robots. In particular, the precondition of T_3 is equal to:
$$\mathbf{pre}_3 = B \wedge ((P(1) \wedge |Mol| = 0) \vee (P(2) \wedge (ParMol = 1 \vee PJR))).$$
Robots must agree on which molecule in F must be formed as first. It corresponds to the molecule fulfilling conditions 2.b, 2.c, and 3.b of the definition of potentially-formable pattern and with the highest position on the disassembling sequence of F. Four robots belonging to one or two orbits O_1, O_2 (according whether $\rho(C) = 4$ or $\rho(C) = 2$, resp.) closest to $c(R)$ are selected. μ is embedded on the grid so that the center of the molecule coincides with $c(R)$.

Move m_3 works as follows:

- if $\rho(C)=2$, then first robots in O_1 move toward $c(R)$ until reaching the minimum reciprocal distance, then robots in O_2 move toward O_1 by suitably form the desired molecule μ;
- if $\rho(C)=4$, robots in O_1 move toward $c(R)$ until forming $\mu = \mathtt{0}$.

The task ends when all the 4 moving robots reach their targets and the molecule is built with its center in $c(R)$. At the end of task T_3, a new configuration C' is obtained with $\rho(C') = 1$. TASK T_4 - MOLECULES AGGREGATION. During this task, the molecules built during T_2 or T_3 move to start forming F' or to be aggregated to F' (created by previous executions of this task). We define **quadrant** any of the four areas into which the square Q is divided by two orthogonal lines parallel to the sides of Q and intersecting in $c(R)$. To test if the pattern creation has already started, robots check whether (1) there exists a sub-pattern F' in one of the four quadrants, or (2) there exists a sub-pattern F' embedded so that it is centered in $c(R)$. This allows robots to evaluate the following precondition of T_4: $\mathtt{pre}_4 = |Mol \setminus F'| > 0$.

During this task, $\rho(C)$ can be 1, 2 or 4. To correctly determine the move to be performed, the algorithm considers four disjoint cases, which are defined according to $\rho(C)$, F', and Mol.

(Case 1) $\rho(C) = 1$, $|F'| = 0$, $Mol = \{\mu\}$, and μ is centered in $c(R)$. It is clear that the current configuration C has been created in T_3. In this case, m_4 breaks the symmetry by simply moving μ away from the center in an arbitrary direction. Notice that, in the formed configuration C' we have $\rho(C') = 1$, $|F'| = 0$, $Mol = \{\mu\}$, and μ is no longer centered in $c(C')$.

(Case 2) $\rho(C) = 1$, $|F'| = 0$, $Mol = \{\mu\}$, and μ is not centered in $c(R)$. The current configuration has been created in T_4 (Case 1), or by T_2. F is meant to be embedded in the quadrant q of Q closest to μ, and m_4 moves μ toward the position in the embedded F corresponding to the minimum position of its shape in the disassembling sequence $S(F)$. Concerning how F is embedded into q: let ℓ be a side of $mbr(F)$ used in the disassembling sequence (cf. Definition 2), and let c be the corner of ℓ with larger label; c is mapped on the vertex in q closest to $c(R)$, and ℓ is mapped on the counter-clockwise internal side of q. Notice that this embedding is used whenever the configuration is asymmetric.

(Case 3) $\rho(C) = 1$ and $|F'| > 0$. In this case, there exists only one molecule μ which is not part of F'. Move m_4 moves μ toward its target identified by comparing F' with the position of μ in the disassembling sequence of F.

(Case 4) $\rho(C) > 1$ and $|Mol \setminus F'| = \rho(C)$. In this case, F' is embedded so that it is centered in $c(R)$. There are exactly $\rho(C)$ molecules which are not part of F', and they must be moved toward their final targets. The final targets are obtained by comparing F with F'. During the movements, each molecule remains in the same region. The last time this task is executed, F is finally formed.

TASK T_5. It refers to the **termination** problem i.e., entities recognize the pattern is formed and no one has to move , $\mathtt{pre}_5 = $ "F is formed".

4.3   Correctness

According to the described algorithm, the possible transitions that can occur from each task are $T_1 \rightarrow \{T_2, T_3\}$, $T_2 \rightarrow T_4$, $T_3 \rightarrow T_4$, $T_4 \rightarrow \{T_2, T_5\}$. The correctness of $\mathcal{A}_{\mathsf{TL}}$ is obtained by proving all the following properties: (1) for each configuration C' generated by $\mathcal{A}_{\mathsf{TL}}$, F remains potentially-solvable from C', (2) no multiplicities are created, (3) for each task T_i, the transitions from T_i are exactly those declared above, (4) each transition occurs within finite time, and (5) possible cycles among transitions are traversed a finite number of times. The detected transitions show that from a given task, only subsequent tasks can be reached, or TL-MPF is solved. The only exception is the cycle among tasks T_2/T_4. However, in this case, each time T_4 is performed, the number of molecules composing the matter F' increases, and since no molecule is moved away from F', the final task T_5 is reached from T_4 within finite time. Along with Theorem 1, this implies the following characterization:

Theorem 2. $\mathcal{A}_{\mathsf{TL}}$ *solves the TL-MPF problem for C and F if and only if F is potentially-formable from C.*

5   Conclusion

In this paper, we have considered the MOBLOT model where robots move along the edges of a graph. We have focused on the Molecular Pattern Formation (MPF) problem where the final configuration is composed by molecules only. For MPF, we have proven a necessary condition for its resolution. As a case study, we have introduced the TL-MPF problem, where robots move along a square grid and the possible molecules to be formed are all the tetrominos. We have identified when TL-MPF is potentially solvable and for all such cases we have provided a resolution distributed algorithm, hence proving a full characterization.

References

1. Cicerone, S., Di Fonso, A., Di Stefano, G., Navarra, A.: Arbitrary pattern formation on infinite regular tessellation graphs. In: Proceedings of the 22nd International Conference on Distributed Computing and Networking (ICDCN), pp. 56–65. ACM, New York, NY, USA (2021). https://doi.org/10.1145/3427796.3427833
2. Cicerone, S., Di Fonso, A., Di Stefano, G., Navarra, A.: MOBLOT: molecular oblivious robots. In: Dignum, F., Lomuscio, A., Endriss, U., Nowé, A. (eds.) AAMAS '21: 20th International Conference on Autonomous Agents and Multiagent Systems, Virtual Event, United Kingdom, 3–7 May 2021, pp. 350–358. ACM (2021)
3. Cicerone, S., Di Stefano, G., Navarra, A.: Asynchronous arbitrary pattern formation: the effects of a rigorous approach. Distrib. Comput. **32**(2), 91–132 (2019). https://doi.org/10.1007/s00446-018-0325-7
4. Cicerone, S., Di Stefano, G., Navarra, A.: Asynchronous robots on graphs: gathering. In: Flocchini, P., Prencipe, G., Santoro, N. (eds.) Distributed Computing by Mobile Entities, Current Research in Moving and Computing. LNCS, vol. 11340, pp. 184–217. Springer, Cham (2019). https://doi.org/10.1007/978-3-030-11072-7_8
5. Cicerone, S., Di Stefano, G., Navarra, A.: Solving the pattern formation by mobile robots with chirality. IEEE Access **9**, 88177–88204 (2021). https://doi.org/10.1109/ACCESS.2021.3089081
6. Cicerone, S., Di Stefano, G., Navarra, A.: A structured methodology for designing distributed algorithms for mobile entities. Inf. Sci. **574**, 111–132 (2021). https://doi.org/10.1016/j.ins.2021.05.043
7. Cieliebak, M., Flocchini, P., Prencipe, G., Santoro, N.: Distributed computing by mobile robots: gathering. SIAM J. Comput. **41**(4), 829–879 (2012)
8. D'Angelo, G., D'Emidio, M., Das, S., Navarra, A., Prencipe, G.: Asynchronous silent programmable matter achieves leader election and compaction. IEEE Access **8**, 207619–207634 (2020)

9. D'Angelo, G., Di Stefano, G., Navarra, A.: Gathering asynchronous and oblivious robots on basic graph topologies under the look-compute-move model. In: Alpern, S., Fokkink, R., Gąsieniec, L., Lindelauf, R., Subrahmanian, V. (eds.) Search Theory: A Game Theoretic Perspective, pp. 197–222. Springer, New York, NY (2013). https://doi.org/10.1007/978-1-4614-6825-7_13

10. Daymude, J.J., et al.: On the runtime of universal coating for programmable matter. Nat. Comput. **17**(1), 81–96 (2018). https://doi.org/10.1007/s11047-017-9658-6

11. Di Stefano, G., Navarra, A.: Optimal gathering of oblivious robots in anonymous graphs and its application on trees and rings. Distrib. Comput. **30**(2), 75–86 (2017). https://doi.org/10.1007/s00446-016-0278-7

12. Flocchini, P., Prencipe, G., Santoro, N.: Self-deployment of mobile sensors on a ring. Theor. Comput. Sci. **402**(1), 67–80 (2008)

13. Flocchini, P., Prencipe, G., Santoro, N.: Moving and computing models: robots. In: Flocchini, P., Prencipe, G., Santoro, N. (eds.) Distributed Computing by Mobile Entities, Current Research in Moving and Computing. Lecture Notes in Computer Science, vol. 11340, pp. 3–14. Springer, Cham (2019). https://doi.org/10.1007/978-3-030-11072-7_1

14. Golomb, S.W., Klarner, D.A.: Polyominoes. In: Handbook of Discrete and Computational Geometry, 2nd Ed., pp. 331–352. Chapman and Hall/CRC, London (2004). https://doi.org/10.1201/9781420035315.ch15

15. Kim, Y., Katayama, Y., Wada, K.: Pairbot: a novel model for autonomous mobile robot systems consisting of paired robots (2020)

16. Prencipe, G.: Pattern formation. In: Flocchini, P., Prencipe, G., Santoro, N. (eds.) Distributed Computing by Mobile Entities, Current Research in Moving and Computing. Lecture Notes in Computer Science, vol. 11340, pp. 37–62. Springer, Cham (2019). https://doi.org/10.1007/978-3-030-11072-7_3

17. Romanishin, J.W., Gilpin, K., Claici, S., Rus, D.: 3D M-Blocks: self-reconfiguring robots capable of locomotion via pivoting in three dimensions. In: Proceedings of the IEEE International Conference on Robotics and Automation (ICRA), pp. 1925–1932 (2015)

18. Rubenstein, M., Ahler, C., Nagpal, R.: Kilobot: a low cost scalable robot system for collective behaviors. In: IEEE International Conference on Robotics and Automation (ICRA), pp. 3293–3298. IEEE (2012). https://doi.org/10.1109/ICRA.2012.6224638

19. Suzuki, I., Yamashita, M.: Distributed anonymous mobile robots: formation of geometric patterns. SIAM J. Comput. **28**(4), 1347–1363 (1999)

Centralised Connectivity-Preserving Transformations by Rotation: 3 Musketeers for All Orthogonal Convex Shapes

Matthew Connor$^{(\boxtimes)}$ and Othon Michail

Department of Computer Science, University of Liverpool, Liverpool, UK
{M.Connor3,Othon.Michail}@liverpool.ac.uk

Abstract. We study a model of programmable matter systems consisting of n devices lying on the cells of a 2-dimensional square grid, which are able to perform the minimal mechanical operation of rotating around each other. The goal is to transform an initial shape of devices A into a target shape B. We are interested in characterising the class of shapes which can be transformed into each other in such a scenario, under the additional constraint of maintaining global connectivity at all times. This was one of the main problems left open by [Michail *et al.*, JCSS'19]. Note that the considered question is about structural feasibility of transformations, which we exclusively deal with via centralised constructive proofs. Distributed solutions are left for future work and form an interesting research direction. Past work made some progress for the special class of colour-consistent *nice* shapes. We here consider the class of *orthogonal convex shapes*, where for any two nodes u, v in a horizontal or vertical line on the grid, there is no empty cell between u and v. We develop a generic centralised transformation and prove that, for any pair A, B of colour-consistent orthogonal convex shapes, it can transform A into B. In light of the existence of *blocked* shapes in the considered class, we use a minimal 3-node *seed* (additional nodes placed at the start) to trigger the transformation. The running time of our transformation is an optimal $O(n^2)$ sequential moves, where $n = |A| = |B|$. We leave as an open problem the existence of a universal connectivity-preserving transformation with a small seed. Our belief is that the techniques developed in this paper might prove useful to answer this.

Keywords: Programmable matter · Transformation · Reconfigurable robotics · Shape formation · Centralised algorithms

1 Introduction

Programmable matter refers to matter which can change its physical properties algorithmically. This means that the change is the result following the procedure

The full paper including all omitted details is available on arXiv at: https://arxiv.org/abs/2207.03062.

© The Author(s), under exclusive license to Springer Nature Switzerland AG 2022
T. Erlebach and M. Segal (Eds.): ALGOSENSORS 2022, LNCS 13707, pp. 60–76, 2022.
https://doi.org/10.1007/978-3-031-22050-0_5

of an underlying program. The implementation of the program can either be a system-level external centralised algorithm or an internal decentralised algorithm executed by the material itself. The model for such systems can be further refined to specify properties that are relevant to real-world applications, for example connectivity, colour [4] and other physical properties.

As the development of these systems continues, it becomes increasingly necessary to develop theoretical models which are capable of describing and explaining the emergent properties, possibilities and limitations of such systems in an abstract and fundamental manner. To this end, models have been developed for programmable matter. For example, algorithmic self-assembly [10,19] focuses on programming molecules like DNA to grow in a controllable way, and the Abstract Tile Assembly Model [20,25], the Kilobot model [21], the Robot Pebbles system [14], and the nubot model [26], have all been developed for this area. Network Constructors [18] is an extension of population protocols [3] that allows for network formation and reconfiguration. The latter model is formally equivalent to a restricted version of chemical reaction networks, which "are widely used to describe information processing occurring in natural cellular regulatory networks" [11,22]. The CATOMS system [12,23,24] is a further implementation which constructs 3D shapes by first creating a "scaffolding structure" as a basis for construction. Finally, there is extensive research into the amoebot model [6–9], where finite automata on a triangular lattice follow a distributed algorithm to achieve a desired goal, including a recent extension [13] to a circuit-based model.

Recent progress in this direction has been made in previous papers, for example [17], covering questions related to a specific model of programmable matter where nodes exist in the form of a shape on a 2D grid and are capable of performing two specific movements: rotation around each other and sliding a node across two other nodes. The authors investigated the problem of transformations with rotations with the restriction that shapes must always remain connected (RotC-Transformability), and left universal RotC-Transformability as an open problem. They hinted at the possibility of universal transformation in an arxiv draft [16]. To the best of our knowledge, progress on this open question has only been made in [5], where, by using a small seed, connectivity-preserving transformations by rotation were developed for a restricted class of shapes. In general, such transformations are highly desirable due to the large numbers of programmable matter systems which rely on the preservation of connectivity and the simplicity of movement, which is not only of theoretical interest but is also more likely to be applicable to real-world systems. Related progress was also made in [1], which used a similar model but with a different type of movement. The authors allowed for a greater range of movement, for example "leapfrog" and "monkey" movements. They accomplished universal transformation in $O(n^2)$ movements using a "bridging" procedure assisted by at most 5 seed-nodes, which they called *musketeers*.

2   Contribution

We investigate the RotC-Transformability problem, introduced in [17], which asks to characterise which families of connected shapes can be transformed into each other via rotation movements without breaking connectivity. The model represents programmable matter on a 2D grid which is only capable of performing rotation movements, defined as the 90° rotation of a node u around a neighbouring edge-adjacent node v, so long as the goal and intermediate cells are empty. As our focus is on the feasibility and complexity of transformations, our approach is naturally based on structural characterisations and *centralised* procedures. Structural and algorithmic progress is expected to facilitate more applied future developments, such as distributed implementations.

We assume the existence of a *seed*, a group of nodes in a shape S which are placed in empty cells neighbouring a shape A to create a new connected shape which is the unification of S and A. Seeds allow shapes which are blocked or incapable of meaningful movement to perform otherwise impossible transformations. The use of seeds was established in [17], leaving open the problem of universal RotC-Transformability. Another work [5] investigated this problem in the context of *nice* shapes, first defined in [2] as a set of shapes containing any shape S which has a central line L, where, for all nodes $u \in S$, either $u \in L$ or u is connected to L by a line of nodes perpendicular to L. Universal reconfiguration in the context of connectivity-preserving transformations using different types of movement has been demonstrated in [1]. That paper calls the seed nodes "musketeers" and their transformation requires the use of 5 such nodes.

The present paper moves towards a solution which is based on connectivity-preservation and the tighter constraints of rotation-only movement of [17] while aiming to (i) widen the characterization of the class of transformable shapes and (ii) minimise the seed required to trigger those transformations. By achieving these objectives for orthogonal convex shapes, we make further progress towards the ultimate goal of an exact characterisation (possibly universal) for seed-assisted RotC-Transformability.

We study the transformation of shapes of size n with *orthogonal convexity* into other shapes of size n with the same property, via the canonical shape of a *diagonal line-with-leaves*. Orthogonal convexity is the property that for any two nodes u, v in a horizontal or vertical line on the grid, there is no empty cell between u and v. A diagonal line-with-leaves is a group of components, the main being a series of 2-node columns where each column is offset such that the order of the nodes is equivalent to a line, and two optional components: two 1-node columns on either end of the shape and additional nodes above each column, making them into 3-node columns. We show that transforming a orthogonal convex shape of n nodes into a diagonal line-with-leaves is possible and can be achieved by $O(n^2)$ moves using a 3-node seed. This bound on the number of moves is optimal for the considered class, due to a matching lower bound from [17] on the distance between a line and a staircase, both of which are orthogonal convex shapes. A seed is necessary due to the existence of blocked orthogonal convex shapes, an example being a rhombus. As [5] shows, any seed with less than 3 nodes is incapable of non-trivial transformation of a line of nodes. Since a line of nodes is orthogonal convex, the 3-node seed employed here is minimal.

The class of orthogonal convex shapes cannot easily be compared to the class of nice shapes. A diagonal line of nodes in the form of a staircase belongs to the former but not the latter. Any nice shape containing a gap between two of its columns is not a orthogonal convex shape. Finally, there are shapes like a square of nodes which belong to both classes. Nevertheless, the nice shapes that are not orthogonal convex have turned out to be much easier to handle than the orthogonal convex shapes that are not nice. We hope that the methods we had to develop in order to deal with the latter class of shapes, will bring us one step closer to an exact characterisation of connectivity-preserving transformations by rotation.

In Sect. 3, we formally define the programmable matter model used in this paper. Section 4 presents some basic properties of orthogonal convex shapes and of their elimination and generation sequences. In Sect. 5, we provide our algorithm for the construction of the diagonal line-with-leaves which, through reversibility, can be used to construct other orthogonal convex shapes and give time bounds for it. In Sect. 6, we conclude and give directions for potential future research.

3   Model

We consider the case of programmable matter on a 2D grid, with each position (or cell) of the grid being uniquely referred to by its (x, y) coordinates. Such a system consists of a set V of n nodes. Each node may be viewed as a spherical module fitting inside a cell of the grid. At any given time, each node occupies a cell, with the positioning of the nodes defining a shape, and no two nodes may occupy the same cell. It also defines an undirected *neighbouring relation* $E \subset V \times V$, where $uv \in E$ iff u and v occupy *horizontally* or *vertically* adjacent cells of the grid. A shape is *connected* if the graph induced by its neighbouring relation is a connected graph.

In general, shapes can *transform* to other shapes via a sequence of one or more movements of individual nodes. We consider only one type of movement: *rotation*. In this movement, a single node moves relative to one or more neighbouring nodes. A single rotation movement of a node u is a 90° rotation of u around one of its neighbours. Let (x, y) be the current position of u and let its neighbour be v occupying the cell $(x, y - 1)$ (i.e., lying below u). Then u can rotate 90° clockwise (counterclockwise) around v iff the cells $(x + 1, y)$ and $(x + 1, y - 1)$ $((x - 1, y)$ and $(x - 1, y - 1)$, respectively) are both empty. By rotating the whole system 90°, 180°, and 270°, all possible rotation movements can be defined.

Let A and B be two connected shapes. We say that A transforms to B via a rotation r, denoted $A \xrightarrow{r} B$, if there is a node u in A such that if u applies r, then the shape resulting after the rotation is B. We say that A transforms in one step to B (or that B is reachable in one step from A), denoted $A \rightarrow B$, if $A \xrightarrow{r} B$ for some rotation r. We say that A transforms to B (or that B is reachable from

A) if there is a sequence of shapes $A = S_1, S_2, \ldots, S_t = B$, such that $S_i \rightarrow S_{i+1}$ for all $1 \leq i \leq t - 1$. Rotation is a reversible movement, a fact that we use in our results. All shapes $S_1, S_2, \ldots, S_t$ must be *edge connected*, meaning that the graph defined by the neighbouring relation E of all nodes in any S_i, where $1 \leq i \leq t$, must be a connected graph.

At the start of the transformation, we will be assuming the existence of a *seed*: a small connected shape M placed on the perimeter of the given shape S to trigger the transformation. This is essential because under rotation-only there are shapes S that are k-blocked, meaning that at most $k \geq 0$ moves can be made before a configuration is repeated. When $k = 0$, no move is possible from S, an example of 0-blocked shape being the rhombus.

For the sake of providing clarity to our transformations, we say that every cell in the 2D grid has a colour from $\{red, black\}$ in such a way that the cells form a black and red checkered colouring of the grid, similar to the colouring of a chessboard. This colouring is fixed so long as there is at least one node on the grid. This represents a property of the rotation movement, which is that any given node in a coloured cell can only enter cells of the same colour. We define $c(u) \in \{black, red\}$ as the colour of node u for a given chessboard colouring of the grid. We represent this in our figures by colouring the nodes red or black. See Fig. 1 for an example and for special notation that we use to abbreviate certain rotations which we perform throughout the paper.

Fig. 1. The rotation on the left is an abbreviated version of the rotations on the right, used throughout the paper. The numbers represent the order of rotations. Red nodes appear grey in print, throughout the paper. (Color figure online)

Any shape S may be viewed as a coloured shape consisting of $b(S)$ blacks and $r(S)$ reds. Two shapes A and B are *colour-consistent* if $b(A) = b(B)$ and $r(A) = r(B)$. For any shape S of n nodes, the *parity* of S is the colour of the majority of nodes in S. If there is no strict majority, we pick any as the parity colour. We use *non-parity* to refer to the colour which is not the parity.

Depending on the context and purpose, the term *node* will be used to refer both to the actual entity that may move between co-ordinates and to the co-ordinates of that entity at a given time.

The *perimeter* of a connected shape S is the minimum-area polygon that completely encloses S in its interior, existence of an interior and exterior directly following from the Jordan curve theorem [15]. The *cell perimeter* of S consists of every cell of the grid not occupied by S that contributes at least one of its edges to the perimeter of S. The *external surface* of S consists of all nodes $u \in S$ such that u occupies a cell defining at least one of the edges of the perimeter of S. The *extended external surface* of S is then defined by adding to the external surface all nodes of S whose cell shares a corner with the perimeter of S. A *line* (of nodes) of length k is a series of consecutive nodes $u_1, u_2, \ldots, u_k$ in a given row or column. For a line $u_1, u_2, \ldots, u_k$, we refer to u_1 and u_k as the *end nodes* or *endpoints* of the line. Our proofs make use of column and row analysis, by dividing connected orthogonal convex shapes into p rows $R_1, R_2, \ldots, R_p$ and q columns $C_1, C_2, \ldots, C_q$. We assume without loss of generality (abbreviated to "w.l.o.g." throughout) that R_1 and C_1 are the bottom-most row and leftmost column, respectively. We use $a \times b$ to refer to a rectangle of a rows and b columns, where all rows and columns are fully occupied.

We use σ and variants to denote sequences of nodes. A *k-sub-sequence* σ' of a sequence σ is any sub-sequence of σ where $|\sigma'| = k$. For a given colouring of the grid, the *colour sequence* $c(\sigma)$ of a sequence of nodes $\sigma = (u_1, u_2, \ldots, u_n)$ is defined as $c(\sigma) = (c(u_1), c(u_2), \ldots, c(u_n))$. A sequence σ' is *colour-order preserving* w.r.t σ if $c(\sigma') = c(\sigma)$. A sequence of nodes $\sigma = (u_1, u_2, \ldots, u_n)$ is called *single-coloured* if $c(\sigma)$ satisfies $c(u_i) = s$ for all $1 \leq i \leq n$ and some $s \in \{black, red\}$.

4 Preliminaries

4.1 Orthogonal Convex Shapes

We now present the class of shapes considered in this paper together with some basic properties about them that will be useful later.

Definition 1. *A shape S is said to belong to the family of orthogonal convex shapes, if, for any pair of distinct nodes $(x_1, y_1), (x_2, y_2) \in S$, $x_1 = x_2$ implies $(x_1, y) \in S$ for all $\min\{y_1, y_2\} < y < \max\{y_1, y_2\}$ while $y_1 = y_2$ implies $(x, y_1) \in S$ for all $\min\{x_1, x_2\} < x < \max\{x_1, x_2\}$.*

Observe now that the perimeter of any connected shape is a cycle drawn on the grid, i.e., a path where its end meets its beginning. The cycle is drawn by using consecutive grid-edges of unit length, each being characterized by a direction from $\{up, right, down, left\}$. For each pair of opposite directions, $(up, down)$ and $(left, right)$, the perimeter always uses an equal number of edges of each of the two directions in the pair and uses every direction at least once. For the purposes of the following proposition, let us denote $\{up, right, down, left\}$ by $\{d_1, d_2, d_3, d_4\}$, respectively. The perimeter of a shape can then be defined as a sequence of moves drawn from $\{d_1, d_2, d_3, d_4\}$, w.l.o.g. always starting with a d_1. Let also N_i denote the number of times d_i appears in a given perimeter.

Proposition 1. *A shape S is a connected orthogonal convex shape if and only if its perimeter satisfies both the following properties:*

- *It is described by the regular expression*

$$d_1(d_1 \mid d_2)^* d_2(d_2 \mid d_3)^* d_3(d_3 \mid d_4)^* d_4(d_4 \mid d_1)^*$$

under the additional constraint that $N_1 = N_3$ and $N_2 = N_4$.
- *Its interior has no empty cell.*

Proof. We begin by considering the forward direction, starting from a connected orthogonal convex shape S. For the first property, the N_i equalities hold for the perimeter of any shape, thus, also for the perimeter of S. In the regular expression, the only property that is different from the regular expressions of more general perimeters is that, for all $i \in \{1, 2, 3, 4\}$, d_{i-2}, where the index is modulo 4, does not appear between the first and the last appearance of d_i.

Assume that it does, for some i. Then d_{i-2} must have appeared immediately after a d_{i-1} or a d_{i+1}, because a d_{i-2} can never immediately follow a d_i. If it is after a d_{i-1}, then this forms the expression $d_i(d_{i-1} \mid d_i)^* d_{i-1} d_{i-2}$, which always has $d_i d_{i-1}^+ d_{i-2}$ as a sub-expression. But for any sub-path of the perimeter defined by the latter expression, the nodes attached to its first and last edges would then contradict Definition 1, as the horizontal or vertical line joining them goes through at least one unoccupied cell, i.e., one of the cells external to the d_{i-1}^+ part of the sub-path. The d_{i+1} case follows by observing that, in this case, the sub-expression satisfied by the perimeter would be $d_{i-2} d_{i+1}^+ d_i$, which would again violate the orthogonal convexity of S.

The second property, follows immediately by observing that if (x, y) is an empty cell within the perimeter's interior, then the horizontal line that goes through (x, y) must intersect the perimeter at two distinct points, one to the left of (x, y) and one to its right. Thus, these three points would contradict the conditions of Definition 1.

For the other direction, let S be a shape satisfying both properties. For the sake of contradiction, assume that S is not orthogonal convex, which means that there is a line, w.l.o.g horizontal and of the form $(x_l, y), (x_l + 1, y), \dots, (x_r, y)$, where (x_l, y) and (x_r, y) are occupied by nodes of S while $(x_l+1, y), \dots, (x_r-1, y)$ are not. Observe first that any gap in the interior would violate the second property, thus $(x_l + 1, y), \dots, (x_r - 1, y)$ must be cells in the exterior of the perimeter of S and (x_l, y), (x_r, y) nodes on the perimeter. There are two possible ways to achieve this: $d_3 d_2^+ d_1$ and $d_1 d_4^+ d_3$. These combinations are impossible to create with the regular expression, thus contradicting that S satisfies the properties. Similarly for vertical gaps. It follows that any shape fulfilling the two properties must belong to the family of connected orthogonal convex shapes. $\square$

Let c_x denote the column of a given shape S at the x coordinate, i.e., the set of all nodes of S at x. Let $y_{max}(x)$ ($y_{min}(x)$) be the largest (smallest) y value in the (x, y) coordinates of the cells which nodes of a column c_x occupy.

Proposition 2. *For any connected orthogonal convex shape S, all the following are true:*

- *Every column c_x of S consists of the consecutive nodes*
  $(x, y_{min}(x)), (x, y_{min}(x) + 1), \dots, (x, y_{max}(x))$.
- *There are no three columns c_{x_1}, c_{x_2}, and c_{x_3} of S, $x_1 < x_2 < x_3$, for which both $y_{max}(x_1) > y_{max}(x_2)$ and $y_{max}(x_3) > y_{max}(x_2)$ hold.*

– *There are no three columns* $c_{x'_1}$, $c_{x'_2}$, *and* $c_{x'_3}$ *of* S, $x'_1 < x'_2 < x'_3$, *for which both* $y_{min}(x'_1) < y_{min}(x'_2)$ *and* $y_{min}(x'_3) < y_{min}(x'_2)$ *hold.*

All the above hold for rows too in an analogous way.

Lemma 1. *For all* $n \geq 3$, *the maximum colour-difference of a connected horizontal-vertical convex shape of size* n *is* $n - 2\lfloor n/3 \rfloor$.

A *staircase* is a shape of the form $(x, y), (x+1, y), (x+1, y+1), (x+2, y+1), \ldots$ or $(x, y), (x, y+1), (x+1, y+1), (x+1, y+2), \ldots$. An *extended staircase* is a staircase $Stairs = \{(x_l, y_d), (x_l, y_d+1), (x_l+1, y_d+1), (x_l+1, y_d+2), \ldots\}$ with a bicolour pair at $(x_l - 1, y_d), (x_l - 1, y_d+1)$ or at $(x_l - 1, y_d - 1), (x_l - 1, y_d)$. Additionally, there are three optional *node-repositories*, $BRep$, $RRep$ and a single-black repository. $BRep = \{(x_l, y_d+2), (x_l+1, y_d+3), (x_l+2, y_d+4), \ldots\}$, $RRep = \{(x_l, y_d-1), (x_l+1, y_d), (x_l+2, y_d+1), \ldots\}$ and the single-black repository at $(x_l - 2, y_d)$.

4.2   Elimination and Generation Sequences

Let S be a connected orthogonal convex shape. A *shape elimination sequence* $\sigma = (u_1, u_2, \ldots, u_n)$ of S defines a sequence $S = S_0[u_1]S_1[u_2]S_2[u_3] \ldots S_{n-1}[u_n]S_n = \emptyset$, where, for all $1 \leq t \leq n$, a connected orthogonal convex shape S_t is obtained by removing the node u_t from the external surface of the shape S_{t-1}. A *row elimination sequence* σ of S is an elimination sequence of S which consists of p sub-sequences $\sigma = \sigma_1\sigma_2\ldots\sigma_p$, each sub-sequence σ_i, $1 \leq i \leq p$, satisfying the following properties. Sub-sequence σ_i consist of the $k = |R_i|$ nodes of row R_i, where $u_1, u_2, \ldots, u_k$ is the line formed by row R_i. Additionally, σ_i is of the form $\sigma_i = \sigma_i^1\sigma_i^2$, where (i) $\sigma_i^1 = (u_1, \ldots, u_k)$ or $\sigma_i^1 = (u_k, \ldots, u_1)$ and σ_i^2 is empty or (ii) there is a $u_j \in R_i$, for $2 \leq j < k$, such that $\sigma_i^1 = (u_1, \ldots, u_j)$ and $\sigma_i^2 = (u_k, \ldots, u_{j+1})$ or (iii) there is a $u_j \in R_i$, for $1 \leq j < k - 1$, such that $\sigma_i^1 = (u_k, \ldots, u_{j+2})$ and $\sigma_i^2 = (u_1, \ldots, u_{j+1})$. We shall call any such sub-sequence σ_i an elimination sequence of row R_i.

Given a connected orthogonal convex shape S of n nodes, a *shape generation sequence* $\sigma = (u_1, u_2, \ldots, u_n)$ of S defines a sequence $\emptyset = S_0[u_1]S_1[u_2]S_2[u_3] \ldots S_{n-1}[u_n]S_n = S$, where, for all $1 \leq t \leq n$, a connected orthogonal convex shape S_t is obtained by adding the node u_t to the cell perimeter of S_{t-1}.

Let S be an extended staircase of n nodes. An *extended staircase generation sequence* $\sigma = (u_1, u_2, \ldots, u_n)$ of S is a generation sequence of S which consists of q sub-sequences $\sigma = \sigma_1\sigma_2\ldots\sigma_q$, where each σ_i contains the nodes of the column C_i of S, ordered such that they do not violate the properties of a shape generation sequence. A *diagonal line-with-leaves generation sequence* can be defined in an analogous way.

Lemma 2. *Every connected orthogonal convex shape* S *has a row (and column) elimination sequence* σ.

Lemma 3. *Let* σ *be a bicoloured sequence of nodes that fulfills all the following conditions:*

– *The set of the first two nodes in σ is not single-coloured.*
– *The third node of σ is black.*
– σ *does not contain a single-coloured 3-sub-sequence.*

Then there is an extended staircase generation sequence $\sigma' = (u'_1, u'_2, \ldots, u'_n)$ which is colour-order preserving with respect to σ.

Lemma 4. *For any connected orthogonal convex shape S of n nodes, given a row elimination sequence $\sigma = (u_1, u_2, \ldots, u_n)$ of S where the set of the first two nodes in σ is not single-coloured and u_3 is black, there is an extended staircase generation sequence $\sigma' = (u'_1, u'_2, \ldots, u'_n)$ which is colour-order preserving w.r.t σ and such that, for all $1 \le i \le |\sigma|$, $D_i = \{u'_1, u'_2, \ldots, u'_i\}$ is a connected orthogonal convex shape.*

The *anchor node* of the shape S of p rows $R_1, R_2, \ldots, R_p$ is the rightmost node in the row R_p, counting rows from bottom to top. *ExtendedStaircase* is an algorithm which creates an extended staircase generation sequence from a row elimination sequence of a connected horizontal-vertical convex shape.

Lemma 5. *Let S be a connected orthogonal convex shape of n nodes divided into p rows $R_1, R_2, \ldots, R_p$, and $\sigma = (u_1, u_2, \ldots, u_n)$ a row elimination sequence from R_1 to R_p of S. If the bottom node of the first two nodes placed by Extended-Staircase is fixed to $(x_c, y_c + 1)$, where (x_c, y_c) are the co-ordinates of the anchor node of S, the shape $T_i = ExtendedStaircase(\sigma_i)$, where $\sigma_i = (u_1, u_2, \ldots, u_i)$, $1 \le i \le n$, fulfills the following properties:*

– $S \cup T_i$ *is a connected shape.*
– $S \cap T = \emptyset$.
– *excluding the single-black repository, $R_p \cup T_i$ is an orthogonal convex shape.*

Lemma 6. *For any extended staircase $W \cup T$ of n nodes, where W is the Stairs, $T \subseteq \{BRep \cup RRep\}$ and $k = |T|$, given a shape elimination sequence $\sigma = (u_1, u_2, \ldots, u_k)$ of T, there is a diagonal line-with-leaves generation sequence $\sigma' = (u'_1, u'_2, \ldots, u'_k)$ which is colour-order preserving w.r.t σ and such that, for all $1 \le i \le |\sigma|$, $D_i = W \cup \{u'_1, u'_2, \ldots, u'_i\}$ is a connected orthogonal convex shape.*

5   The Transformation

In this section, we present the transformation of *orthogonal convex* shapes, via an algorithm (Algorithm 1) for constructing a diagonal line-with-leaves from any orthogonal convex shape S. For the first step of the algorithm, we generate a 6-robot from the seed and the shape, which we then use to transport nodes. By using a row elimination sequence of S and an extended staircase generation sequence, we convert the initial shape S into an extended staircase. We then use appropriate elimination and generation sequences focused on the repositories of the extended staircase, to convert the latter into a diagonal line-with-leaves.

Given any two colour-consistent orthogonal convex shapes A and B and their diagonal line-with-leaves D, our algorithm can be used to transform both A into D and B into D and, thus, A into B, by reversing the latter transformation. This transformation applies to all orthogonal convex shapes with 3 nodes. A 2-node shape can trivially transform by rotating one node around the other and a 1-node shape cannot transform at all.

Algorithm 1. OConvexToDLL(S, M)

Input: shape $S \cup M$, where S is a connected orthogonal convex shape of n nodes and M is a 3-node seed on the cell perimeter of S, row elimination sequence $\sigma = (u_1, u_2, \ldots, u_n)$ of S, extended staircase generation sequence of $W \cup T = \sigma' = (u'_1, u'_2, \ldots, u'_n)$ which is colour-order preserving w.r.t. σ, shape elimination sequence $\sigma = (u_1, u_2, \ldots, u_{|T|})$ of T, shape generation sequence of $X = \sigma' = (u'_1, u'_2, \ldots, u'_{|T|})$ which is colour-order preserving w.r.t. σ

Output: shape $G = W \cup X \cup M$, where G is a diagonal line-with-leaves and M is a connected 3-node shape on the cell perimeter of S.

$R \leftarrow$ GenerateRobot(S, M)
$\sigma \leftarrow$ rowEliminationSequence(S)
$\sigma' \leftarrow$ ExtendedStaircase(σ)
$W \cup T \leftarrow$ HVConvexToExtStaircase(S, R, σ, σ')
$\sigma \leftarrow$ repsEliminationSequence$(W \cup T)$
$\sigma' \leftarrow$ stairExtensionSequence$(W \cup T)$
$G \leftarrow$ ExtStaircaseToDLL$(W \cup T, R, \sigma, \sigma')$
TerminateRobot(G, R)

Algorithm 2. OConvexToExtStaircase(S, R, σ, σ')

Input: shape $S \cup R$, where S is a connected orthogonal convex shape of n nodes and R is a 6-node robot on the cell perimeter of S, row elimination sequence $\sigma = (u_1, u_2, \ldots, u_n)$ of S, extended staircase generation sequence $\sigma' = (u'_1, u'_2, \ldots, u'_n)$ which is colour-order preserving w.r.t. σ

Output: shape $T \cup R$, where T is the extended staircase generated by σ'

for all $1 \le i \le n$ do
    source $\leftarrow \sigma_i$, *dest* $\leftarrow \sigma'_i$
    while R cannot extract source **do**
        if R can climb **then** $Climb(R)$
        else $Slide(R)$
    end while
    $Extract(R, source)$
    while R cannot place its load in dest **do**
        if R can climb **then** $Climb(R)$
        else $Slide(R)$
    end while
    $Place(R, dest)$
end for

Algorithm 3. ExtStaircaseToDLL(W, R, σ, σ')

Input: extended staircase $W = Stairs \cup \{BRep \cup RRep\}$ and a 6-robot R on its cell
perimeter, shape elimination sequence $\sigma = (u_1, u_2, \ldots, u_{|T|})$ of $T \subseteq \{BRep \cup RRep\}$,
shape generation sequence $\sigma' = (u'_1, u'_2, \ldots, u'_{|T|})$ which is colour-order preserving
w.r.t. σ

Output: shape $Stairs' \cup R'$, where $Stairs' \setminus Stairs$ is an extension of $Stairs$ generated
by σ' and R' is a 6-robot which is colour-consistent with R.

    for all $1 \leq i \leq |T|$ **do**
        $source \leftarrow u_i$
        $dest \leftarrow u'_i$
        while R not at $source$ **do**
            if R can climb **then**
                $ClimbTowards(R, source)$
            else
                $SlideTowards(R, source)$
            end if
        end while
        $Extract(R, source)$
        while R not at $dest$ **do**
            if R can climb **then**
                $ClimbTowards(R, dest)$
            else
                $SlideTowards(R, dest)$
            end if
        end while
        $Place(R, dest)$
    end for

5.1 Robot Traversal Capabilities

6-Robot Movement. We first show that for all S in the family of orthogonal
convex shapes, a connected 6-robot is capable of traversing the perimeter of S.
We prove this by first providing a series of scenarios which we call *corners*, where
we show that the 6-robot is capable of making progress past the obstacle that
the corner represents. We then use Proposition 1 to show that the perimeter of
any S is necessarily made up of a sequence of such corners, and therefore the
6-robot is capable of traversing it.

We begin by considering the *up-right* quadrant, that is any cells which neighbour the section of the perimeter defined by the regular expression $d_1(d_1 \mid d_2)^* d_2$
$(d_2 \mid d_3)^* d_3$, where d_1, d_2 and d_3 are *up*, *right* and *down* respectively, as our base
case. We define progress as the movement of the 6-robot upwards and to the
right of its starting position. Our goal is to show that attaining the maximum
progress for each corner is possible. Since we can construct a series of corners
where every corner follows from the point of maximum progress of the previous
corner, it follows that for such a series we can make progress indefinitely.

Let $\mathcal{C}$ be a set of orthogonal convex shapes, where each shape is a corner
scenario for the $up - right$ quadrant, depicted in Fig. 2. Given a corner-shape

scenario $C \in \mathcal{C}$ consisting of a horizontal line $(x_l, y_d), (x_l+1, y_d), \ldots, (x_r, y_d)$ and a vertical line $(x_r, y_d), (x_r, y_d + 1), \ldots, (x_r, y_u)$, as depicted in Fig. 2, we define its *width* $w(C) = |x_r - x_l|$, i.e., equal to the length of its horizontal line, and its *height* $h(C) = |y_u - y_d|$, i.e., equal to the length of its vertical line, excluding in both cases the corner node (x_r, y_d).

(a) The height 1 cases, with widths 1 and 2+.

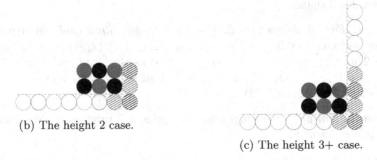

(b) The height 2 case.

(c) The height 3+ case.

Fig. 2. The four basic corner scenarios of $\mathcal{C}$. Filled circles represent the 6-robot. Striped circles represent the nodes on the exterior of the shape. Hollow circles represent potential space for additional nodes for corner scenarios which are not in this set.

Lemma 7. *For any orthogonal convex shape S, the extended external surface defined by the regular expression $d_1(d_1 \mid d_2)^*d_2 (d_2 \mid d_3)^*d_3$ of the shape can be divided into a series of shapes $S_0, S_1, \ldots$, where all $S_i \in \mathcal{C}$.*

Given that the quadrant is made up of cases from $\mathcal{C}$, if the 6-robot is able to move from one vertical to another for all $S_i \in \mathcal{C}$, it is able to do so for any upright quadrant of the perimeter until it runs into the d_3 line. We now show that this movement is possible, first for this quadrant and later for all four quadrants.

Lemma 8. *For all shapes $C \in \mathcal{C}$, if a 2×3 shape (the 6-robot) is placed in the cells $(x_l - 2, y_d + 1), (x_l - 1, y_d + 1), (x_l, y_d + 1), (x_l - 2, y_d + 2), (x_l - 1, y_d + 2), (x_l, y_d + 2)$, it is capable of translating itself to $(x_r - 2, y_u + 1), (x_r - 1, y_u + 1), (x_r, y_u + 1), (x_r - 2, y_u + 2), (x_r - 1, y_u + 2), (x_r, y_u + 2)$.*

Theorem 1. *For any orthogonal convex shape S, a 6-robot is capable of traversing the perimeter of S.*

7-Robot Movement. We consider once again the *up-right* quadrant, and generalise to other quadrants later. We say a cell $c = (x, y)$ is *behind* the robot if x is smaller than the x-coordinate of every node in the robot.

The *load* of a 7-robot S is any node u such that $S \setminus \{u\}$ is a 2×3 shape. The *position* of the robot is an offset of the y axis for the purpose of the initial positioning of the 7-robot. For our transformations, we maintain the invariant that the 7-robot, after any of its high-level movements, will return to the structure of a 2×3 shape with a load. For this invariant, we assume that the load is always *behind* the 2×3 shape (while remaining connected). The situation where the load is positioned differently does not need to be considered. We therefore use $(x, y|y')$ to refer to the co-ordinates of the two cells (x, y) and (x, y') *behind* the robot which can contain the load, keeping it attached to the robot while the latter is a 2×3 shape.

Lemma 9. *For all shapes $C \in \mathcal{C}$, if a 2×3 shape with a load (the 7-robot) is placed in the cells $(x_l - 3, y_d + 1|y_d + 2), (x_l - 2, y_d + 1), (x_l - 1, y_d + 1), (x_l, y_d + 1), (x_l - 2, y_d + 2), (x_l - 1, y_d + 2), (x_l, y_d + 2)$, it is capable of translating itself to $(x_r - 3, y_u + 1|y_u + 2), (x_r - 2, y_u + 1), (x_r - 1, y_u + 1), (x_r, y_u + 1), (x_r - 2, y_u + 2), (x_r - 1, y_u + 2), (x_r, y_u + 2)$.*

Theorem 2. *For any orthogonal convex shape S, a 7-robot is capable of traversing the perimeter of S.*

Repository Traversal. Whenever the single-black repository is occupied, the robot may need to traverse a non-convex region when moving between S and the extended staircase. The following lemma shows that this is not an issue.

Lemma 10. *If the single-black repository of the extended staircase is occupied, then both the 6-robot and the 7-robot are able to traverse past it.*

5.2 Initialisation

Robot Generation. We now prove that we can generate a 6-robot from the orthogonal convex shape S with the help of the 3 musketeers.

Lemma 11. *Let S be a connected orthogonal convex shape. Then there is a connected shape M of 3 nodes (the 3 musketeers) and an attachment of M to the bottom-most row of S, such that $S \cup M$ can reach a configuration $S' \cup M'$ satisfying the following properties. $S' = S \setminus \{u_1, u_2, u_3\}$, where $\{u_1, u_2, u_3\}$ is the 3-prefix of a row elimination sequence σ of S starting from the bottom-most row of S. M' is a 6-robot on the perimeter of S'.*

Prefix Construction. To construct the extended staircase from an orthogonal convex shape S, we must first retrieve a sequence of 3 nodes u_1, u_2, u_3 from S, where u_3 is black. We assume w.l.o.g. that S is a black parity shape. We now show with the following lemma that this is possible. We consider the edge case where S is a rhombus in the full version of our paper.

Lemma 12. *For any shape $S \cup M$, where S is a non-red parity connected orthogonal convex shape of n nodes divided into p rows, $R_1, R_2, \ldots, R_p$ and M is a 6-robot, it is possible for M to extract a sequence of nodes (u_1, u_2, u_3) from S, where u_1, u_2 is a bicolour pair, u_3 is black, and $S \setminus \{u_1, u_2, u_3\}$ is a connected orthogonal convex shape.*

5.3 Transformations Between Shapes

In this section, we show that, given our previous results, we are now in the position to convert an orthogonal convex shape into another such shape. We begin with the conversion of an extended staircase into a diagonal line-with-leaves, then the orthogonal convex shape to the diagonal line-with-leaves, and then our main result follows by reversibility.

Lemma 13. *Let S be a connected orthogonal convex shape with n nodes divided into p rows $R_1, R_2, \ldots, R_p$. Given a row elimination sequence $\sigma = (u_1, u_2, \ldots, u_n)$ of S, an extended staircase generation sequence $\sigma' = (u'_1, u'_2, \ldots, u'_n)$ which is colour-order preserving w.r.t. σ, and a 6-robot placed on the external surface of S, for all $1 \leq i < n$ the 6-robot is capable of picking up the node u_i, moving as a 7-robot to the empty cell u'_i and placing it, and then returning as a 6-robot to u_{i+1}.*

Proof. We follow the procedure of Algorithm 2. By Theorem 1 and Theorem 2, the 6-robot R and 7-robot $R \cup u_i$ can climb and slide around the external surface of S. We use this to move to each u_i, extract it, move to the cell for u'_i and then place a node of the same colour as u_i in it, substituting u_i for a node in R as necessary to create a new 6-robot. By Lemma 5, so long as we approach T_i from R_p, we can climb onto and off T_i to place the nodes using the same movements as the previous theorems. By Lemma 10, placing a black node in the repository cell does not inhibit movement. $\square$

Lemma 14. *Let $W \cup T \cup R$ be the union of the Stairs of an extended staircase W, $T \subseteq \{BRep \cup RRep\}$ from the extended staircase and a 6-node robot R on the cell perimeter of $S \cup T$. Given a shape elimination sequence $\sigma = (u_1, u_2, \ldots, u_n)$ of T, a diagonal line-with-leaves generation sequence σ' which is colour-order preserving w.r.t. σ and a 6-robot placed on the external surface of S, for all $1 \leq i \leq n$ the 6-robot is capable of picking up the node u_i, moving as a 7-robot to u'_i and placing it, and then returning as a 6-robot to u_{i+1}.*

Proof. We follow the procedure of Algorithm 3. By Theorem 1 and Theorem 2, the 6-robot R and 7-robot $R \cup u_i$ can climb and slide around the external surface of $S \cup T$. We use this to move to each u_i, extract it, move to the cell for u'_i and then place a node of the same colour as u_i in it, substituting u_i for a node in R as necessary to create new 6-robot. Since the placement of u'_i is extending *Stairs*, the resulting shape is always orthogonal convex for all $1 \leq i \leq n$. $\square$

Lemma 15. *Let S be a connected orthogonal convex shape. Then there is a connected shape M of 3 nodes (the 3 musketeers) and an attachment of M to the bottom-most row of S, such that $S \cup M$ can reach the configuration D, where D is a diagonal line-with-leaves which is colour-consistent with S.*

Proof. We follow the procedure of Algorithm 1. By Lemma 11 we can form a 6-robot from $S \cup M$. By Lemma 13, we can build an extended staircase from the resulting shape. By Lemma 14, we can then build a diagonal line-with-leaves. Finally, by reversibility, we can place R such that the removal of 3 nodes leaves a larger diagonal line-with-leaves D which is colour-consistent with S.   □

Lemma 16. *There exists a connected orthogonal convex shape of n nodes S and a diagonal line-with-leaves T and such that any strategy which transforms S into T requires $O(n^2)$ time steps in the worst case.*

Proof. To construct T, we must transfer nodes using the robot to the anchor node. In the worst case, S is a staircase, and the robot must move nodes from one end to the other. It must therefore make $O(cn^2)$ moves, where c is the maximum number of rotations needed for the robot to move one step. When the extended staircase has been constructed, it must be converted into a diagonal line-with-leaves. In the worst case every column in the staircase has 4 nodes, and the robot must extend *Stairs* until one repository has a single node. Therefore, the robot must make $O(2cn^2)$ moves to travel on both sides of *Stairs*. Combining the worst cases of both procedures therefore takes $O(3cn^2) = O(n^2)$ time steps. □

Theorem 3. *Let S and S' be connected colour-consistent orthogonal convex shapes. Then there is a connected shape M of 3 nodes (the 3 musketeers) and an attachment of M to the bottom-most row of S, such that $S \cup M$ can reach the configuration S' in $O(n^2)$ time steps.*

Proof. By Lemma 15, we can convert S into a diagonal line-with-leaves T. By reversibility, we can convert T into S'. By Lemma 16, this procedure takes $O(n^2)$ time steps.   □

6   Conclusions

There are some open problems which follow from the findings of our work. The most obvious is expanding the class of shapes which can be constructed to achieve universal transformation. An example of a bad case is the "double spiral", which is a line forming two connected spirals. In this case, preserving connectivity after the removal of a node requires the robot to get to the centre of a spiral, which may not be possible without a special procedure to "dig" into it without breaking connectivity. Finally, successfully switching to a decentralised model of transformations will greatly expand the utility of the results, especially because most programmable matter systems which model real-world applications implement programs in this way. This in turn could lead to real-world applications for the efficient transformation of programmable matter systems.

References

1. Akitaya, H.A., et al.: Universal reconfiguration of facet-connected modular robots by pivots: the $O(1)$ musketeers. Algorithmica **83**(5), 1316–1351 (2021). https://doi.org/10.1007/s00453-020-00784-6

2. Almethen, A., Michail, O., Potapov, I.: Pushing lines helps: efficient universal centralised transformations for programmable matter. Theor. Comput. Sci. **830–831**, 43–59 (2020). https://doi.org/10.1016/j.tcs.2020.04.026

3. Angluin, D., Aspnes, J., Diamadi, Z., Fischer, M.J., Peralta, R.: Computation in networks of passively mobile finite-state sensors. Distrib. Comput. **18**(4), 235–253 (2006). https://doi.org/10.1007/s00446-005-0138-3

4. Chen, X., et al.: Magnetochromatic polydiacetylene by incorporation of Fe3O4 nanoparticles. Angew. Chem. Int. Ed. **50**(24), 5486–5489 (2011). https://doi.org/10.1002/anie.201100064

5. Connor, M., Michail, O., Potapov, I.: Centralised connectivity-preserving transformations for programmable matter: a minimal seed approach. Theor. Comput. Sci. **936**, 77–91 (2022). https://doi.org/10.1016/j.tcs.2022.09.016, https://www.sciencedirect.com/science/article/pii/S0304397522005527

6. Daymude, J.J., et al.: On the runtime of universal coating for programmable matter. Nat. Comput. **17**(1), 81–96 (2017). https://doi.org/10.1007/s11047-017-9658-6

7. Derakhshandeh, Z., Dolev, S., Gmyr, R., Richa, A.W., Scheideler, C., Strothmann, T.: Amoebot - a new model for programmable matter. In: Proceedings of the 26th ACM Symposium on Parallelism in Algorithms and Architectures, pp. 220–222. SPAA 2014, Association for Computing Machinery, Prague (2014). https://doi.org/10.1145/2612669.2612712

8. Derakhshandeh, Z., Gmyr, R., Richa, A.W., Scheideler, C., Strothmann, T.: An algorithmic framework for shape formation problems in self-organizing particle systems. In: Proceedings of the Second Annual International Conference on Nanoscale Computing and Communication, pp. 1–2. NANOCOM 2015, Association for Computing Machinery, Boston (2015). https://doi.org/10.1145/2800795.2800829

9. Derakhshandeh, Z., Gmyr, R., Richa, A.W., Scheideler, C., Strothmann, T.: Universal shape formation for programmable matter. In: Proceedings of the 28th ACM Symposium on Parallelism in Algorithms and Architectures, pp. 289–299. SPAA 2016, Association for Computing Machinery, Pacific Grove (2016). https://doi.org/10.1145/2935764.2935784

10. Doty, D.: Theory of algorithmic self-assembly. Commun. ACM **55**(12), 78–88 (2012). https://doi.org/10.1145/2380656.2380675

11. Doty, D.: Timing in chemical reaction networks. In: Proceedings of the 2014 Annual ACM-SIAM Symposium on Discrete Algorithms (SODA), pp. 772–784. Proceedings, Society for Industrial and Applied Mathematics (2013). https://doi.org/10.1137/1.9781611973402.57

12. Fekete, S.P., Keldenich, P., Kosfeld, R., Rieck, C., Scheffer, C.: Connected Coordinated Motion Planning with Bounded Stretch. Technical report (2021). http://arxiv.org/abs/2109.12381arXiv:2109.12381

13. Feldmann, M., Padalkin, A., Scheideler, C., Dolev, S.: Coordinating amoebots via reconfigurable circuits. J. Comput. Biol.: J. Comput. Mol. Cell Biol. **29**(4), 317–343 (2022). https://doi.org/10.1089/cmb.2021.0363

14. Gilpin, K., Knaian, A., Rus, D.: Robot pebbles: one centimeter modules for programmable matter through self-disassembly. In: 2010 IEEE International Conference on Robotics and Automation, pp. 2485–2492 (2010). https://doi.org/10.1109/ROBOT.2010.5509817,iSSN: 1050-4729

15. Jordan, C.: Cours d'analyse de l'École polytechnique, vol. 1. Gauthier-Villars et fils (1893)

16. Michail, O., Skretas, G., Spirakis, P.G.: On the Transformation Capability of Feasible Mechanisms for Programmable Matter. Tech. Rep. (2017), http://arxiv.org/abs/1703.04381, arXiv:1703.04381

17. Michail, O., Skretas, G., Spirakis, P.G.: On the transformation capability of feasible mechanisms for programmable matter. J. Comput. Syst. Sci. **102**, 18–39 (2019). https://doi.org/10.1016/j.jcss.2018.12.001

18. Michail, O., Spirakis, P.G.: Simple and efficient local codes for distributed stable network construction. Distrib. Comput. **29**(3), 207–237 (2015). https://doi.org/10.1007/s00446-015-0257-4

19. Rothemund, P.W.K.: Folding DNA to create nanoscale shapes and patterns. Nature **440**(7082), 297–302 (2006). https://doi.org/10.1038/nature04586

20. Rothemund, P.W.K., Winfree, E.: The program-size complexity of self-assembled squares (extended abstract). In: Proceedings of the thirty-second annual ACM symposium on Theory of computing, pp. 459–468. STOC 2000, Association for Computing Machinery, Portland (2000). https://doi.org/10.1145/335305.335358

21. Rubenstein, M., Cornejo, A., Nagpal, R.: Programmable self-assembly in a thousand-robot swarm. Science **345**(6198), 795–799 (2014). https://doi.org/10.1126/science.1254295

22. Soloveichik, D., Cook, M., Winfree, E., Bruck, J.: Computation with finite stochastic chemical reaction networks. Nat. Comput. **7**(4), 615–633 (2008). https://doi.org/10.1007/s11047-008-9067-y

23. Thalamy, P., Piranda, B., Bourgeois, J.: Distributed self-reconfiguration using a deterministic autonomous scaffolding structure. In: Proceedings of the 18th International Conference on Autonomous Agents and MultiAgent Systems, pp. 140–148. AAMAS 2019, International Foundation for Autonomous Agents and Multiagent Systems, Montreal QC (2019)

24. Thalamy, P., Piranda, B., Bourgeois, J.: 3D coating self-assembly for modular robotic scaffolds. In: 2020 IEEE/RSJ International Conference on Intelligent Robots and Systems (IROS), pp. 11688–11695 (Oct 020). https://doi.org/10.1109/IROS45743.2020.9341324, iSSN: 2153-0866

25. Winfree, E.: Algorithmic Self-assembly of DNA. Ph.D. thesis, California Institute of Technology (1998)

26. Woods, D., Chen, H.L., Goodfriend, S., Dabby, N., Winfree, E., Yin, P.: Active self-assembly of algorithmic shapes and patterns in polylogarithmic time. In: Proceedings of the 4th Conference on Innovations in Theoretical Computer Science, pp. 353–354. ITCS 2013, Association for Computing Machinery, Berkeley (2013). https://doi.org/10.1145/2422436.2422476

Triangle Evacuation of 2 Agents in the Wireless Model

(Extended Abstract)

Konstantinos Georgiou[(⊠)] and Woojin Jang

Department of Mathematics, Toronto Metropolitan University,
Toronto, ON M5B 2K3, Canada
{konstantinos,woojin.jang}@ryerson.ca

Abstract. The input to the *Triangle Evacuation* problem is a triangle *ABC*. Given a starting point *S* on the perimeter of the triangle, a feasible solution to the problem consists of two unit-speed trajectories of mobile agents that eventually visit every point on the perimeter of *ABC*. The cost of a feasible solution (evacuation cost) is defined as the supremum over all points *T* of the time it takes that *T* is visited for the first time by an agent plus the distance of *T* to the other agent at that time.

Similar evacuation type problems are well studied in the literature covering the unit circle, the ℓ_p unit circle for $p \geq 1$, the square, and the equilateral triangle. We extend this line of research to arbitrary non-obtuse triangles. Motivated by the lack of symmetry of our search domain, we introduce 4 different algorithmic problems arising by letting the starting edge and/or the starting point *S* on that edge to be chosen either by the algorithm or the adversary. To that end, we provide a tight analysis for the algorithm that has been proved to be optimal for the previously studied search domains, as well as we provide lower bounds for each of the problems. Both our upper and lower bounds match and extend naturally the previously known results that were established only for the equilateral triangle.

Keywords: Search · Evacuation · Triangle · Mobile agents

1 Introduction

Search Theory is concerned with the general problem of retrieving information in some search domain. Seemingly simple but mathematically rich problems pertaining to basic geometric domains where studied as early as the 1960's, see for example [6] and [7], then popularized in the Theoretical Computer Science community in the late 1980's by the seminal works of Baeza-Yates et al. [4], and then recently re-examined under the lens of mobile agents, e.g. in [13].

In search problems closely related to our work, a hidden item (exit) is placed on a geometric domain and can only be detected by unit speed searchers (mobile agents

---

The full version of this paper appears on arXiv [20].

K. Georgiou—Research supported in part by NSERC.

© The Author(s), under exclusive license to Springer Nature Switzerland AG 2022
T. Erlebach and M. Segal (Eds.): ALGOSENSORS 2022, LNCS 13707, pp. 77–90, 2022.
https://doi.org/10.1007/978-3-031-22050-0_6

or robots) when any of them walks over it. When the exit is first visited by an agent, its location is communicated instantaneously to the remaining agents (wireless model) so that they all gather to the exit along the shortest path in the underlying search domain. The time it takes for the last agent to reach the exit, over all exit placements, is known as the *evacuation time* of the (evacuation) algorithm.

Optimal evacuation algorithms for 2 searchers are known for a series of geometric domains, e.g. the circle [13], ℓ_p circles [24], and the square and the equilateral triangle [17]. For all these problems, a plain-vanilla algorithm is the optimal solution: the two searchers start from a point on the perimeter of the geometric domain and search the perimeter in opposite directions at the same unit speed until the exit is found, at which point the non-finder goes to the exit along the shortest path.

In this work we consider the 2 searcher problem in the wireless model over non-obtuse triangles. The consideration of general triangles comes with unexpected challenges, since even the worst-case analysis of the plain-vanilla algorithm becomes a technical task due to the lack of symmetry of the search domain. But even more interestingly, the consideration of general triangles allows for the introduction of 4 different algorithmic problems pertaining to the initial placement of the searchers. Indeed, in all previously studied domains, the optimal algorithm had the searchers start from the same point on the perimeter. Motivated by this, we consider 4 different algorithmic problems that we believe are interesting in their own right. These problems are obtained by specifying whether the algorithm or the adversary chooses the starting edge and/or the starting point on that edge for the 2 searchers. In our results we provide upper bounds for all 4 problems, by giving a technical and tight analysis of the plain-vanilla algorithm that we call OPPOSITESEARCH. We also provide lower bounds for arbitrary search algorithms for the same problems.

It is worth noting that the results of [17] for the equilateral triangle were presented in the form of evaluating the evacuation time of the OPPOSITESEARCH algorithm for any starting point on the perimeter for the purpose of finding only the best starting point. It is an immediate corollary to obtain optimal results for all 4 new algorithmic problems, but only for the equilateral triangle. Both our upper and lower bounds for general triangles match and extend the aforementioned results for the equilateral triangle. To that end, one of our surprising findings is that for some of the algorithmic problems, the evacuation time is more than half the perimeter of the search domain, even though the induced searchers' trajectories stay exclusively on the perimeter of the domain and the searchers cover the entire triangle perimeter for the worst placements of the exit (which would be the same trajectory, should the exit was found only at the very end of the search). This is despite that two agents can search the entire domain in time equal to half the triangle perimeter.

2   Related Work

Search problems have received several decades of treatment that resulted in some interesting books [1,2], in a relatively recent survey [25], and in an exposition of mobile agent-based (and hence more related to our work) results in [19]. A primitive, and maybe the most well-cited search-type problem is the so-called cow-path or linear-search [3] in which a mobile agent searches for hidden item on the infinite line. Numerous variations of the problem have been studied, ranging from different domains to different searchers specifications to different objectives. The interested reader may consult any of the aforementioned resources for problem variations. Below we give a representative outline of results most relevant to our new contributions, and pertaining primarily to wireless evacuation from geometric domains.

The problem of evacuating 2 or more mobile agents from a geometric domain was consider by Czyzowicz et al. [13] on the circle. The authors considered the distinction between the wireless (our communication model), where searchers exchange information instantaneously, and the face-to-face model, where information cannot be communicated from distance. The results pertaining to the wireless model were optimal, while improved algorithms for the face-to-face model followed in [8,16,18]. A little later, the work of [10] also considered trade-offs to multi-objective evacuations costs. Since the first study of [13] a number of variations emerged. Different searchers' speeds were considered in [26], faulty robots were studied in [14,22], evacuation from multiple exits was introduced in [12], searching with advice was considered in [23], and search-and-fetch type evacuation was studied in [21].

The work most relevant to our new contributions are the optimal evacuation results in the wireless model of Czyzowicz et al. [17] pertaining to the equilateral triangle. In particular, Czyzowicz et al. considered the problem of placing two unit speed wireless agents on the perimeter of an equilateral triangle. If the starting point is x away from the middle point of any edge (assumed to have unit length, hence $x \leq 1/2$), they showed that the optimal worst-case evacuation cost equals $3/2 + x$. As a corollary, the overall best evacuation cost is $3/2$ if the algorithm can choose the starting point, even if an adversary chooses first an edge for where the starting point will be placed. Similarly, the evacuation cost is 2 when an adversary chooses the searchers' starting point even if the algorithm can choose the starting edge. These are the results that we extend to general triangles by obtaining formulas that are functions of the triangle edges. Notably, the search domains of [17] were later re-examined in the face-to-face model [9] and with limited searchers' communication range [5].

One of the main features of our results is that we quantify the effectiveness of choosing the starting point of the searchers. When the search domain is the circle [17], the starting point is irrelevant as long as both agents start from the same point (and turns out it is optimal to have searchers initially co-located on the perimeter). Nevertheless, strategic starting points based on the searchers' relative distance have been considered in [11,15]. Apart from [17], the only other result we are aware of where the (same) starting point of the searchers has to be chosen strategically is that of [24] that considered evacuation from ℓ_p unit discs, with $p \geq 1$. Nevertheless, a key difference in our own result is that the geometry of the underlying search domain, that is a triangle, allows us to quantify how good an evacuation solution can be when choosing the searchers' and the exit's placement. In particular the order of decisions for the problems studied here, once one fixes an arbitrary triangle, are obtained by fixing (i) the starting edge of the searchers, then (ii) the starting point on that edge, then (iii) the searchers' evacuation algorithm, and then (iv) the placement of the exit, in that order. Item (iii) is always an algorithmic choice while (iv) is always an adversarial choice.

3   Problem Definition, Motivation and Results

We begin with the problem definition and some motivation. Two unit speed mobile agents start from the same point on the perimeter of some non-obtuse triangle ABC. Somewhere on the perimeter of ABC there is a hidden object, also referred to as the *exit*, that an agent can see only if it is collocated with the exit. When an agent identifies the location of the exit, the information reaches the other agent instantaneously (wireless model). A feasible solution to the problem consists of agents' trajectories that ensure that regardless of the placement of the exit, both agents eventually reach the exit. For this reason such solutions/algorithms are also known as evacuation algorithms. The time it takes the last agent to reach the exit is known as the *evacuation time* of the algorithm for the specific exit placement. As it is common for worst-case analysis, in this work we are concerned with the calculation of the *worst-case evacuation cost* of an algorithm (or simply evacuation cost), that is, the supremum of the evacuation time over all possible placements of the exit. Note that the worst-case evacuation cost of an algorithm is a function of the agents' starting point, and of course the size of the given triangle ABC.

The 2-agent evacuation problem in the wireless model has been studied on the circle, the square and the equilateral triangle. Especially when the search domain enjoys the symmetry of the circle, the starting point of the agents is irrelevant. In other cases when the search domain exhibits enough symmetries, e.g. for the square and the equilateral triangle, the exact evaluation of the worst-case evacuation cost (as a function of the agents' starting point) for a natural (and optimal algorithm) is an easy exercise, and due to the underlying symmetries not all starting points need to be considered. Interestingly, things are quite different in our problem when the search domain is a general non-obtuse triangle; indeed, not only the worst-case evacuation cost depends (in a strong sense) on the agents' starting point, but also its' exact evaluation (as a function of the starting point, and the triangle's edges) is a non-trivial task even for a plain-vanilla evacuation algorithm.

Due to the asymmetry of a general triangle, we are motivated to identify efficient evacuation algorithms when the agents' starting point is chosen in two steps:

Step 1: Choose a starting edge (the largest, or the second largest, or the smallest), and
Step 2: Choose the starting point on that edge.

Each of the two choices can be either *algorithmic or adversarial*, giving rise to 4 different interesting algorithmic questions, summarized in the next table, that also introduces notation for the best possible evacuation time, over all evacuation algorithms. Note that after a starting edge and a starting point on that edge are fixed, the performance (evacuation cost) of an evacuation algorithm is quantified as the worst-case evacuation time over all adversarial placements of the exit. To that end, we are after algorithms that minimize the evacuation cost in the underlying algorithmic/adversarial choice of a starting point, as a function of the edge lengths $a \geq b \geq c$. All our contributions are summarized next in Theorem 1. We emphasize that our findings generalize some of the results in [17] about the equilateral triangle evacuation problem. Indeed, if the searchers' starting point is x away from the middle

Choose edge	Choose starting point	Optimal evacuation cost
Algorithm	Algorithm	$\underline{\mathscr{L}}(a,b,c)$
Adversary	Algorithm	$\overline{\mathscr{L}}(a,b,c)$
Algorithm	Adversary	$\underline{\mathscr{U}}(a,b,c)$
Adversary	Adversary	$\overline{\mathscr{U}}(a,b,c)$

point of an equilateral triangle with edges $a = b = c = 1$, the authors of [17] proved that the optimal evacuation cost equals $3/2 + x$, showing this way that $\underline{\mathscr{L}}(a,a,a) = \overline{\mathscr{L}}(a,a,a) = 3a/2$ and $\underline{\mathscr{U}}(a,a,a) = \overline{\mathscr{U}}(a,a,a) = 2a$. The claims of Theorem 1 imply the exact same bounds by setting $a = b = c$.

Theorem 1. *For non-obtuse triangle ABC with edges $a \geq b \geq c$, we have that*

$$\underline{\mathscr{L}}(a,b,c) = \frac{a+b+c}{2},$$

$$\frac{a+b+c}{2} \leq \overline{\mathscr{L}}(a,b,c) \leq \min\left\{b+c, \frac{(a+b)^2 - c^2 + 4\sqrt{3}\tau}{4b}\right\},$$

$$\min\left\{\frac{1}{2}\sqrt{\frac{2b^2(a-c)-(a-2c)(a+c)^2}{a}} + b, a+c\right\} \leq \underline{\mathscr{U}}(a,b,c) \leq \min\left\{\frac{a}{2}+b+\frac{c}{2}, a+c\right\},$$

$$a + \frac{1}{2}\sqrt{\frac{2a^2(b-c)-(b-2c)(b+c)^2}{b}} \leq \overline{\mathscr{U}}(a,b,c) \leq a + \frac{b+c}{2},$$

where τ is the area of the triangle.

4   Preliminaries for Our Upper Bound Arguments

In this section we introduce some notation, we recall some useful past results, as well as we make some technical observations that we use repeatedly in our arguments. Line segments with endpoints A, B are denoted as AB. By abusing notation, and whenever it is clear from the context, we also use AB to refer to the length of the line segment. We use $\angle BAC$ to refer to the angle of vertex A of triangle ABC, or simply as $\angle A$ (or even more simply A), whenever it is clear from the context.

Our upper bounds for all 4 algorithmic problems we consider are obtained by analyzing the plain-vanilla algorithm that has been proved to be optimal for other search domains in the wireless model, e.g. the circle and the equilateral triangle. We refer to this algorithm as OPPOSITESEARCH.

The OPPOSITESEARCH Algorithm: The algorithm is executed once the two agents are placed at any point on the perimeter of the given geometric search domain. The two agents search the perimeter of the domain in opposite directions at the same unit speed until one of them reports the exit. Then the non-finder, who is notified instantaneously, goes to the exit along the shortest line segment. Consequently, the evacuation cost, for any exit placement, is the time that the non-finder reaches the exit. Note also that due to the symmetry of the communication model, it does not matter who is the exit finder, rather only when the exit is found.

Our upper bounds rely on a tight analysis of the OPPOSITESEARCH algorithm. Our proofs use a monotonicity criterion of [15] that we present next. The lemma refers to arbitrary unit-speed trajectories $S(t), R(t) \in \mathbb{R}^2$, $t \geq 0$, assumed to be continuous and differentiable at $t = 0$. Let also $S = S(0)$ and $R = R(0)$. We think of S, R as the locations of the two robots where one of them reports the exit. We define the *critical angle* of robot $S(t)$ (similarly of robot $R(t)$) as the angle that the velocity vector $S'(0)$ forms with segment SR (and as the angle that velocity vector $R'(0)$ forms with segment SR, for robot $R(t)$). The following lemma characterizes the monotonicity of the evacuation time, assuming that the exit is found in one of the two points S, R.

Lemma 1 (Theorem 2.6 in [15]). *Let ϕ, θ denote the critical angles of robots $S(t), R(t)$ at time $t = 0$. Then, the evacuation cost, assuming that the exit is at S or R, is strictly increasing if $\cos(\phi) + \cos(\theta) < 1$, strictly decreasing if $\cos(\phi) + \cos(\theta) > 1$, and constant otherwise.*

Intuitively, the proof of Lemma 1 relies on that the rate by which the two agents approach each other is $\cos(\phi) + \cos(\theta)$, while the rate by which the time goes by is 1. Lastly, our arguments often reduce to the solutions of Non-Linear Programs (NLPs). Whenever we do not provide a theoretical solution to the NLPs, we solve them using computer assisted symbolic (non-numerical) calculations on MATHEMATICA [27].

4.1 Evacuation Cost for Two Line Segments

In this section we analyze the performance of OPPOSITESEARCH under a special scenario, see Fig. 1(a) on page 8. We consider a configuration according to which a portion of the search domain has already been explored, and currently the two agents reside at points B, C, both moving towards point A at unit speed. Conditioning that the exit is somewhere on segments AB, AC, we calculate the evacuation cost, e.g. the worst-case time it takes the last agent to reach the exit, over all placements of the exit. The next lemma relies on Lemma 1.

Lemma 2. *Consider two unit speed robots starting at points B, C simultaneously, and moving toward point A along the corresponding line segments. Assuming that an exit is placed anywhere on segments AB, AC, and $\angle A \leq \pi/2$, then the worst case evacuation time equals $\max\{AB, AC, BC\}$.*

5 Evacuation Cost Bounds Starting from Anywhere on the Perimeter

Fix a triangle ABC with edges $a \geq b \geq c$. For evacuation algorithm OPPOSITESEARCH, and for each $i \in \{a, b, c\}$, we denote by $l_i(a, b, c)$ and $u_i(a, b, c)$ the smallest possible and largest possible worst-case evacuation cost, respectively, when the evacuation algorithm is restricted to start agents anywhere on edge i (where the worst-case cost is over all placements of the exit). From the definition of the four algorithmic problems we introduced, we have that

$\underline{\mathscr{L}}(a,b,c) \leq \min_{i \in \{a,b,c\}} l_i(a,b,c)$ *(Overall smallest worst-case cost),*

$\overline{\mathscr{L}}(a,b,c) \leq \max_{i \in \{a,b,c\}} l_i(a,b,c)$ *(Worst starting-edge for best starting-point worst-case cost),*

$\underline{\mathscr{U}}(a,b,c) \leq \min_{i \in \{a,b,c\}} u_i(a,b,c)$ *(Best starting-edge for worst starting-point worst-case cost),*

$\overline{\mathscr{U}}(a,b,c) \leq \max_{i \in \{a,b,c\}} u_i(a,b,c)$ *(Overall largest worst-case cost).*

In this section we are concerned with the exact evaluation of $l_i(a,b,c)$ and $u_i(a,b,c)$ of algorithm OPPOSITESEARCH, i.e. the smallest possible and highest possible worst-case evacuation cost, respectively, when starting anywhere on edge $i \in \{a,b,c\}$ of a non-obtuse triangle ABC, where $a \geq b \geq c$.

The backbone of the lengthy and technical analysis appears in the full version of the paper [20]. At a high level, the analysis proceeds by considering the evacuation cost of OPPOSITESEARCH for searching triangle ABC with edge lengths α, β, γ. In the proof we present in the full version of the paper, we assume that the starting point S of the agents lies on edge BC (of length α), and that it is x away from the middle point N of BC on the side of B, i.e. $BS = \alpha/2 - x$ and $NS = x$, where $0 \leq x \leq \alpha/2$, see also Fig. 1(b) on page 8. If $T(x)$ denotes the worst-case evacuation time (over all placements of the exit) starting from S, we calculate

$$\max_{0 \leq x \leq \alpha/2} T(x), \quad \min_{0 \leq x \leq \alpha/2} T(x),$$

that is, the worst and best starting points on segment NB (inducing worst possible and best possible worst-case costs).

The best starting point can be thought of as an algorithmic choice, whereas the worst starting point can be thought of as an adversarial choice. We note here that $T(x)$ denotes the worst-case evacuation cost for the starting point induced by point $S = S(x)$, which is determined by the adversarial placement of the exit anywhere on the perimeter of the triangle. That is, for each x, $T(x)$ denotes the supremum of the evacuation cost of the algorithm that has agents start from S and given that the exit is at I, where the supremum is taken over all I.

Next we give an outline of the performance analysis as it reads in the full version of the paper [20]. A critical consideration in the analysis pertains to which of the two vertices A, C is reached first by an agent, for the given starting point S (see Fig. 1(b)). Indeed, if x is "big enough", then vertex A is visited no later than vertex C (see Fig. 1(c) on page 8) while if x is "small enough", then vertex C is visited no later than vertex A (see Fig. 1(d) on page 8). In either case, when A or C is visited first, the two agents start moving towards the same vertex, and hence Lemma 2 applies. In particular the evacuation cost, past the moment that the first vertex among A, C is visited, is also a function of the distance of the two agents $R_1 R_2$, which is also a function of x. To that end, an important property is that $R_1 R_2(x)$ is convex in its domain, which allows us to simplify the formulas obtained by Lemma 2. We note that even though the starting point S, in the corresponding proof of the full version of the paper [20] is restricted to be on segment BN, we do the performance analysis for all $3! = 6$ cases regarding the relative lengths of α, β, γ. That allows us next to deduce the worst possible and best possible worst-case costs starting anywhere on the perimeter of a triangle with edges

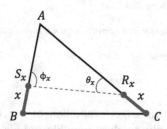

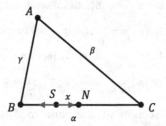

(a) Two agents start from points B, C and move towards A. The exit is placed somewhere on line segments AB, AC. Their critical angles, after searching for time x are denoted as ϕ_x, θ_x, respectively.

(b) The starting point S of the two robots.

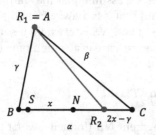

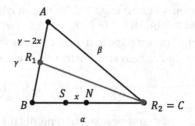

(c) The positions of the two robots in Configuration 1. Both R_1, R_2 move towards C.

(d) The positions of the two robots in Configuration 2. Both R_1, R_2 move towards A.

Fig. 1. Different configurations of searchers' starting points.

$a \geq b \geq c$ for algorithm OPPOSITESEARCH. Overall, the analysis allow us to obtain the following bounds (see Lemmata 3, 4 and 5).

Lemma 3. *For the smallest and largest possible worst-case evacuation cost of* OPPO-SITESEARCH, *when starting from the largest edge* a, *we have*

$$l_a(a, b, c) = \min\left\{ b + c, \frac{(a+b)^2 - c^2 + 4\sqrt{3}\tau}{4b} \right\}$$

$$u_a(a, b, c) = \frac{a}{2} + b + \frac{c}{2},$$

where τ *is the area of the given triangle.*

It is worthwhile mentioning here that $l_a(a, b, c)$ cannot be further simplified. Indeed, for $a = \sqrt{2}, b = c = 1$, the formula is given by $l_a(a, b, c) = b + c = 2$. On the other hand, when $a = b = c = 1$, we have that $l_a(a, b, c) = \frac{(a+b)^2 - c^2 + 4\sqrt{3}\tau}{4b} = 3/2$ (while formula $b + c$ would evaluate to 2).

Lemma 4. *For the smallest and largest possible worst-case evacuation cost of* OPPO-SITESEARCH, *when starting from the second largest edge* b, *we have*

$$l_b(a,b,c) = \max\left\{\frac{a+b+c}{2}, \frac{(a+b)^2 - c^2 + 4\sqrt{3}\tau}{4a}\right\}$$

$$u_b(a,b,c) = a + \frac{b}{2} + \frac{c}{2},$$

where τ *is the area of the given triangle.*

We note that the formula for $l_b(a,b,c)$ simplifies to a piece-wise function conditioning on whether $B \geq \pi/3$ or not.

Lemma 5. *For the smallest and largest possible worst-case evacuation cost of* OPPO-SITESEARCH, *when starting from the smallest edge* c, *we have*

$$l_c(a,b,c) = \frac{a+b+c}{2}, \quad u_c(a,b,c) = a+c.$$

We are now ready to prove the upper bounds for $\mathcal{L}(a,b,c), \overline{\mathcal{L}}(a,b,c), \underline{\mathcal{U}}(a,b,c)$ and $\overline{\mathcal{U}}(a,b,c)$ as stated in Theorem 1

Proof (of the Upper bounds of Theorem 1). By Lemmata 3, 4 and 5, we know all $l_i(a,b,c), u_i(a,b,c)$ for $i \in \{a,b,c\}$. Therefore we compute

$$\overline{\mathcal{U}}(a,b,c) \leq \max_{i\in\{a,b,c\}} u_i(a,b,c)$$

$$= \max\left\{\frac{a}{2} + b + \frac{c}{2}, a + \frac{b+c}{2}, a+c\right\}$$

$$= a + a + \frac{b+c}{2}.$$

We also have

$$\underline{\mathcal{U}}(a,b,c) \leq \min_{i\in\{a,b,c\}} u_i(a,b,c)$$

$$= \min\left\{\frac{a}{2} + b + \frac{c}{2}, a + \frac{b+c}{2}, a+c\right\}$$

$$= \min\left\{\frac{a}{2} + b + \frac{c}{2}, a+c\right\}$$

Next we calculate $\min_{i\in\{a,b,c\}} l_i(a,b,c)$, which is an upper bound to $\underline{\mathcal{L}}(a,b,c)$. By the already established results, we have that $\underline{\mathcal{L}}(a,b,c)$ is at most

$$\min\left\{\begin{matrix} b+c \\ \frac{(a+b)^2 - c^2 + 4\sqrt{3}\tau}{4b} \\ \frac{a+b+c}{2} \\ \max\left\{\frac{a+b+c}{2}, \frac{(a+b)^2 - c^2 + 4\sqrt{3}\tau}{4a}\right\} \end{matrix}\right\} = \min\left\{\begin{matrix} b+c \\ \frac{(a+b)^2 - c^2 + 4\sqrt{3}\tau}{4b} \\ \frac{a+b+c}{2} \end{matrix}\right\} = \min\left\{\begin{matrix} \frac{(a+b)^2 - c^2 + 4\sqrt{3}\tau}{4b} \\ \frac{a+b+c}{2} \end{matrix}\right\},$$

where the last equality is due to that $b + c \geq (a + b + c)/2$, by the triangle inequality.

Next we show that $\frac{(a+b)^2 - c^2 + 4\sqrt{3}\tau}{4b} \geq \frac{a+b+c}{2}$, which will conclude our claim about $\mathscr{L}(a, b, c)$ (but we will use this inequality in our last argument too). To see why we calculate

$$\frac{(a+b)^2 - c^2 + 4\sqrt{3}\tau}{4b} - \frac{a+b+c}{2}$$
$$= \frac{a^2 + \sqrt{3}\sqrt{-((a-b-c)(a+b-c)(a-b+c)(a+b+c))} - (b+c)^2}{4b}.$$

Clearly it is enough to show that the next expression is non-negative

$$3(b+c-a)(a+b-c)(a-b+c)(a+b+c) - \left((a+b)^2 - c^2\right)^2 = 4(b+c-a)(a+b+c)\left(a^2 - b^2 + bc - c^2\right).$$

The last expression is indeed non-negative, since $b + c - a \geq 0$ by the triangle inequality, and since by the Cosine Law $a^2 - b^2 + bc - c^2 = bc(1 - 2\cos(A)) \geq 0$, where the last inequality is because a is the largest edge, hence $A \geq \pi/3$, hence $\cos(A) \leq 1/2$.

Finally, we calculate $\max_{i \in \{a,b,c\}} l_i(a, b, c)$ which is an an upper bound to $\overline{\mathscr{L}}(a, b, c)$. For this, we have

$$\overline{\mathscr{L}}(a, b, c) \leq \max \begin{cases} \min\left\{b + c, \frac{(a+b)^2 - c^2 + 4\sqrt{3}\tau}{4b}\right\} \\ \frac{a+b+c}{2} \\ \max\left\{\frac{a+b+c}{2}, \frac{(a+b)^2 - c^2 + 4\sqrt{3}\tau}{4a}\right\} \end{cases} = \max \begin{cases} \min\left\{b + c, \frac{(a+b)^2 - c^2 + 4\sqrt{3}\tau}{4b}\right\} \\ \frac{a+b+c}{2} \\ \frac{(a+b)^2 - c^2 + 4\sqrt{3}\tau}{4a} \end{cases}$$

From the discussion above we know that $b + c \geq (a + b + c)/2$ and

$$\frac{a+b+c}{2} \leq \frac{(a+b)^2 - c^2 + 4\sqrt{3}\tau}{4b},$$

and hence $(a + b + c)/2 \leq \min\left\{b + c, \frac{(a+b)^2 - c^2 + 4\sqrt{3}\tau}{4b}\right\}$. So, we have

$$\overline{\mathscr{L}}(a, b, c) \leq \max \begin{cases} \min\left\{b + c, \frac{(a+b)^2 - c^2 + 4\sqrt{3}\tau}{4b}\right\} \\ \frac{(a+b)^2 - c^2 + 4\sqrt{3}\tau}{4a} \end{cases}.$$

Lastly, we recall that $a \geq b$, and hence $\frac{(a+b)^2 - c^2 + 4\sqrt{3}\tau}{4b} \geq \frac{(a+b)^2 - c^2 + 4\sqrt{3}\tau}{4a}$. Our main claim pertaining to $\overline{\mathscr{L}}(a, b, c)$ will follow once we show that $b + c \geq \frac{(a+b)^2 - c^2 + 4\sqrt{3}\tau}{4a}$. To that end we consider the non-linear program

$$\min \ (b + c) - \frac{(a+b)^2 - c^2 + 4\sqrt{3}\tau}{4a}$$
$$s.t. \ a = 1$$
$$(a, b, c) \in \Delta.$$

whose optimal value is 0, attained among others at $a = b = 1, c = 0$.   ∎

6 Lower Bounds

This section is concerned with proving the lower bounds for $\mathcal{L}(a,b,c)$, $\overline{\mathcal{L}}(a,b,c)$, $\mathcal{U}(a,b,c)$ and $\overline{\mathcal{U}}(a,b,c)$ as stated in Theorem 1. In all our arguments below, we denote by A, B, C the vertices opposite to edges $a \geq b \geq c$, respectively.

The Lower Bound for $\mathcal{L}(a,b,c)$: The proof follows by observing that $(a+b+c)/2$ is half the perimeter of the geometric object where the exit is hidden. Indeed, consider any algorithm for the triangle evacuation problem, where agents can possibly choose even distinct starting location on the perimeter of the given triangle. In time $(a+b+c)/2-\epsilon/2$, the two agents can search at most $a+b+c-\epsilon$, and hence there will also be, at that moment, an unexplored point. In other words, for every $\epsilon > 0$, the evacuation time is at least $(a+b+c)/2-\epsilon$.

The Lower Bound for $\overline{\mathcal{L}}(a,b,c)$: In this problem, the adversary chooses a starting edge, and then the algorithm may deploy the two robots on any point on that edge before attempting to evacuate the given triangle (from an exit that is again chosen by the adversary). An adversary who also allows the algorithm to choose the starting edge is even weaker, and therefore the lower bound for $\mathcal{L}(a,b,c)$ is a lower bound to $\overline{\mathcal{L}}(a,b,c)$ too.

The Lower Bound for $\mathcal{U}(a,b,c)$: Recall that in the underlying algorithmic problem, the algorithm chooses the starting edge, while the adversary chooses the starting point on the edge. So we consider some cases as to which starting edge an algorithm may choose. If the starting edge is either b or c, then the adversary can choose starting point A. Consequently, the adversary can wait until at the first among B, C is visited, and place the exit in the other vertex (the argument works even if vertices are visited simultaneously). But then, the evacuation time would be $\min\{AB, AC\} + BC = \min\{b,c\} + a = c + a$. In the last case, the algorithm may choose to start from edge a. In that case the adversary may choose starting point D which is $(a-c)/2$ away from B, i.e. for which $BD = (a-c)/2$ and $DC = (a+c)/2$. For that starting point, an adversary can wait until the first vertex among A, C is visited. If C is the first (which happens at time at least $DC = (a+c)/2$), the exit can be placed at A, then the induced running time would be at least $b+(a+c)/2$. Overall that would mean that the performance of the arbitrary algorithm would be $\min\{c+a, b+(a+c)/2\}$, which also equals our upper bound. If, on the other hand, A, is visited before C, then that can happen in time at least $AD = \left(c^2 + (a-c)^2/4 - c(a-c)\cos(B)\right)^{1/2}$, where also $\cos(B) = \frac{-b^2+a^2+c^2}{2ac}$ (note that $AD \leq (a+c)/2$ by the triangle inequality). Then, placing the exit at C induces evacuation time at least $AD + b$. Overall, since the algorithm can choose the starting edge, the induced lower bound to $\mathcal{U}(a,b,c)$ is at least

$$\min\{a+c, AD+b\} = \min\left\{a+c, \frac{1}{2}\sqrt{\frac{2b^2(a-c)-(a-2c)(a+c)^2}{a}} + b\right\}.$$

If we call the latter expression $f(a,b,c)$, then a Non-Linear Program can establish that

$$f(a,b,c) \geq \frac{1}{10}\left(\sqrt{10}+5\right)\min\{c+a, b+(a+c)/2\}$$

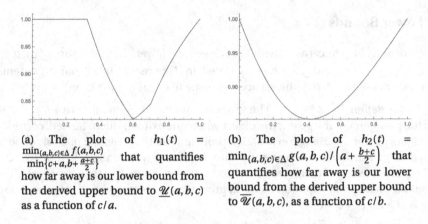

(a) The plot of $h_1(t) = \frac{\min_{(a,b,c)\in\Delta} f(a,b,c)}{\min\{c+a,b+\frac{a+c}{2}\}}$ that quantifies how far away is our lower bound from the derived upper bound to $\underline{\mathcal{U}}(a,b,c)$ as a function of c/a.

(b) The plot of $h_2(t) = \min_{(a,b,c)\in\Delta} g(a,b,c)/\left(a+\frac{b+c}{2}\right)$ that quantifies how far away is our lower bound from the derived upper bound to $\overline{\mathcal{U}}(a,b,c)$, as a function of c/b.

Fig. 2. Upper and lower bound gaps over all triangles.

(over all triangles with $A \le \pi/2$), meaning that our lower bound is off by at most $(\sqrt{10}+5) \approx 0.816228$ from our upper bound. By letting also denote by $h_1(t)$ the smallest ratio

$$f(a,b,c)/\min\{c+a,b+(a+c)/2\},$$

over all triangles non-obtuse triangles), condition on $c/a = t \in (0,1]$, we can also derive that our lower bound is much better than 0.816228 times our upper bound, for the various values of t, see Fig. 2(a)

The Lower Bound for $\overline{\mathcal{U}}(a,b,c)$: For this problem, the adversary can choose the agents' starting point on the perimeter of the triangle ABC. Consider the starting point D, on edge b, such that $AD = (b-c)/2$, and note that by the Cosine Law in triangle ADB we have that $BD = \left(c^2 + (b-c)^2/4 - c(b-c)\cos(A)\right)^{1/2}$, where also $\cos(A) = \frac{-a^2+b^2+c^2}{2bc}$ (note that $BD \le (b+c)/2$ by the triangle inequality). Now, with starting point D, we let an arbitrary algorithm run until the first point among B,C is visited (our argument works even if the points are visited simultaneously). If C is visited first, and since $DC = (b+c)/2$, this does not happen before time $(b+c)/2$, and so by placing the exit at B, the evacuation time would be at least $a+(b+c)/2$ (and that would be equal to the established upper bound). If on the other hand B is discovered before C, then we can place the exit C (when B is visited by any robot), and that would induce running time at least

$$BD + a = \frac{1}{2}\sqrt{\frac{2a^2(b-c)-(b-2c)(b+c)^2}{b}} + a.$$

If we call the last expression $g(a,b,c)$, then a Non-Linear Program can establish that $g(a,b,c) \ge^1 0.852\left(a+\frac{b+c}{2}\right)$. By denoting the smallest ratio $g(a,b,c)/\left(a+\frac{b+c}{2}\right)$ (over all triangles) condition on that $c/b = t \in (0,1]$ as $h_2(t)$, we can also derive that our

---

[1] 0.852 is the third smallest (also second largest) real root of polynomial $20x^6-68x^5+671x^4-2776x^3+2550x^2-516x-25$ (the polynomial has 4 real and 2 complex roots).

lower bound is much better than 0.852 times our upper bound, for the various values of t, see Fig. 2(b).

This completes the proof of all the lower bounds claims of Theorem 1.

7 Discussion

We provided upper and lower bounds to the 2 searcher evacuation problem from triangles in the wireless model, extending results previously known only for equilateral triangles. Our main contribution is a technical analysis of a plain-vanilla algorithm that has been proven to be optimal for various search domains in the wireless model. Our analysis covers 4 novel algorithmic problems pertaining to who is choosing the starting point of the searchers. We also provided lower bounds that depending on the given triangle could range from being tight to having a gap of at most .8 depending on the considered algorithmic problem and the given triangle. Providing tight upper and lower bounds for the entire spectrum of triangles is an open problem We also see the study of the same problem in the face-to-face model as the next natural direction to consider, but definitely more challenging.

References

1. Alpern, S., Fokkink, R., Gasieniec, L., Lindelauf, R., Subrahmanian, V.S.: Search Theory: A Game Theoretic Perspective. Springer, Heidelberg (2013). https://doi.org/10.1007/978-1-4614-6825-7

2. Alpern, S., Gal, S.: The Theory of Search Games and Rendezvous. Kluwer, Alphen aan den Rijn (2003)

3. Baezayates, R.A., Culberson, J.C., Rawlins, G.J.: Searching in the plane. Inf. Comput. **106**(2), 234–252 (1993)

4. Baeza-Yates, R.A., Culberson, J.C., Rawlins, G.J.E.: Searching with uncertainty extended abstract. In: Karlsson, R., Lingas, A. (eds.) SWAT 1988. LNCS, vol. 318, pp. 176–189. Springer, Heidelberg (1988). https://doi.org/10.1007/3-540-19487-8_20

5. Bagheri, I., Narayanan, L., Opatrny, J.: Evacuation of equilateral triangles by mobile agents of limited communication range. In: Dressler, F., Scheideler, C. (eds.) ALGOSENSORS 2019. LNCS, vol. 11931, pp. 3–22. Springer, Cham (2019). https://doi.org/10.1007/978-3-030-34405-4_1

6. Beck, A.: On the linear search problem. Israel J. Math. **2**(4), 221–228 (1964). https://doi.org/10.1007/BF02759737

7. Bellman, R.: An optimal search. SIAM Rev. **5**(3), 274 (1963)

8. Brandt, S., Laufenberg, F., Lv, Y., Stolz, D., Wattenhofer, R.: Collaboration without communication: evacuating two robots from a disk. In: Fotakis, D., Pagourtzis, A., Paschos, V.T. (eds.) CIAC 2017. LNCS, vol. 10236, pp. 104–115. Springer, Cham (2017). https://doi.org/10.1007/978-3-319-57586-5_10

9. Chuangpishit, H., Mehrabi, S., Narayanan, L., Opatrny, J.: Evacuating equilateral triangles and squares in the face-to-face model. Comput. Geom. **89**, 101624 (2020)

10. Chuangpishit, H., Georgiou, K., Sharma, P.: A multi-objective optimization problem on evacuating 2 robots from the disk in the face-to-face model; trade-offs between worst-case and average-case analysis. Information **11**(11), 506 (2020)

11. Czyzowicz, J., et al.: Priority evacuation from a disk: the case of $n \geq 4$. Theoret. Comput. Sci. **846**, 91–102 (2020)
12. Czyzowicz, J., Dobrev, S., Georgiou, K., Kranakis, E., MacQuarrie, F.: Evacuating two robots from multiple unknown exits in a circle. In: ICDCN, pp. 28:1–28:8. ACM (2016)
13. Czyzowicz, J., Gąsieniec, L., Gorry, T., Kranakis, E., Martin, R., Pajak, D.: Evacuating robots via unknown exit in a disk. In: Kuhn, F. (ed.) DISC 2014. LNCS, vol. 8784, pp. 122–136. Springer, Heidelberg (2014). https://doi.org/10.1007/978-3-662-45174-8_9
14. Czyzowicz, J., et al.: Evacuation from a disc in the presence of a faulty robot. In: Das, S., Tixeuil, S. (eds.) SIROCCO 2017. LNCS, vol. 10641, pp. 158–173. Springer, Cham (2017). https://doi.org/10.1007/978-3-319-72050-0_10
15. Czyzowicz, J., et al.: Priority evacuation from a disk: the case of n= 1, 2, 3. Theoret. Comput. Sci. **806**, 595–616 (2020)
16. Czyzowicz, J., Georgiou, K., Kranakis, E., Narayanan, L., Opatrny, J., Vogtenhuber, B.: Evacuating robots from a disk using face-to-face communication. Discrete Math. Theoret. Comput. Sci. **22**(4) (2020)
17. Czyzowicz, J., Kranakis, E., Krizanc, D., Narayanan, L., Opatrny, J., Shende, S.: Wireless autonomous robot evacuation from equilateral triangles and squares. In: Papavassiliou, S., Ruehrup, S. (eds.) ADHOC-NOW 2015. LNCS, vol. 9143, pp. 181–194. Springer, Cham (2015). https://doi.org/10.1007/978-3-319-19662-6_13
18. Disser, Y., Schmitt, S.: Evacuating two robots from a disk: a second cut. In: Censor-Hillel, K., Flammini, M. (eds.) SIROCCO 2019. LNCS, vol. 11639, pp. 200–214. Springer, Cham (2019). https://doi.org/10.1007/978-3-030-24922-9_14
19. Flocchini, P., Prencipe, G., Santoro, N. (eds.): Distributed Computing by Mobile Entities, Current Research in Moving and Computing. Lecture Notes in Computer Science, vol. 11340. Springer, Heidelberg (2019). https://doi.org/10.1007/978-3-030-11072-7
20. Georgiou, K., Jang, W.: Triangle evacuation of 2 agents in the wireless model. CoRR, abs/2209.08544 (2022)
21. Georgiou, K., Karakostas, G., Kranakis, E.: Search-and-fetch with 2 robots on a disk: Wireless and face-to-face communication models. Discret. Math. Theoret. Comput. Sci. **21** (2019)
22. Georgiou, K., Kranakis, E., Leonardos, N., Pagourtzis, A., Papaioannou, I.: Optimal circle search despite the presence of faulty robots. In: Dressler, F., Scheideler, C. (eds.) ALGO-SENSORS 2019. LNCS, vol. 11931, pp. 192–205. Springer, Cham (2019). https://doi.org/10.1007/978-3-030-34405-4_11
23. Georgiou, K., Kranakis, E., Steau, A.: Searching with advice: robot fence-jumping. J. Inf. Process **25**, 559–571 (2017)
24. Georgiou, K., Leizerovich, S., Lucier, J., Kundu, S.: Evacuating from ℓ_p unit disks in the wireless model. In: Gąsieniec, L., Klasing, R., Radzik, T. (eds.) ALGOSENSORS 2021. LNCS, vol. 12961, pp. 76–93. Springer, Cham (2021). https://doi.org/10.1007/978-3-030-89240-1_6
25. Hohzaki, R.: Search games: literature and survey. J. Oper. Res. Soc. Japan **59**(1), 1–34 (2016)
26. Lamprou, I., Martin, R., Schewe, S.: Fast two-robot disk evacuation with wireless communication. In: Gavoille, C., Ilcinkas, D. (eds.) DISC 2016. LNCS, vol. 9888, pp. 1–15. Springer, Heidelberg (2016). https://doi.org/10.1007/978-3-662-53426-7_1
27. Wolfram Research. Minimize (2021). https://reference.wolfram.com/language/ref/Minimize.html. Accessed 19 May 2022

Resource Time-Sharing for IoT Applications with Deadlines

George Karakostas[1]([✉]) and Stavros G. Kolliopoulos[2]

[1] Department of Computing and Software, McMaster University,
Hamilton, ON, Canada
karakos@mcmaster.ca
[2] Department of Informatics and Telecommunications,
National and Kapodistrian University of Athens, Athens, Greece
sgk@di.uoa.gr

Abstract. Motivated by time-sharing systems with deadlines, such as
2-way synchronization of Digital Twins, we introduce the study of a very
natural problem which can be abstracted as follows. We are given m
machines and n jobs, as well as a set of *tolerance capacities* $u_{ij} \geq 0$ for
every job j and machine i. Can we assign the jobs so that, if job j ends up
on machine i, at most u_{ij} jobs in total are processed on i? We define two
natural optimization versions: (i) Maximize the total weight of jobs that
can be assigned without violating the tolerance capacities u_{ij}, and (ii)
minimize the amount $\rho \geq 1$, by which capacities have to be scaled so that
all jobs can be assigned. For the first problem and its generalizations we
provide an $(1 - 1/e)$-approximation algorithm. For the second problem
we show that it is $n^{1/2-\varepsilon}$-inapproximable and provide linear integrality
gap lower bounds for two key relaxations.

Keywords: Time-sharing · Deadlines · Tolerance capacities ·
Scheduling

1 Introduction

An ever increasing number of applications within the framework of the Internet-
of-Things (IoT) depend on *real-time* response times, i.e., the ability of delivering
data to and from the application, as well as processing data, with acceptable
delays [24]. These delay requirements can apply to almost all different components of an IoT architecture. For example, the need for fast delivery of the
'freshest' available sensor data to cyber-physical systems has lead to the recent
concept of the Age-of-Information [25], i.e., the scheduling of data transmission
so that the largest latency between data generation at a source and its delivery to
the application is minimized. A different approach to the requirement for timely
data delivery and processing is the imposition of delay constraints (as opposed to
delay as objective in AoI), that can guarantee the real-time nature of the system.
An example of this latter approach is the concept of *Digital Twins (DT)* [17,21].

G. Karakostas—Research supported by an NSERC Discovery grant.

© The Author(s), under exclusive license to Springer Nature Switzerland AG 2022
T. Erlebach and M. Segal (Eds.): ALGOSENSORS 2022, LNCS 13707, pp. 91–107, 2022.
https://doi.org/10.1007/978-3-031-22050-0_7

These are virtual replicas of physical systems (PS), which capture a subset of the PS's features, maintain a 2-way synchronization of DT and PS states, and can store data relevant to the PS in order to perform computationally-heavy tasks, such as prediction and data analytics.

The 2-way synchronization requires that a DT performs periodically its data transmission and task processing, and is expected to finish both within a given period, thus assuring the data 'freshness'. With the proliferation of DTs, the time-sharing of critical resources, such as wireless channels and CPUs, by many DTs simultaneously puts a strain on the satisfaction of these timing requirements, and motivates the scheduling problem we introduce in this work as follows: A DT j with a synchronization period T_j, needs c_j CPU cycles in order to complete its data processing task (for simplicity we assume the data transmission time is negligible). DT j's task is executed on a server i of CPU frequency f_i together with the tasks of K other DTs, which share the CPU equally and continuously with j. In order for j's task to finish on time, the inequality $\frac{Kc_j}{f_i} \leq T_j$ must hold (j gets every K-th cycle of the CPU), which implies that $K \leq \frac{f_iT_j}{c_j}$, i.e., DT j's task can co-execute with at most $u_{ij} := \frac{f_iT_j}{c_j}$ (including itself) DTs on server i. A similar situation arises when several DTs share a wireless channel with their PSs, using TDMA. The natural question then is how to schedule a set of tasks with deadlines on a set of servers, when Round-Robin time-sharing is applied, and so that all deadlines are respected.

Although time-sharing scheduling with deadlines has been the motivation, we can move one level of abstraction higher, ignore the provenance of u_{ij} above, and ask the following general question, which is a very natural one and can apply to settings well beyond IoT. Given a set of n distinct balls, a set of m distinct bins, and a set of nm nonnegative integers u_{ij}, can the balls be placed in the bins so that if the j-th ball is placed in bin i, at most u_{ij} balls in total are placed in bin i? Note that some tolerance capacities u_{ij} can be equal to 0, i.e., job j cannot be assigned to machine i. The formal definition of the problem we examine is the following.

MACHINE-SHARING WITH TOLERANCE CAPACITIES (MSTC)

Input: Set of n jobs $\mathcal{J}$, set of m machines $\mathcal{M}$, tolerance capacities $u_{ij} \in \mathbb{Z}_{\geq 0}$ for all $(i, j) \in \mathcal{M} \times \mathcal{J}$.

Output: An assignment $\sigma : \mathcal{J} \to \mathcal{M}$ such that $|\sigma^{-1}(\sigma(j))| \leq u_{\sigma(j)j}$ $\forall j \in \mathcal{J}$, or NO if no such assignment exists.

For job $j \in \mathcal{J}$, $\mathcal{M}(j)$ denotes the set of machines on which j can be assigned, i.e., $\mathcal{M}(j) = \{i \in \mathcal{M} \mid u_{ij} > 0\}$. Similarly, for $i \in \mathcal{M}$, $\mathcal{J}(i) = \{j \in \mathcal{J} \mid u_{ij} > 0\}$. With this notation in place, MSTC can be equivalently formulated as finding a feasible solution to the following quadratic program:

$$\sum_{i \in \mathcal{M}(j)} x_{ij} \geq 1 \qquad \forall j \in \mathcal{J} \qquad\qquad (\text{QP})$$

$$x_{ij} \cdot \sum_{k \in \mathcal{J}(i)} x_{ik} \leq u_{ij} \quad \forall j \in \mathcal{J}, \forall i \in \mathcal{M}(j)$$

$$x_{ij} \in \{0, 1\} \qquad\qquad \forall i \in \mathcal{M}, \forall j \in \mathcal{J}(i)$$

MSTC can be easily seen to be NP-complete (e.g., via a reduction from SAT). To the best of our knowledge, this is the first time that the problem has been studied. The coverage problem with group budget constraints defined and studied in [4] comes perhaps closest to the spirit of MSTC. Assignment problems with forbidden *pairs* of assignments have been studied in the literature (e.g., [8]), but are incomparable to MSTC.

Problem MSTC gives rise to two natural optimization versions. Let every job j have a weight $w_j \geq 0$. One can ask for a *maximum-weight* set of jobs that can be assigned to machines without violating any tolerance capacities, together, possibly, with additional constraints. An immediate additional constraint is to require that no more than k machines can be used, but more natural constraints include job costs and a budget that should not be exceeded, or resource augmentation (e.g., more UAVs used as relays at a location to increase the number of available channels [18]), or bundles of jobs that *have* to be executed on a machine, or combinations of the above. We call this general family of problems the MAXIMUM MACHINE-SHARING WITH TOLERANCE CAPACITIES (MMSTC). The second problem derived from MSTC is a *congestion* version of the original that asks for the smallest scaling factor that one can multiply all tolerance capacities with, so that there is a feasible assignment for all jobs.

Definition 1. *For $\rho \geq 1$, an assignment σ is ρ-feasible if for all $j \in \mathcal{J}$, $|\sigma^{-1}(\sigma(j))| \leq \rho \cdot u_{\sigma(j)j}$.*

The SCALED MACHINE-SHARING WITH TOLERANCE CAPACITIES (SMSTC) asks for the minimum scaling factor ρ, such that there is a ρ-feasible assignment. The case of SMSTC where the tolerance capacities u_{ij} are equal to a common value T_i, for all $j \in \mathcal{J}(i)$, is the famous scheduling problem with machine deadlines problem for which Lenstra et al. gave a 2-approximation [16]. Our problem is more general, as every job has its own upper bound on the completion time of machine i, namely u_{ij}. The algorithm of [16] assumes a size p_{ij} for every job j and machine i. In the negative results we provide for SMSTC every job j has unit size on the set of machines $\mathcal{M}(j)$ it can be assigned to.

MMSTC in its simplest form (only tolerance capacities constraints) via an appropriate reformulation (see Sect. 2) can be efficiently reduced to the Separable Assignment Problem (SAP) of [9], and also to Maximum Coverage with Group Budgets, defined in [4], with an implicit set system that describes feasible packings of jobs. The simple randomized rounding of [9] yields an $(1 - \frac{1}{e})$-approximation, but cannot handle the additional constraints mentioned above. Based on an equivalent formulation of MSTC presented in Sect. 2, we also design an $(1 - \frac{1}{e})$-approximation algorithm for the simplest version of MMSTC (cf. Theorem 2), using the more sophisticated dependent rounding technique of [10,22] on a configuration LP relaxation. Unlike [9] though, the dependent rounding and the results presented in Sect. 3.2 can be extended to include the additional constraints. The requirement that no more than k machines are used can still be $(1 - \frac{1}{e})$-approximated by the algorithms of [2,5] that generalize [9] to matroidal constraints. In Sect. 3.3 we show how dependent rounding can be extended to also give a $(1 - \frac{1}{e})$-approximation for this case (cf. Theorem 4), as a template to deal with job costs, resource augmentation, required job bundles, or combinations of the above. Our algorithm can be extended to handle arbitrary integer job sizes p_{ij}, for $j \in \mathcal{J}$ and $i \in \mathcal{M}(j)$, at the cost of a $(1 + \varepsilon)$ scaling of the capacities.

Unfortunately, SMSTC turns out to be much harder to approximate. Using a reduction from 3D-MATCHING, we show that there is no polynomial-time $(n^{1/2-\varepsilon})$-approximation algorithm for SMSTC, unless P = NP (cf. Theorem 7). Here $n = |\mathcal{J}|$. The bound holds even when every job j has the same tolerance capacity $u_{ij} = u_j$ on every machine in $\mathcal{M}(j)$. In order to tackle the problem algorithmically, we explore two key relaxations. First, we study the configuration LP, a powerful linear relaxation that was introduced in the context of the cutting stock problem [6,12] and has been used among other for bin packing [15,19] and scheduling problems with assignment restrictions (e.g., [1,14,23]). Applied to the SMSTC problem, it is strictly stronger than the natural LP that has assignment variables x_{ij} for job-machine pairs. We prove that the configuration LP has an integrality gap of $\Omega(n)$ for congestion even when there are only two distinct tolerance capacity values, every job j has the same tolerance capacity u_j on every machine, and each job can be assigned to at most two machines (cf. Theorem 5). The second relaxation we consider is the formulation resulting from the quadratic program (QP) by relaxing the integrality constraints. Notably, this is a non-convex program. Still we show that it has an integrality gap of at least m, the number of machines. The lower bound holds again when every job has a machine-independent tolerance capacity (cf. Theorem 6). Hence, rounding the fractional solution of these two key formulations cannot give a non-trivial approximation factor. We leave the closing of the gap between Theorem 7 and Theorem 5 (or Theorem 6) as an open problem.

2   An Equivalent Formulation of MSTC

In this section we give an equivalent formulation of the MSTC problem. Recall that we are given as input a set $\mathcal{M}$ of machines, a set $\mathcal{J}$ of jobs and a set $\{u_{ij} \in \mathbb{Z}_{\geq 0} \mid (i,j) \in \mathcal{M} \times \mathcal{J}\}$. For $i \in \mathcal{M}$, let $d(i)$ denote $|\mathcal{J}(i)|$. Sort the capacities u_{ij}, $j \in \mathcal{J}(i)$, in non-decreasing order $u_{ij_1} \leq u_{ij_2} \leq \ldots \leq u_{ij_{d(i)}}$. Let m_i denote the number of distinct values in the sequence $u_{ij_1}, u_{ij_2}, \ldots, u_{ij_{d(i)}}$. Denote these distinct values in increasing order as $\bar{u}_{i1} < \bar{u}_{i2} < \ldots < \bar{u}_{im_i}$. Each machine $i \in \mathcal{M}$ consists of a set S_i of m_i submachines where submachine $k \in S_i$ has capacity $\bar{u}_{ik}$. The set $\mathcal{J}(i,k)$ of jobs that can be assigned to submachine $k \in S_i$ consists of

$$\{j \in \mathcal{J}(i) \mid u_{ij} \geq \bar{u}_{ik}\}.$$

Similarly, the set of submachines of machine i to which job j can be assigned is denoted $\mathcal{M}(i,j)$.

A *submachine assignment* of the jobs in $S \subseteq \mathcal{J}$ is a mapping $\psi : S \to \cup_{i \in \mathcal{M}} S_i$ such that (i) $\forall j \in S$, $\psi(j) \in \mathcal{M}(i,j)$ and (ii) for all $i \in \mathcal{M}$, at most one of the sets $\psi^{-1}(k)$, $k \in S_i$, is nonempty. In words, every job j in S is assigned to a submachine of a machine in $\mathcal{M}(j)$ and for every machine $i \in \mathcal{M}$, at most one of the submachines in S_i can be "open". In analogy to Definition 1, the submachine assignment ψ is ρ-feasible, for $\rho \geq 1$, if $\forall i \in \mathcal{M}, \forall k \in S_i, \ |\psi^{-1}(k)| \leq \rho \bar{u}_{ik}$.

Clearly the two problem formulations are equivalent, i.e., there is a ρ-feasible assignment σ if and only if there is ρ-feasible submachine assignment ψ. In the following sections we will choose each time the problem formulation (with or without submachines) that is more convenient.

3 Approximation Algorithms for MMSTC

In this section we consider the family of MMSTC problems. The simplest version is the following: Given input $\{u_{ij} \in \mathbb{Z}_{\geq 0} \mid (i,j) \in \mathcal{M} \times \mathcal{J}\}$, and a function $w : \mathcal{J} \to \mathbb{Q}_{\geq 0}$ that assigns weights to jobs, find a maximum-weight $S \subseteq \mathcal{J}$ for which there is a 1-feasible assignment.

3.1 Linear Relaxation with Configurations

For machine i and submachine $k \in S_i$, a subset $C \subseteq \mathcal{J}(i,k)$ is a *configuration* if $|C| \leq \bar{u}_{ik}$. The set of these configurations is denoted $\mathcal{C}(i,k)$. The configuration LP, denoted (CLP), has a variable x_{i,C_k} for each machine i, submachine $k \in S_i$, and configuration $C_k \in \mathcal{C}(i,k)$:

$$\max \sum_{j \in \mathcal{J}} w_j \left(\sum_{i \in \mathcal{M}} \sum_{k \in S_i} \sum_{C_k : j \in C_k} x_{i,C_k} \right) \tag{CLP}$$

$$\sum_{k \in S_i} \sum_{C_k} x_{i,C_k} \leq 1 \qquad \forall i \in \mathcal{M} \tag{1}$$

$$\sum_{i \in \mathcal{M}} \sum_{k \in S_i} \sum_{C_k : j \in C_k} x_{i,C_k} \leq 1 \qquad \forall j \in \mathcal{J} \tag{2}$$

$$x_{i,C_k} \geq 0 \qquad \forall i \in \mathcal{M}, \forall k \in S_i, \forall C_k \in \mathcal{C}(i,k) \tag{3}$$

The set of constraints (1) ensures that each machine is assigned at most one configuration and that at most one submachine is open. Constraints (2) ensure that each job is assigned at most once. Clearly, an integer solution to (CLP) corresponds to a 1-feasible assignment for a maximum-weight subset of $\mathcal{J}$. For a configuration C_k, let $w(C_k) := \sum_{j \in C_k} w_j$. The dual of (CLP) is the following:

$$\min \sum_{i \in M} y_i + \sum_{j \in \mathcal{J}} z_j \tag{D-CLP}$$

$$y_i + \sum_{j \in C_k} z_j \geq w(C_k) \qquad \forall i \in \mathcal{M}, \forall k \in S_i, \forall C_k \in \mathcal{C}(i,k) \tag{4}$$

$$y, z \geq 0 \tag{5}$$

A solution for (D-CLP) (and, therefore, (CLP)) can be computed using the ellipsoid algorithm as follows: Given a candidate solution (y^*, z^*) to (D-CLP), its separation oracle has to solve $\sum_{i \in \mathcal{M}} |S_i|$ instances of a knapsack-like problems, which we denote KPN. Fix $i \in \mathcal{M}$, $k \in S_i$. Consider a KPN instance with $\mathcal{J}(i, k)$ being the set of items and knapsack capacity $\bar{u}_{ik}$. Every item j has a size $s_j = 1$ and a (possibly negative) value $v_j = w_j - z_j$. The oracle returns a violated inequality iff there is a feasible packing in the knapsack with total value that exceeds y_i. The KPN instance can be solved by the obvious greedy algorithm in $O(n \log n)$ time.

3.2   Dependent-Rounding Algorithm

In this section we present our dependent rounding for the simplest version of MMSTC, i.e., finding and integral solution of (CLP). Although the approximation result we obtain in Theorem 2 can also be obtained by the simple randomized rounding for SAP in [9], this section provides the algorithmic foundations for the extensions of Sect. 3.3.

Let x^* be an optimal solution of (CLP). Without loss of generality we can assume that

$$\sum_{k \in S_i} \sum_{C_k} x^*_{i, C_k} = 1, \quad \forall i \in \mathcal{M}.$$

The vector x^* induces on each machine a probability distribution on the sub-machines in S_i. We will use dependent rounding to choose one configuration per machine and ensure that a near-optimal fraction of jobs is scheduled.

Srinivasan [22] (see also [10]) has provided a technique to sample algorithmically from a distribution with the following properties. Consider any sequence of t reals $P = (p_1, \ldots, p_t)$ such that $p_i \in [0, 1]$ and $\sum_i p_i$ is an integer l. F_t is defined as a family of distributions over vectors in $\{0, 1\}^t$. A member $D(t; P)$ of the family F_t guarantees the following properties on any vector $(X_1, \ldots, X_t)$ sampled from $D(t; P)$.

(A1) *(probability preservation)* $\forall i, \Pr[X_i = 1] = p_i$.
(A2) *(degree preservation)* $\Pr[|\{i : X_i = 1\}| = l] = 1$.
(A3) *(negative correlation)* For all $S \subseteq [t]$ we have $\Pr[(\bigwedge_{i \in S}(X_i = 0)] \leq \prod_{i \in S} \Pr[X_i = 0]$ and $\Pr[(\bigwedge_{i \in S}(X_i = 1)] \leq \prod_{i \in S} \Pr[X_i = 1]$.

Theorem 1 ([22]). *Given $P = (p_1, \ldots, p_t)$ there is a linear-time algorithm that generates a sample from distribution $D(t; P)$.*

Let $\mathcal{C}_i$ denote the disjoint union of the sets of configurations in $\bigsqcup_{k \in S_i} \mathcal{C}(i, k)$ whose corresponding variable has a nonzero value in the solution x^* of (CLP). Every configuration in $\mathcal{C}_i$ belongs to a unique $\mathcal{C}(i, k)$. Denote by $x^*|i$ the restriction of vector x^* to the entries corresponding to the configurations in $\mathcal{C}_i$. To simplify notation, set $t_i = |\mathcal{C}_i|$. We define a distribution $D(t_i; x^*|i)$ that satisfies properties (A1), (A2), (A3) for each machine $i \in \mathcal{M}$. Observe that in our setting $l = 1$. The rounding algorithm is the following.

ALGORITHM DEPROUND

For all $i \in \mathcal{M}$, do independently:

1. Using the algorithm of Theorem 1, sample from $D(t_i; x^*|i)$ to obtain vector $X^{(i)} \in \{0,1\}^{t_i}$. By Property (A2), $X^{(i)}$ has a unique entry equal to 1.
2. Assign the configuration C that corresponds to the nonzero entry of $X^{(i)}$ to machine i.

Theorem 2. *Algorithm* DEPROUND *runs in polynomial-time and outputs a 1-feasible assignment for a set of jobs S whose expected total weight is at least $(1 - 1/e)$ times the optimum of the (CLP) relaxation.*

Proof. Let $\mathcal{C}$ denote the disjoint union $\bigsqcup_{i \in \mathcal{M}} \mathcal{C}_i$. That is, every configuration in $\mathcal{C}$ corresponds to a unique (i,k) pair. For $j \in \mathcal{J}$, let z_j be the random variable that takes value 1 if job j is assigned by Algorithm DEPROUND and zero otherwise. Our analysis is quite similar to the analysis in [22] for Maximum Coverage versions of Set Cover. We slightly abuse notation and index the entries of the vectors $X^{(i)}$ by the corresponding configurations. Since every configuration C belongs to a unique $\mathcal{C}_i$ we omit the superscript i as well.

$$\Pr[z_j = 1] = 1 - \Pr\Big[\bigwedge_{C \in \mathcal{C}: C \ni j} (X_C = 0)\Big]$$

$$\geq 1 - \prod_{C \in \mathcal{C}: C \ni j} \Pr[X_C = 0] \qquad (6)$$

$$= 1 - \prod_{C \in \mathcal{C}: C \ni j} (1 - x_C^*) \qquad (7)$$

Inequality (6) follows from the "negative correlation" property (A3) and Equality (7) from property (A1). Define $z_j^* := \sum_{C \in \mathcal{C}: C \ni j} x_C^*$. Thus the fractional amount by which job j is scheduled and the objective value of the solution x^* is equal to $\sum_{j \in \mathcal{J}} w_j z_j^*$. Using the AM-GM inequality and the fact that $z_j^* \leq 1$, it is easy to see that

$$\prod_{C \in \mathcal{C}: C \ni j} (1 - x_C^*) \leq (1 - z_j^*/s)^s$$

where s is the maximum number of configurations in the support of x^* that a job belongs to. By calculus, $1 - (1 - z_j^*/s)^s \geq (1 - (1 - 1/s)^s) \cdot z_j^* > (1 - 1/e) \cdot z_j^*$. $\square$

The results in this section can be easily extended to the case where every job j has an integer size $p_{ij} \geq 1$ for $i \in \mathcal{M}(j)$ and an assignment σ of set $S \subseteq \mathcal{J}$ is ρ-feasible if

$$\forall j \in S, \quad \sum_{k \in \sigma^{-1}(\sigma(j))} p_{\sigma(j)k} \leq \rho \cdot u_{\sigma(j)j}.$$

By rounding the job sizes as explained in [1] we can solve in polynomial time the Configuration LP while using configurations whose size is at most $(1 + \varepsilon)$

the capacity of the corresponding submachine. As an alternative, standard techniques [3,13] can be used to bring the capacity violation factor into the approximation factor instead. Applying the algorithm DEPROUND yields the following (also by simple randomized rounding [9]):

Theorem 3. *If every job j in $\mathcal{J}$ has an integer size p_{ij}, for $i \in \mathcal{M}(j)$, one can in polynomial-time compute a set of jobs S whose expected total weight is at least $(1 - 1/e)$ times the optimum of the (CLP) relaxation and an assignment for S that is $(1 + \varepsilon)$-feasible for any arbitrary constant $\varepsilon > 0$.*

3.3   Constraint Extensions of MMSTC

The techniques of the previous section can be extended to derive a good approximation for the extensions of MMSTC, as mentioned in Sect. 1. More specifically, an $(1 - \frac{1}{e})$-approximation of the objective can be obtained for the following additional constraints:

Coverage: No more than k machines can be used.

Bundles of required jobs: Given k bundles of jobs $C_1, \ldots, C_k$, maximize the total scheduled job weight, while scheduling all bundles on machines.

Required machines: Given a set of machines $A \subseteq \mathcal{M}$, the machines in A *must* be used.

Resource augmentation: Given integers $l_1, \ldots, l_{|\mathcal{M}|}$, the schedule can use at most l_i copies of the i-th machine.

Budget: Given assignment costs c_{ij} for all jobs j on machines i, and a budget B, the total cost of scheduled jobs cannot exceed the budget B.

In the full version of this abstract, we show that the dependent rounding of Sect. 3.2 can be extended to $(1 - \frac{1}{e})$-approximate these versions, or their combinations, while not violating the the coverage, resource augmentation, bundles of required jobs constraints, required machines, and not violating the budget and capacity constraints by much (or, alternatively, not at all with an ε cost to the approximation factor, for any $\varepsilon > 0$). As a template for dealing with the extra constraints, in this abstract we show how this can be done for the COVERAGE-MMSTC, which requires that no more than k machines can be used. Since this constraint by itself happens to be matroidal, the algorithms of [2,5] also achieve an approximation factor of $(1 - \frac{1}{e})$.

  To simplify our exposition, we will assume that we have guessed the exact number of machines $k_0 \leq k$ used by the optimal solution (by 'guessing' we mean the exhaustive enumeration of k_0 values, and the output of the maximum obtained solution). Formulation (CLP) can be extended by adding a special empty configuration $C_\emptyset$:

$$\max \sum_{j \in \mathcal{J}} w_j \left(\sum_{i \in \mathcal{M}} \sum_{k \in S_i} \sum_{C_k \,:\, j \in C_k} x_{i,C_k} \right) \qquad \text{(CovCLP)}$$

$$\sum_{i \in \mathcal{M}} x_{i,C_\emptyset} = m - k_0 \tag{8}$$

$$\sum_{k \in S_i} \sum_{C_k} x_{i,C_k} + x_{i,C_\emptyset} = 1 \qquad \forall i \in \mathcal{M} \tag{9}$$

$$\sum_{i \in \mathcal{M}} \sum_{k \in S_i} \sum_{C_k : j \in C_k} x_{i,C_k} \leq 1 \qquad \forall j \in \mathcal{J} \tag{10}$$

$$x_{i,C_k} \geq 0 \qquad \forall i \in \mathcal{M}, k \in S_i, C_k \in \mathcal{C}(i,k) \cup \{\mathcal{C}_\emptyset\} \tag{11}$$

Note that it can still be the case of assigning an empty configuration in $\mathcal{C}_i$ to i, but that doesn't matter (it means that eventually fewer than k_0 machines are used by the solution).

If w is the (unrestricted) dual variable corresponding to (8), then the objective of (D-CLP) becomes $\sum_{i \in \mathcal{M}} y_i + \sum_{j \in \mathcal{J}} z_j + (m - k_0)w$, and the constraints $w + y_i \geq 0$, $\forall i \in \mathcal{M}$ are added. The separation oracle of (D-CLP) can be easily extended to solve the new dual LP, and, therefore compute the optimal solution x^* to (CovCLP). The dependent rounding of Sect. 3.2 becomes the rounding procedure of [10] on a bipartite graph $G = (A, B, E)$, constructed as follows: Each distribution $D(t_i; x^*|i)$ gives rise to a star with machine i at its center, and the configurations of $\mathcal{C}_i$ in the support of x^* at the leaves. Side A contains the machines/centers of these stars, while the leaves of the stars are vertices in side B. We add another vertex $C_\emptyset$ to B, and connect all vertices $i \in A$ with $x^*_{i,C_\emptyset} > 0$ to $C_\emptyset$.

Note that variable x^*_{i,C_k} corresponds to edge (i, C_k). We require a rounding of these variables that achieves degree 1 for all vertices in A, and degree k_0 for vertex $C_\emptyset$ in B (we don't care about the degrees of the rest of the nodes in B). The dependent randomized rounding of [10] satisfied these requirements with probability 1 (property (A2)). Moreover, as is proven in Theorem 4.4 of [20], the configurations in B are negatively correlated (property (A3)), i.e., the indicator random variables X_C of configurations C being picked or not are negatively correlated, and this for arbitrary fractional degree bounds on the vertices of B ([20, p. 684]). Hence, (6) carries through, and, together with the known lower bound for the Maximum Coverage problem [7], we have the following (also by the algorithms of [2,5]):

Theorem 4. *A solution for problem* COVERAGE-MMSTC *that is 1-feasible and assigns in expectation at least* $(1 - 1/e)$ *times the optimal weight of jobs can be computed in polynomial time. This factor is best possible, unless* P = NP.

Similarly to Theorem 3, Theorem 4 can be extended to the case where job j has an integer size p_{ij}, for $i \in \mathcal{M}(j)$.

4   Minimizing Congestion

In this section we consider the SMSTC problem. Given input $\{u_{ij} \in \mathbb{Z}_{\geq 0} \mid (i,j) \in \mathcal{M} \times \mathcal{J}\}$, find the minimum $\rho \geq 1$ for which there is a ρ-feasible assignment for the set $\mathcal{J}$. We show integrality gap lower bounds in Sect. 4.1 and a hardness of approximation result in Sect. 4.2.

4.1   Integrality Gaps for SMSTC

Let P be a valid mathematical programming relaxation for computing an assignment for the jobs in $\mathcal{J}$. For $f \geq 1$, we say that P has an *integrality gap of at least f for congestion* if there is an instance $I = \{u_{ij} \mid (i,j) \in \mathcal{M} \times \mathcal{J}\}$ for which P is feasible, but P has no integer feasible solution for any instance $I_\rho = \{\rho \cdot u_{ij} \mid (i,j) \in \mathcal{M} \times \mathcal{J}\}$ with $\rho < f$.

We start by showing an integrality gap for the Configuration LP relaxation. We define an instance Ξ where each job will have the same capacity on each machine it can be assigned to. The set of machines consists of three blocks of machines, blocks A, B and C. Each machine has two submachines, one with large and one with small capacity. Accordingly we refer to the *big* and the *small* submachine of a given machine. All machines within the same block X have the same large and small capacities at their two submachines. These capacity values are denoted U_X and u_X respectively.

Block A consists of a single machine with $U_A = 2k$ and $u_A = 2$, where $k \geq 2$ is a positive integer of our choice. We refer to this single machine as machine A.

Block B consists of 2 machines, B_1 and B_2. The submachine capacities are $U_B = 2k$ and $u_B = 2$.

Block C consists of 2 machines, C_1 and C_2. The submachine capacities are $U_C = 2k$ and $u_C = 2$.

All jobs have processing time (height) 1. They are partitioned into two sets, those that can only be assigned to small submachines and those that can be assigned to big and small submachines. By slightly abusing terminology we refer to the corresponding sets as *small* and *large* jobs respectively. In what follows when we say that a job may be assigned to the big submachine of machine x it is implied that it can also be assigned to the small submachine of x.

The set of large jobs consists of the disjoint union of two sets F and G. Set F contains $2k$ jobs divided into 2 groups F_1, F_2 each containing k jobs. G consists of k jobs.

- The jobs of F can be assigned to the big submachine of machine A. The jobs of F_i, can be assigned to the big submachine of machine B_i, $i = 1, 2$.
- The jobs of G can be assigned to the big submachines of machines C_1, C_2.

The set of small jobs consists of the disjoint union of two sets P and Q.

- P contains 2 jobs p_1, p_2 that can be scheduled on the small submachine of machine A. Moreover p_i can be assigned on the small submachine of machine C_i, $i \in \{1, 2\}$.

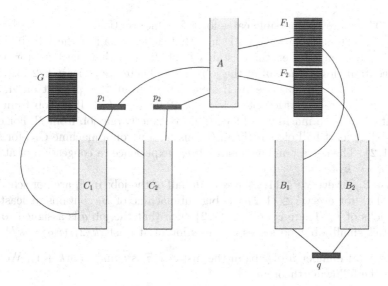

Fig. 1. Instance Ξ used in the integrality gap construction.

– Set Q contains 1 job, call it q. Job q can be scheduled on the small submachine of machines B_1, B_2.

See Fig. 1 for a depiction of the instance Ξ. The Configuration LP for congestion minimization is the following.

$$\sum_{k \in S_i} \sum_{C_k} x_{i,C_k} \leq 1 \qquad \forall i \in \mathcal{M} \qquad \text{(CCLP)}$$

$$\sum_{i \in \mathcal{M}} \sum_{k \in S_i} \sum_{C_k : j \in C_k} x_{i,C_k} \geq 1 \qquad \forall j \in \mathcal{J}$$

$$x_{i,C_k} \geq 0 \qquad \forall i \in \mathcal{M}, \forall k \in S_i, \forall C_k \in \mathcal{C}(i,k)$$

Lemma 1. *Linear program (CCLP) has a feasible half-integral solution x for the instance Ξ.*

Proof. There is a feasible half-integral solution where to every submachine a configuration of x-value $1/2$ is assigned. The jobs in $F \cup G \cup P \cup Q$ can be assigned exactly to two machines each and in x they are split equally among these two machines. It is easy to see that these split jobs (of width $1/2$ and height 1) can be packed into configurations of width $1/2$ and height that does not exceed the capacity of the corresponding submachine. □

Lemma 2. *Any integer solution for the instance Ξ that leaves no job unassigned has a congestion of at least $k/4$.*

Proof. There are two possible cases for a feasible solution.

Case 1. There is an $i \in \{1, 2\}$ such that at least half of the jobs in F_i are not scheduled on B_i. I.e., there is an $i \in \{1, 2\}$ such that the big submachine of B_i contains less than half of the jobs in F_i. Therefore at least $k/2$ jobs from F_i are scheduled on machine A. If some job p_j from P is present on A, then p_j experiences a congestion of at least $(k/2)/(u_A) = k/4$. If no job from P is present on A, each machine of block C hosts exactly one job from P. For every $i \in \{1, 2\}$ at least half of the jobs in G must end up on a machine C_{i^*}, for some $i^* \in \{1, 2\}$. The corresponding small job p_{i^*} experiences a congestion of at least $(k/2)/u_C = k/4$.

Case 2. For every $i \in \{1, 2\}$, less than half of the jobs in F_i are not scheduled on B_i. I.e., for every $i \in \{1, 2\}$ the big submachine of B_i contains at least half of the jobs of F_i. There is an $i^* \in \{1, 2\}$ such that the job q is assigned to B_{i^*}. Then this small job experiences a congestion of at least $(k/2)/(u_B) = k/4$. $\square$

The total number n of jobs in the instance Ξ is equal to $3(k + 1)$. We have proved the following theorem.

Theorem 5. *The integrality gap of the Configuration LP (CCLP) for minimizing congestion on an instance of n jobs is at least $(n - 3)/12$ even when (i) there are only two distinct capacity values (ii) every job j has the same tolerance capacity on every machine in $\mathcal{M}(j)$ (iii) each job can be assigned to at most two machines.*

Define (QP-F) to be the relaxation of (QP) where the integrality constraints are replaced by

$$x_{ij} \geq 0 \quad \forall i \in \mathcal{M}, \forall j \in \mathcal{J}(i).$$

The instance Ξ we used in Theorem 5 is infeasible for (QP-F). We define a new instance Υ. Let $m = U$ be the number of machines, for some integer $U \geq 2$. The number n of jobs is $m(U - 1) + 1$. Recalll that for a positive integer t, $[t]$ denotes the set $\{1, 2, \ldots, t\}$. Each machine $i \in [m]$, has a cluster $J_i = \{j_l^i \mid l \in [U - 1]\}$ of $U - 1$ "private" clients that can only be assigned to i and have each tolerance capacity U. The remaining single job out of the n, call it job 1, can be assigned to all machines, with tolerance capacity $u_{i1} = 1$, for all i. The set of jobs is $\mathcal{J} = \{1\} \cup \bigcup_{i=1}^m J_i$. In any feasible integer solution, there is a machine $i^* \in [m]$ that processes job 1. In order to service the jobs in J_{i^*} a congestion of U has to be incurred.

There is a feasible fractional solution to (QP-F). For every $i \in [m]$ and for every job $d = j_l^i \in \mathcal{J}_i$, set $x_{i,d} = 1$. For every $i \in [m]$, set $x_{i1} = 1/U$. Because $U = m$, job 1 is completely serviced. It is easy to see that all capacity constraints are met.

Theorem 6. *The integrality gap of (QP-F) with respect to congestion is at least m, where m is the number of machines in the instance. This holds even when (i) there are only two distinct capacity values (ii) every job j has the same tolerance capacity on every machine in $\mathcal{M}(j)$.*

4.2   Hardness of Approximation for SMSTC

It is well-known that the following problem is NP-complete [11].

BOUNDED 3D-MATCHING
Input: Set of triples $M \subseteq A \times B \times C$, where A, B, and C are pairwise disjoint sets having the same number q of elements. Every element of $A \cup B \cup C$ occurs in at most 3 triples.
Question: Does M contain matching, i.e., a subset $M' \subseteq M$ such that $|M'| = q$ and no two elements of M' agree in any coordinate?

Recall Definition 1. An instance of SMSTC which has an f-feasible assignment is called an *f-feasible instance*.

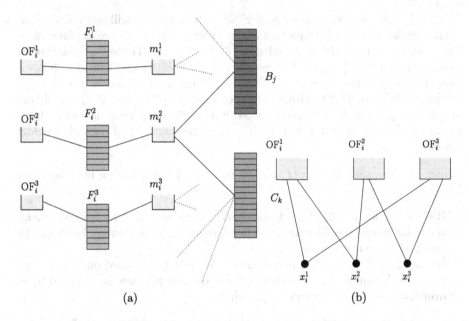

Fig. 2. The construction for the hardness reduction of SMSTC. (a) Example of a group M_i of size 3 and the jobs that can be assigned to the triple-machines in M_i. Machine m_i^2 corresponds to the triple (a_i, b_j, c_k). (b) Allowed assignments for the three placeholder jobs x_i^p, $p \in \{1, 2, 3\}$.

Given an instance I of BOUNDED 3D-MATCHING we construct an instance $\phi(I)$ of SMSTC. For every triple in M we have in $\phi(I)$ a dedicated *triple-machine*. For every $i \in [q]$, group together all machines that correspond to triples whose first coordinate is $a_i \in A$ in a group M_i. For every such group, add $|M_i|$ *overflow machines* OF_i^p, $p \in [|M_i|]$. Without loss of generality we may assume that $|M_i| > 1$. The reader is invited to bear in mind from now on that $|M_i| \in \{2, 3\}$. The total number of machines in the instance $\phi(I)$ is $|M| + \sum_{i=1}^{q} |M_i| \leq 12q$.

For $i \in [q]$, we create $|M_i|$ blocks of "dummy" jobs F_i^p, $p \in [|M_i|]$. Every block contains f jobs where $f > 1$ is an integer we will define later. The jobs of block F_i^p can be scheduled only on machine $m_i^p \in M_i$ and on the overflow machine OF_i^p. The tolerance capacity of every dummy job is f on both machines it can be assigned to. Observe that if a block of dummies ends up on a machine, nothing else can be assigned there without incurring congestion larger than 1.

For every $b_j \in B$ we create a set B_j of f' jobs b_j^r, $r \in [f']$, each of which can only be scheduled on the triple-machines that correspond to triples on which b_j is the second component. The quantity f' is an integer larger than f and will be defined later. For every $c_k \in C$ we create a set C_k of f' jobs c_k^r, $r \in [f']$, each of which can only be scheduled on the triple-machines that correspond to triples on which c_k is the third component. The tolerance capacity of these jobs is $2f'$. See Fig. 2a.

Finally, there is a set of "placeholder" jobs whose mission will be to block some of the overflow machines. In particular, for every $i \in [q]$, there are d_i placeholder jobs with $d_i = 1$ if $|M_i| = 2$ and $d_i = 3$ if $|M_i| = 3$. The set of placeholder jobs is denoted as $\{x_i^p\}_{p \in [d_i]}$. The assignment possibilities are defined as follows. *Case 1: $d_i = 1$.* The single placeholder job x_i^1 can be assigned to the overflow machines OF_i^p, $p \in \{1, 2\}$, with a tolerance capacity of 1. *Case 2: $d_i = 3$.* Every placeholder job can be assigned to exactly two of the overflow machines OF_i^p, $p \in [3]$, in the way shown in Fig. 2b. The tolerance capacity of each placeholder job is 2.

Remark 1. In a solution to $\phi(I)$ with congestion 1 the following hold for every $i \in [q]$.

- If Case 1 holds for d_i, at least one overflow machine must be reserved exclusively for the placeholder job x_i^1. Therefore at most one dummy block can be assigned to an overflow machine.
- If Case 2 holds for d_i, the placeholder jobs must be assigned on at least two overflow machines. No more than a single dummy job may be assigned to an overflow machine that carries a placeholder.

Lemma 3. *If I is a "YES"-instance of* BOUNDED 3D-MATCHING, *then $\phi(I)$ is a 1-feasible instance of* SMSTC.

Proof. For all $i \in [q]$ perform the following. Let $\tau = (a_i, b_j, c_k)$ be the triple in the matching that contains element a_i. For all $r \in [f']$ assign the jobs b_j^r and c_k^r to the machine $m_i^p \in M_i$ that corresponds to the triple τ. The dummy jobs of block F_i^p are assigned to the overflow machine OF_i^p. The remaining dummy jobs $F_i^{p'}$, $p' \neq p$, are assigned each to their corresponding machine in M_i. There are $|M_i| - 1$ available overflow machines and we can schedule the d_i placeholders on them. □

Define ρ so that the following relations are satisfied

$$2 \cdot \rho < f \text{ and } \rho \cdot f < f'/3. \tag{12}$$

Lemma 4. *If I is a "NO'-instance of BOUNDED 3D-MATCHING, then $\phi(I)$ is not a ρ-feasible instance of SMSTC.*

Proof. Assume to the contrary that there is a ρ-feasible assignment σ. Fix a $j \in [q]$. Consider the jobs b_j^r, $r \in [f']$. By the structure of the instance I there are at most 3 triple-machines to which these f' jobs can be assigned. Therefore in σ there is a machine that carries at least $f'/3$ jobs from B_j. By (12) a triple machine that carries even one dummy job can tolerate a total of at most $\rho \cdot f < f'/3$ jobs. Therefore among the triple-machines that can accept the jobs of B_j at least one must have no dummy assigned. The above holds for all j, and in each triple-machine m only jobs from the same set $B_{m(j)}$ can be assigned. Hence there must be at least q machines in M that are empty from dummy so that each receives a job from a distinct B_j, $j \in [q]$.

Claim. In a ρ-feasible assignment σ, for every $i \in [q]$, exactly one triple-machine in group M_i is empty from dummy.

Proof (of claim). We have shown that at least q machines in M must be empty from dummy. We will show that for each i at most one machine in M_i can be empty from dummy. This will establish the claim. We distinguish two cases.

Case 1: $d_i = 1$. Assume that in σ both machines m_i^1, m_i^2 in M_i are empty from dummy. Then the two overflow machines OF_i^1, OF_i^2 take each one block of dummy jobs. The placeholder job x_i^i must live on the same machine with f other jobs. By (12) this incurs a congestion larger than ρ, a contradiction.

Case 2: $d_i = 3$. Assume that in σ at least two among the three machines in M_i are empty from dummy. Then at least two overflow machines $OF_i^p, OF_i^{p'}$ take each one block of dummy jobs. At least one of the three placeholder jobs x_i^1, x_i^2, x_i^3 must live in σ on the same machine with f other jobs. By (12) this incurs a congestion larger than ρ, a contradiction. $\square$

By the claim, exactly one machine from each of the q groups M_i must be empty from dummy. Let M' be the set of these machines. Each machine in M' gets at least one member from a distinct B_j. M' induces a 2D perfect matching of $A \times B$. Similarly, a triple machine that carries a dummy job can tolerate at most $\rho \cdot f < f'/3$ jobs from C_k, for any $k \in [q]$. Since σ is ρ-feasible, for every $k \in [q]$ at least one job from C_k is assigned to a machine that is empty of dummy, i.e., to a machine of M'. Clearly, no two jobs from different $C_k, C_{k'}$ sets, with $k \neq k'$, can appear on the same triple-machine. The q machines of M' that are empty from dummy induce a feasible 3D-Matching of $A \times B \times C$. We have reached a contradiction. As long as f' is larger than a suitable constant, setting $\rho = \frac{\sqrt{f'}}{4}$ and $f = \lceil \sqrt{f'}/2 \rceil + 1$ satisfies (12). $\square$

We conclude that unless P = NP there is no polynomial-time algorithm that on input $\phi(I)$ can output a solution with congestion at most $\sqrt{f'}/4$ times the optimum. Given that the number n of jobs in $\phi(I)$ is equal to $2f'q + f \cdot |M| + \sum_{i=1}^{q} d_i$ and that $q \leq |M| \leq 9q$, we have that $n = \Theta(f'q)$. To keep the reduction polynomial-time it must be that $f' = O(q^c)$ for some constant $c > 0$. In other words, $f' = n^{1-\varepsilon}$ for an arbitrary constant $\varepsilon > 0$ of our choice.

Theorem 7. *For any constant $\varepsilon > 0$, there is no polynomial-time $(n^{1/2-\varepsilon})$-approximation algorithm for* SMSTC, *unless* P $=$ NP. *The result holds even when each job j has the same tolerance capacity on each machine in $\mathcal{M}(j)$.*

References

1. Bansal, N., Sviridenko, M.: The Santa Claus problem. In: Proceedings of the 38th Annual ACM Symposium on Theory of Computing (STOC), pp. 31–40 (2006)
2. Călinescu, G., Chekuri, C., Pál, M., Vondrák, J.: Maximizing a monotone submodular function subject to a matroid constraint. SIAM J. Comput. **40**(6), 1740–1766 (2011)
3. Carr, R.D., Vempala, S.S.: Randomized metarounding. Random Struct. Algorithms **20**(3), 343–352 (2002)
4. Chekuri, C., Kumar, A.: Maximum coverage problem with group budget constraints and applications. In: Jansen, K., Khanna, S., Rolim, J.D.P., Ron, D. (eds.) APPROX/RANDOM -2004. LNCS, vol. 3122, pp. 72–83. Springer, Heidelberg (2004). https://doi.org/10.1007/978-3-540-27821-4_7
5. Chekuri, C., Vondrák, J.: Randomized pipage rounding for matroid polytopes and applications. CoRR abs/0909.4348 (2009)
6. Eisemann, K.: The trim problem. Manage. Sci. **3**(3), 279–284 (1957)
7. Feige, U.: A threshold of ln n for approximating set cover. J. ACM **45**(4), 634–652 (1998)
8. Ficker, A.M.C., Spieksma, F.C.R., Woeginger, G.J.: The transportation problem with conflicts. Ann. Oper. Res. **298**, 1–21 (2018). https://doi.org/10.1007/s10479-018-3004-y
9. Fleischer, L., Goemans, M.X., Mirrokni, V.S., Sviridenko, M.: Tight approximation algorithms for maximum separable assignment problems. Math. Oper. Res. **36**(3), 416–431 (2011)
10. Gandhi, R., Khuller, S., Parthasarathy, S., Srinivasan, A.: Dependent rounding and its applications to approximation algorithms. J. ACM **53**(3), 324–360 (2006)
11. Garey, M.R., Johnson, D.S.: Computers and Intractability: A Guide to the Theory of NP-Completeness. W.H. Freeman and Company, New York (1979)
12. Gilmore, P.C., Gomory, R.E.: A linear programming approach to the cutting-stock problem. Oper. Res. **9**, 849–859 (1961)
13. Jain, K., Mahdian, M., Salavatipour, M.R.: Packing steiner trees. In: Proceedings of the Fourteenth Annual ACM-SIAM Symposium on Discrete Algorithms, 12–14 January 2003, Baltimore, Maryland, USA, pp. 266–274. ACM/SIAM (2003)
14. Jansen, K., Rohwedder, L.: A quasi-polynomial approximation for the restricted assignment problem. SIAM J. Comput. **49**(6), 1083–1108 (2020)
15. Karmarkar, N., Karp, R.: An efficient approximation scheme for the one-dimensional bin-packing problem. In: Proceedings of the 23rd Annual IEEE Symposium on Foundations of Computer Science (FOCS), pp. 312–320 (1982)
16. Lenstra, J.K., Shmoys, D.B., Tardos, E.: Approximation algorithms for scheduling unrelated parallel machines. Math. Program. A **46**, 259–271 (1990)
17. Minerva, R., Lee, G.M., Crespi, N.: Digital twin in the IoT context: a survey on technical features, scenarios, and architectural models. Proc. IEEE **108**(10), 1785–1824 (2020)
18. Oteafy, S.M.A.: Resource augmentation in heterogeneous internet of things via UAVs. In: 2021 IEEE Global Communications Conference (GLOBECOM), pp. 1–6 (2021)

19. Rothvoss, T.: Better bin packing approximations via discrepancy theory. SIAM J. Comput. **45**(3), 930–946 (2016)
20. Saha, B., Srinivasan, A.: A new approximation technique for resource-allocation problems. Random Struct. Algorithms **52**(4), 680–715 (2018)
21. Sharma, A., Kosasih, E.E., Zhang, J., Brintrup, A., Calinescu, A.: Digital twins: state of the art theory and practice, challenges, and open research questions. CoRR abs/2011.02833 (2020)
22. Srinivasan, A.: Distributions on level-sets with applications to approximation algorithms. In: Proceedings of 42nd IEEE Annual Symposium on Foundations of Computer Science (FOCS), pp. 588–597 (2001)
23. Svensson, O.: Santa Claus schedules jobs on unrelated machines. SIAM J. Comput. **41**(5), 1318–1341 (2012)
24. Verma, S., Kawamoto, Y., Fadlullah, Z., Nishiyama, H., Kato, N.: A survey on network methodologies for real-time analytics of massive IoT data and open research issues. IEEE Commun. Surv. Tutor. **19**(3), 1457–1477 (2017)
25. Yates, R.D., Sun, Y., Brown, D.R., Kaul, S.K., Modiano, E., Ulukus, S.: Age of information: an introduction and survey. IEEE J. Sel. Areas Commun. **39**(5), 1183–1210 (2021)

Fault-Tolerant Graph Realizations
in the Congested Clique

Manish Kumar[⊠] [ID], Anisur Rahaman Molla[ID], and Sumathi Sivasubramaniam[ID]

Indian Statistical Institute, Kolkata, India

manishsky27@gmail.com, anisurpm@gmail.com, sumathive189@gmail.com

Abstract. In this paper, we study the graph realization problem in the Congested Clique model of distributed computing under crash faults. We consider *degree-sequence realization*, in which each node v is associated with a degree value $d(v)$, and the resulting degree sequence is realizable if it is possible to construct an overlay network with the given degrees. Our main result is a $O(f)$-round deterministic algorithm for the degree-sequence realization problem in a n-node Congested Clique, of which f nodes could be faulty ($f < n$). The algorithm uses $O(n^2)$ messages. We complement the result with lower bounds to show that the algorithm is tight w.r.t the number of rounds and the messages simultaneously. We also extend our result to the Node Capacitated Clique (NCC) model, where each node is restricted to sending and receiving at-most $O(\log n)$ messages per round. In the NCC model, our algorithm solves degree-sequence realization in $O(nf/\log n)$ rounds and $O(n^2)$ messages. For both settings, our algorithms work without the knowledge of f, the number of faults. To the best of our knowledge, these are the first results for the graph realization problem in the crash-fault distributed network.

Keywords: Graph realizations · Congested-Clique · Distributed algorithm · Fault-tolerant algorithm · Crash fault · Time complexity · Message complexity

1 Introduction

Graph Realization problems have been studied extensively in the literature, mainly in the sequential setting. In general, graph realization problems deal with constructing graphs that satisfy certain predefined properties (such as a degree sequence). While the area was mostly focused on realizing graphs with specified degrees [33], other properties, such as connectivity [24–26], flow [31] and eccentricities [12,42] have also been studied.

The *degree-sequence* realization problem has been explored widely in the centralized setting. Typically, the problem consists of the following. Given a sequence of non-negative numbers $D = (d_1, d_2, \ldots, d_n)$, the degree-sequence problem asks if D is *realizable*. A sequence D is said to be *realizable* if there is a graph of n nodes whose sequence of degrees matches D. The first complete characterization of the problem was established in 1960, when Erdös and Gallai [21] showed that D is realizable if and only if $\sum_{i=1}^{k} d_i \leq k(k-1) + \sum_{i=k+1}^{n} \min(d_i, k)$ for every $k \in [1, n]$ following which, the

© The Author(s), under exclusive license to Springer Nature Switzerland AG 2022
T. Erlebach and M. Segal (Eds.): ALGOSENSORS 2022, LNCS 13707, pp. 108–122, 2022.
https://doi.org/10.1007/978-3-031-22050-0_8

definitive solution was independently found by Havel and Hakimi [32,33], a recursive sequential algorithm that takes $O(n)$ time (see Sect. 3 for more detail). Non-centralized versions of realizing degree sequences have also been studied, albeit to a lesser extent. Arikati and Maheshwari [2] provide an efficient technique to realize degree sequences in the PRAM model.

Recently, Augustine et al. [5] studied the graph realization problem in distributed networks. They approach the graph realization from the perspective of Peer-to-Peer (P2P) overlay construction. P2P overlay networks are virtual networks built on top of the underlying network, e.g., Internet. Given the increasing popularity of P2P networks (in the key areas like, cryptocurrencies, blockchain, etc.), research on P2P networks, particularly in the construction of P2P overlays, has become a crucial part in distributed computing.

In [5], the authors build overlay networks by adapting graph realization algorithms. Briefly, given a network of n nodes $V = \{v_1, \ldots, v_n\}$, where each v_i is assigned a degree d_i, the goal is to create an overlay graph $G(V, E)$ such that $d(v_i) = d_i$ in G, and for any edge $e \in E$, at least one of e's end points knows the existence of e (referred to as an *implicit realization*). Note that, for any edge it is only required that one end point must be aware of its existence, which means that a node may be aware of only a small part of the realized graph. In the best case, the nodes know only their neighbors in the final realization. However, in most of the P2P overlay applications, it is crucial to know the entire overlay graph. Furthermore, the network is assumed to be fault-free.

In this work, we extend the graph realization problem in faulty setting where node may fail by crashing. In addition, we consider the graph realization from the approach of learning degrees so that the nodes may recreate the degree sequence locally, i.e., they know the entire overlay graph. To be precise, we develop fault-tolerant algorithm which ensures that each node learns the degree of all the non-crashed nodes (at least) in the network. This allows the nodes to use the sequential Havel-Hakimi algorithm [32,33] to build the overlay graph G locally. Note that, since every (non-crashed) node learns the degree sequence and creates the realization, all of them know the entire overlay graph.

Our work is primarily in the Congested Clique (CC) model, a well studied model in distributed networks [43]. The Congested Clique model has been explored widely for many fundamental distributed problems [10,11,14,20,28,29,34,35,38,39]. Distributed networks are faulty by nature; nodes crash, links fail, nodes may behave maliciously, etc. In the node failure settings, the two fundamental problems, namely, agreement and leader election has been studied extensively [1,7,13,19,22,27,30,36,37,41]. The main challenge in a faulty setting is to ensure that no two nodes have a different view of a value, which may lead to an increase in the number of rounds or messages or both. Thus, in our work, we focus on developing an algorithm that minimizes the time complexity and the message complexity simultaneously in the Congested Clique with faulty nodes.

In order to make our algorithm more suited for the networks with message overhead limitation (such as peer-to-peer networks), we also extend the algorithm to the Node Capacitated Clique (NCC) model, introduced by Augustine et al. [6]. In the NCC, nodes are restricted to send and receive only $O(\log n)$ messages per round, making it ideal for more realistic settings (e.g., less or no overhead at nodes). The authors in [5] restrict their graph realization algorithms primarily to the NCC model. While our main algorithm considers the CC model, we extend it to the NCC model also. For both the settings (CC and NCC), our algorithms do not require any prior knowledge of f—the number of faulty nodes.

As a byproduct, our algorithms solve fault-tolerant reliable broadcast or consensus [15–17,49] in a congested clique. Reliable broadcast algorithms ensure that both senders and receivers agree on a value m sent by a correct process. That is, either all correct processes decide on the value m being sent or decide the sender is faulty. While this is similar to our problem, in our case we extend the basic premise to ensure that all nodes agree on the same degree sequence, which consists of ensuring that the network agrees on at most $O(n)$ values (degrees). This causes a significant challenge to the broadcast protocols in a faulty setting. To the best of our knowledge, the best known for consensus protocol in the crash failure setting has $O(f)$ time complexity and $O(n)$ message complexity [16]. Since there could be $O(n)$ values to be agreed to make sure that all the non-crashed nodes have the same degree sequence, the best known reliable broadcast or consensus protocol won't give better bounds if applies to solve the graph realization problem in the congested clique.

Paper Organization: The rest of the paper is organized as follows. In the rest of the section, we first present our results, followed by a brief description of the model and a formal definition of our problem. In Sect. 2, we discuss various related works in the field. Section 3 provides a brief description of the sequential Havel-Hakimi solution for the graph realization problem. The Sect. 4 presents the main result, which is an efficient solution for the fault-tolerant graph realization problem and also provides matching lower bounds. In Sect. 5, we extend the graph realization algorithm to the NCC model. And finally, in Sect. 6 we conclude with some interesting open problems.

1.1   Our Contributions

We present an efficient algorithm and matching lower bounds for the distributed graph realization problem in the Congested Clique and Node Capacitated Clique model in the presence of node failures. Specifically, our results are:

(1) An $O(f)$-round deterministic algorithm for the graph realization problem in an n-node Congested Clique with at most $f < n$ node failures. The message complexity of the algorithm is $O(n^2)$, where the size of each message is $O(\log n)$ bits.
(2) We show a matching lower bound for both the time and the message bounds–which demonstrates the simultaneous time and message bounds optimality of our algorithm.
(3) We extend the algorithm for the Congested Clique to the Capacitated Clique, and present a $O(nf/\log n)$-round and $O(n^2)$-message complexity algorithm.

1.2   Model and Definitions

We consider the message passing model of distributed computing. The underlying network is a Congested Clique (CC) [39,43]. A Congested Clique consists of n nodes which are identified by unique IDs from $\{u_1, u_2, \ldots, u_n\}$. Communication among the nodes happens in synchronous rounds, where in each round a node can communicate with any of the other $n - 1$ neighbors by sending a message of size $O(\log n)$ bits. This was first introduced in [47]. Nodes know the ID of the other nodes and the port connecting to the IDs. This assumption is known as the KT_1 model [47]. We assume that an arbitrary subset of the nodes in the clique of size up to $f < n$ may fail by crashing. A faulty node may crash in any round during the execution of the algorithm. If a node crashes in a round, then an arbitrary subset (possibly all) of its messages for that round may be lost (as determined by an adversary) and may not have reached the destination (i.e., neighbors). The crashed node halts (inactive) in the further rounds of the algorithm. If a node does not crash in a round, then all the messages that it sends in that round are delivered to the destination.

We assume an *adaptive* adversary controls the faulty nodes, which selects the faulty nodes at any time during the execution of the algorithm. Also, the adversary chooses when and how a node crashes, which is unknown to the nodes.

The time complexity of an algorithm is the number of rounds from the start until the termination of the algorithm. The message complexity of an algorithm is the total number of messages sent by all the nodes throughout the execution of the algorithm.

In the interest of being useful in the Peer-to-Peer context, we also consider the Node Capacitated Clique (NCC) [6] model. NCC limits each node to send or receive a bounded number of messages, which, interestingly, makes NCC quite distinct from CC. In this model, any node, say, u can send or receive $O(\log n)$ messages, each of size $O(\log n)$ bits.

We will now formally define the distributed graph realization problem (with and without faults). We say that an overlay graph $G = (V, E)$ is constructed if, for every $e = (u, v) \in E$, at least one of the endpoints is aware of the ID of the other and also aware that $e \in E$. We say that the overlay graph is *explicit* if, for every edge $e \in E$ in the graph both endpoints know each other's ID and are aware of that $e \in E$.

Definition 1 (Distributed Graph Realization [5]). *Let $V = \{v_1, \ldots, v_n\}$ be the set of nodes in the network. Let $D = (d_1, d_2, \ldots, d_n)$ be an input degree sequence such that each d_i is only known to the corresponding node v_i. The distributed degree realization problem requires that the nodes in V construct a graph realization of D such that in the resulting overlay graph G, the following conditions hold:*

(i) The degree sequence of G is precisely D.
(ii) The degree of v_i is d_i, $\forall i \in \{1, \ldots, n\}$.

Thus, in the case of the distributed graph realization problem, a solution should output the graph G if D is a realizable degree sequence; otherwise, output "unrealizable".

Definition 2 (Distributed Graph Realization with Faults). *Let $V = \{v_1, \ldots v_n\}$ be the set of nodes in the network and $D = (d_1, d_2, \ldots, d_n)$ be an input degree sequence such that each d_i is only known to the corresponding node v_i. Let $F \subset V$ be an arbitrary subset of faulty nodes in the network, such that $|F| = f \leq n - 1$. Let us define $D' \subseteq D$ be the modified degree sequence after losing the degrees of some faulty nodes and G' be the corresponding overlay graph over D'. The distributed degree realization with faults problem requires that the non-faulty nodes in V construct a graph realization of D' such that in the resulting overlay graph G', the following conditions hold:*

(i) $|D'| \geq n - |F|$.
(ii) $D - D'$ *is the degree sequence corresponding to some nodes that crashed.*
(iii) *For any edge* $e = (u, v) \in G'$, *either* u *or* v *(or both) knows of the existence of* e.

The required output is an overlay graph G' *if* D' *is realizable; otherwise, output "unrealizable".*

2   Related Work

Fault tolerant computation has always been a popular area of research in distributed computation, only becoming more popular with the prevalence of P2P networks that encourage for high decentralization. Often the focus of such research is on maintaining connectivity [9], recovery, or on ensuring that the network can tolerate a certain number of faults [52]. We refer interested readers to [50] for more information on models and techniques for designing such systems. In our work, we focus mainly on ensuring that all the (non-faulty) nodes have the same view of the information in-spite of the presence of numerous faults.

In lieu of this, our goal in this work is to solve the distributed degree sequence problem, which is a graph realization problem. Graph realization problems have been well studied in the literature, focusing on problems such as realizing graphs with specified degrees [33] as well as other properties, like connectivity and flow [24–26,31] or eccentricities [12,42]. Arikati and Maheshwari [2] provide an efficient technique to realize degree sequences in the PRAM model, and in [5], the authors explored graph realization from a distributed setting. However, both of these works assumed a fault-free setting. Here we extend the model to a faulty setting. In [5], Augustine et al. discussed distributed graph realizations on a path (both implicit and explicit). However, in their work, a node is only required to learn its neighbors in the final realization, in our work, the nodes are aware of the entire graph.

In the area of P2P overlays, there is a great deal of existing literature. In particular, a large amount of research exists to create overlays that provide structure and stability. This is best captured by overlays such as Chord [51], CAN [48], and Skip Graphs [3]. Overlays have also been specifically designed to tolerate faults [8,23]. For a more detailed survey on P2P overlays and their properties, we refer interested readers to the following excellent surveys [44,45].

Our network is modeled using the Congested Clique model. The congested clique model, first introduced by Lokter et al. [43] has been well studied, in both the faulty and non-faulty settings [18,46]. Problems such as agreement and leader election have also been well studied in this model [1,7,30,40]. To the best of our knowledge, this is the first time graph realization problems have been studied in the faulty setting of Congested Clique.

While the results for the Congested Clique are interesting in and of itself, in order to make our work more applicable to P2P settings, we also explore how to solve the graph realization problem in the NCC [6]. In the NCC, unlike the CC, a node is allowed to send/receive at most $O(\log n)$ messages in a round, this makes gathering information in a faulty-setting slightly more challenging.

3 Preliminary: The Sequential Havel-Hakimi Algorithm for Graph Realization

We will now briefly introduce the sequential Graph Realization problems that inspired our distributed version of the same. Graph realization problems are fairly simple in characterization. The basic premise is as follows: given a particular degree sequence $D = (d_1, d_2 \ldots d_n)$, can we create a graph G whose degree sequence is precisely D? The most well known characterization is given independently by Havel [33] and Hakimi [32], which can be stated concisely as follows.

Theorem 1 (Based on [33] and [32]). *A non-increasing sequence* $D = (d_1, d_2, \ldots, d_n)$ *is graphic (i.e., graph is realizable) if and only if the sequence* $D' = (d'_2, \ldots, d'_n)$ *is graphic, where* $d'_j = d_j - 1$, *for* $j \in [2, d_1 + 1]$, *and* $d'_j = d_j$, *for* $j \in [d_1 + 2, n]$

This characterization directly implies a $O\left(\sum_{i=1}^{n} d_i\right)$ time (in terms of number of edges) sequential algorithm, known as the Havel-Hakimi algorithm, for constructing a realizing graph $G = (V, E)$ where $V = \{v_1, \ldots v_n\}$ and $d(v_i) = d_i$, or deciding that no such graph exists. The algorithm works as follows. Initialize $G = (V, E)$ to be an empty graph on V. For $i = 1$ to n, in step i do the following:

1. Sort the remaining degree sequence in non-increasing order ($d_i \geq d_{i-1} \geq \ldots d_n$).
2. Remove d_i from D, and set $d_j = d_j - 1$ for all $j \in [i + 1, d_i + i + 1]$.
3. Set the neighborhood of the node v_i to be $\{v_{i+1}, v_{i+2}, \ldots v_{i+1+d_i}\}$.

If, at any step, D contains a negative entry, the sequence is not realizable.

4 Fault-Tolerant Graph Realization

In this section, we present an efficient solution for graph realization with faults. Recall that we are given a n-node Congested Clique, in which at most $f < n$ nodes may crash arbitrarily at any time. Also, a vector of degree sequence $(d_1, d_2, \ldots, d_n)$ is given as an input such that each d_i is only known to one node in the clique. Our goal is to construct an overlay graph of size at least $n - f$ if realizable; otherwise output unrealizable. We present an algorithm that guarantees, despite $f < n$ faulty nodes, that (i) all the (non-crashed) nodes learn and recreate a degree sequence whose size is at least $n - f$, and (ii) this degree sequence is the same for all the nodes as a requirement of the graph realization (see Definition 2). This allows the non-crashed nodes to locally realize the overlay graph with the help of Havel-and-Hakimi's algorithm, described in Sect. 3. We note that the algorithm does not require any knowledge of f. Our algorithm crucially uses only a few number of nodes to be involved in propagating the information about crashed nodes to the other nodes in the network– which helps to minimize the message complexity and round complexity of the algorithm.

At a high level, the algorithm runs in two phases. In the first phase, which consists of only two rounds, each node sends the message containing its ID and input-degree twice (in two consecutive rounds). Based on the frequency of the received message, i.e., zero or one or two times, the receiver node considers the sender node's status as faulty or non-faulty. Then each node locally creates an initial faulty list and a degree sequence (known only to itself). In the second phase, through sharing the information about faulty nodes present in the faulty list, the nodes rectify the degree sequence and create a final degree sequence D', which is guaranteed to be the same for all the non-crashed nodes. The non-crashed nodes then realize the overlay graph using D' as the degree sequence via the Havel-and-Hakimi algorithm.

Let us recall a few basic assumptions. For simplicity, we assume the KT_1 version of the Congested Clique model, in which all the nodes know the IDs of the nodes in the clique and the corresponding link or port connecting to the IDs. Thus, in the KT_1 version, a node can sort all the nodes in the clique according to their distinct IDs. W.l.o.g, let us assume the IDs are $U = \{u_1, \ldots u_n\}$ in the sorted order, i.e., $u_i < u_j$ for $i < j$. A node knows its position in the sorted order. Notice that a node u_i can track whether it has received any messages from a node u_j. However, the algorithm also works in the KT_0 version of the Congested Clique model where only the IDs are known, but the corresponding links are unknown (i.e., a node doesn't know which neighbor has which ID).

We will now explain the algorithm in detail, whose terminologies and definitions are summarized in Table 1. The first phase (which we call the *initialization phase*) consists of two rounds. In both the rounds, every node broadcasts their input degree value to reach all the nodes in the clique. After the two rounds, each node u_i creates a *faulty-list* F_{u_i} and a *degree sequence* D'_{u_i} as follows. F_{u_i} consists of n cells corresponding to all the nodes $u_j \in U$ (in the sorted order). For any u_j ($j \neq i$), if u_i hears from u_j in both the rounds, u_i includes u_j's degree value $d(u_j)$ in its final degree sequence D'_{u_i} (and correspondingly u_j's entry in the faulty-list is empty, i.e., $F_{u_i}(u_j) = null$). If u_i hears from u_j only in the first round (i.e., u_j crashed during the initialization phase), then u_j is included as a *faulty-node* in its corresponding entry. If u_i did not hear from u_j in both the rounds (i.e., u_j crashed in the first round itself), then u_j is additionally marked as a *smite-node* in u_i's *faulty-list*. At the end of the algorithm, we show that $D'_{u_i} = D'_{u_j}$ for all i, j, which represents the final *non-faulty-list* D'.

In the second phase, nodes update their faulty-list locally. Nodes are divided into two groups based on the two states– *active* state and *listening* state. A node in the active state transmits messages, whereas a node in the listening state only receives messages. Nodes may update their faulty-list according to the information received from the active nodes. Initially, all the nodes start in the listening state. A node u_i in listening state continues to be in that state as long as there is another active node in the network. Let u_j be the ID of the last active node (if there is none, let $j = 1$). A node u_i changes its status from listening state to active state if and only if u_i has not received any message from the last $3(i - j)$ rounds where j is the index of last heard node, i.e., u_j. Then u_i becomes active in the $(3(i - j) + r)^{th}$ round; r is the round when u_i heard from u_j.

After the initialization phase (i.e., from the 3rd round), the node with the minimum ID (or minimum index) becomes the active node, say the node u_1 (if present). If F_{u_1} is non-empty, then u_1 sends the $\langle ID, d(ID) \rangle$ from the first non-empty cell in F_{u_1} twice (in two consecutive rounds). If there is no $d(ID)$ then u_1 sends only ID. This situation may arise when an ID crashed such that u_1 doesn't receive $d(ID)$ in initialization phase (in first two rounds). u_1 continues sending $\langle ID, d(ID) \rangle$ from its F_{u_1} one by one from minimum ID to maximum ID and for each message $\langle ID, d(ID) \rangle$ it sends twice in consecutive rounds. When u_1 finishes sending all the non-null entries in F_{u_1}, it switches to the exit state (which we will explain shortly). If at any point in time, u_1 crashed then u_2 will become the next active node after $3(2 - 1) = 3$ rounds. The exit state for any node u_j consists of two tasks, (i) move all the F_{u_j} (if any) into D'_{u_j}. (ii) Send out "all-okay" message to all other nodes and exit the algorithm. Sending or receiving "all-okay" message conveys that all the known faulty-nodes have been addressed. All other nodes who hear the message (those who are in the listening state) "all-okay" also enter the exit state.

Let us now discuss the update process of nodes in active and listening states in detail. Suppose u_i is a node which is currently in its active state and F_{u_i} is non-empty. Then u_i sends the first non-null entry, say s, twice in consecutive rounds. If s was a *smite-node* then u_i permanently removes s from the F_{u_i}. If s was a *faulty-node*, then u_i moves $d(s)$ to D'_{u_i}. If F_{u_i} is empty, then u_i enters the exit state.

If instead the node u_j happened to be in its listening state, then let i be the index of the last node heard by the node u_j. If u_j has not heard from any node during the last $3(j - i)$ rounds, then u_j sets its state to active. Since each node needs to send the message twice, we maintain a gap of one extra round (total three) to prevent two or more nodes from being active at the same time. But if u_j is currently receiving messages from an active node u_i then it does the following. Let s be the ID it heard from u_i. u_j now updates its faulty-list F_{u_j} based on how many times u_j heard about s from the active node u_i.

If u_j heard about s twice, and s was a *smite-node* then u_j permanently removes s from its faulty-list F_{u_j}. However, if s was a *faulty-node* then u_j moves s to D'_{u_j} (if not in D'_{u_j}) and permanently removes $F_{u_j}(s)$ (if any). Notice that u_j might have received s earlier two times, in that case $F_{u_j}(s)$ will be null and there will be a corresponding entry in the D'_{u_j}. If u_j heard about s only once, then if s had been a *smite-node* (or respectively a *faulty-node*) then $F_{u_j}(s)$ is marked as a *smite-node* (respectively *faulty-node*). All non-null entries in F_{u_j} below s's index are included in D'_{u_j} if the entries correspond to faulty-nodes, otherwise they are set to null.

Throughout the algorithm, inclusion of the degree in D' is permanent. Therefore, the corresponding node entries in *faulty-list* remain null. At last, all the non-faulty nodes have the same view of *non-faulty-list* i.e., D'. Therefore, the graph can be realized locally by the Havel-Hakimi's algorithm (see Sect. 3). Let us call this algorithm as FT-GRAPH-REALIZATION.

We will now show the correctness of the algorithm using the following lemmas and then analyze the time and the message complexity. Lemma 1, Lemma 2 and Lemma 3 show that the final degree sequence D' of all the non-crashed nodes are the same. Thus, the algorithm correctly solves the distributed graph realization with faults in the Congested Clique. Finally, Lemma 4 analyzes the time complexity and Lemma 5 analyzes the message complexity of the algorithm.

The *view* of a node s at u is the classification of s as a *smite-node* or *faulty-node* at u. We will now show that for any node s, the view of s is same across all the nodes at the end of the protocol.

Lemma 1. *Let s be an ID for which there are conflicting views at the beginning of second phase. Then at the end of the protocol, i.e., when all nodes have reached the exit state, all nodes are guaranteed to have the same view of s.*

Proof. We prove this in cases. Suppose s is sent by some node. We look at the possible scenarios for both the heard-twice and the heard-once.

Heard Twice: For the trivial case when a good node successfully broadcasts s twice to all nodes, the statement follows immediately. For the other case when a faulty node successfully broadcasts s in the first round, but crashes in the second round, there is a possibility that some nodes may have heard about s twice, but the others may have not. In this case, all the nodes are still guaranteed to have heard s at least once (in the first round of transmission) and thus would have the same view, as they would have all updated their views simultaneously.

Heard Once: Let us consider the two cases.

Case 1: Node crashed sending s during the second round. This scenario is equivalent to the second scenario in the heard-twice case, and thus follows the same logic.

Case 2: Node crashed sending s during the first round. In this case, let u_i and u_j be two nodes that survived until the end, then there must exist a round in which u_i (or respectively u_j) informed each other about their view of s. Then, based on the received values, they updated their views to match.   □

Lemma 2. *Let s be an ID that was successfully transmitted twice by an active node u_i during the second phase of the algorithm. Then for any pair of nodes u_j, u_k $(j, k \geq i)$, all the (non-null) entries below s are the same in their faulty-list. That is, for any non-null entry, $F_{u_j}(p) = F_{u_k}(q)$ for all $p, q < s$.*

Proof. Suppose not. Let there be a node r $(r < s)$ such that for two nodes u_j, u_k, $F_{u_j}(r)$ reads as *smite-node* while $F_{u_k}(r)$ reads as *faulty-node*. If r had crashed during the second round of phase 1, this immediately contradicts our claim as all nodes can only have r as either *null* or *faulty-node*. In case it crashed during the first round, consider the following. Since r's cell in u_i is null (otherwise $r's$ value would have been transmitted first by u_i), u_i must have heard r successfully twice at a previous round of either phase. Which implies that all other nodes would have heard about r at least once, hence would share the same view of r.   □

Lemma 3. *If a node u_i decides to exclude an entry from its faulty-list then all other nodes u_j $(j \neq i)$ will also eventually exclude that entry. Conversely, if u_i moves an entry from its fault-list to D_{u_i}, then eventually all other nodes u_j will also move that entry to their D_{u_j}.*

Proof. If a node s is excluded from u_i's *faulty-list* then u_i must have heard s as a *smite-node* twice, which indicates that all other nodes must have received s at least once (as a *smite-node*). So all the nodes exclude s from their faulty-list. The same logic applies in case of moving an entry to D_{u_i}.   □

Table 1. Terminology and their definition used throughout the algorithms in the paper. * represent the terminology's definition for Phase 1.

Terminology at a Glance for a node u	
Terminology	Definition
Smite-node*	Node $v \neq u$ is classified as *smite-node* if u did not receive v's degree in the first two rounds
Smite-node (Phase 2)	Node $v \neq u$ is classified as *smite-node* if u receives a message from any node (even once) which classifies v as a *smite-node*
Faulty-node	Node $v \neq u$ is classified as a *faulty-node* if u receives v's degree only once
Faulty-list (F_u)	List of known faulty IDs (and their corresponding degrees if present) at u
Listening State	A node is in the listening state if it is waiting for its turn (to send entries from its faulty-list) or to receive an "all-okay" message
Active State	A node is in the active state if it is transmitting the entries from its faulty-list
"all-okay"	Reception of "all-okay" at u acts as a signal for u to terminate the algorithm
Degree Sequence (D'_u)	D'_u keeps track of all the degrees heard from other nodes in the network. At termination, it contains the final degree sequence used for graph realization at u

Lemma 4. *The time complexity of the* FT-GRAPH-REALIZATION *algorithm is* $O(f)$ *rounds.*

Proof. The first phase takes exactly two rounds. For the finalization of D', any non-faulty node would require at most f messages in $O(f)$ rounds. In case of faults, there can be at most f node-crashes, which can introduce a delay of at most f rounds. During phase 2, a node may take at most $O(f)$ rounds to inform the network of the entries in its fault-list (including delay due to faults). Therefore, round complexity is $O(f)$. □

Lemma 5. *The message complexity of the* FT-GRAPH-REALIZATION *algorithm is* $O(n^2)$, *where each message is at most* $O(\log n)$ *bits in size.*

Proof. The first phase of the algorithm uses $O(n^2)$ messages, since all the nodes broadcast in two rounds. In the second phase, each faulty node's ID is broadcast only twice by a single (non-faulty) node. Since there are at most f faulty nodes, $O(nf)$ messages incur. Therefore, total message complexity is $O(n^2)$, since $f < n$. Since both the value of degree and the ID can be encapsulated using $O(\log n)$ bits, messages are at most $O(\log n)$ bits in length. □

Thus, we get the following main result of fault-tolerant graph realization.

Theorem 2. *Consider an n-node Congested Clique, where $f < n$ nodes may crash arbitrarily at any time. Given an n-length graphic sequence $D = (d_1, d_2, \ldots, d_n)$ as an* *input such that each d_i is only known to one node in the clique, there exists an algorithm* (FT-GRAPH-REALIZATION) *which solves the fault-tolerant graph realization problem in $O(f)$ rounds and using $O(n^2)$ messages.*

4.1 Lower Bound

In the graph realization with faults problem, the nodes are required to learn the degrees assigned to the other nodes in the network and recreate a degree sequence which must be the same for all the nodes. If two nodes have a different view of the final degree sequence D', then their output would be different. It essentially reduces to a *consensus* problem where all the nodes agree on the degrees in D'. In the consensus problem, all nodes start with some input value and the nodes are required to agree on a common value (among all the input values to the nodes). In the presence of faulty nodes, all non-faulty nodes must agree on a common value. Therefore, any t-round solution of the graph realization with faults problem can be used to solve the consensus problem in $O(t)$ rounds. Now, a lower bound of $f + 1$ on the number of rounds required for reaching consensus in the presence of f crash failures is a well-known result (see Chap. 5: Fault-Tolerant Consensus of Attiya-Welch's book [4]). Thus, this $f + 1$ lower bound on the round complexity also applies to the graph realization with faults problem. Hence, we get the following result.

Theorem 3. *Any algorithm that solves the distributed graph realization with faults in an n-node Congested Clique with f crash failures requires $\Omega(f)$ rounds in some admissible execution.*

We now argue that graph realization with faults, where nodes construct the entire overlay graph, requires $\Omega(n^2)$ messages in the Congest model [47]. Consider a graph realization algorithm $\mathcal{A}$ that constructs the entire overlay graph in a n-node Congested Clique. The algorithm $\mathcal{A}$ must correctly output the overlay graph for any inputs.

First consider the fault-free case, i.e., no faulty nodes in the Congested Clique. Since every node constructs the entire overlay graph, the n degree-values (for all the nodes) need to be propagated to all the nodes. The size of a degree can be $O(\log n)$ bits. In the Congest model, the size of each message is $O(\log n)$ bits. Hence, a node can send at most a constant number of degree-values in one message packet. Now, it requires $n - 1$ messages to send one degree-value from a node to all the nodes. Thus, it requires at least $n(n - 1) = O(n^2)$ messages to propagate n degree-values to all the nodes.

Consider the faulty case. The following situation may occur in some execution of $\mathcal{A}$. A faulty node may crash in a round by sending $O(n)$ messages in that round. Further, any message of a crashed node that has not reached to all the nodes may need to be rectified to make it consistent throughout the network. This requires that the message may need to be propagated to all the nodes. Hence, we require at least $O(n^2)$ messages in the worst case. Thus, we get the following result.

Theorem 4. *In the* Congest *model, any graph realization algorithm, in which nodes construct the entire overlay graph, in a n-node network (with or without faults) requires $\Omega(n^2)$ messages in some admissible execution.*

Therefore, the above two theorems prove that the FT-GRAPH-REALIZATION algorithm is tight simultaneously with respect to the time and the message complexity.

5   Fault-Tolerant Graph Realization in the NCC Model

In this section we extend the above fault-tolerant algorithm to the Node Capacitated Clique (a.k.a NCC) model. To the best of our knowledge, distributed versions of graph realization problem (without faults) were first studied by the authors in [5]. In the original work, the authors attempted to solve the distributed degree sequence problem in two versions of the NCC model introduced by the authors in [6], namely the NCC_0 and the NCC_1. In this section, we present how we may extend our ideas for solving the graph realizations with faults problem in the Congested Clique to NCC_1.

Briefly, the NCC_1 is exactly like the KT_1 version of the Congested Clique (CC) model with one clear difference, which is a constraint on the number of messages a node is allowed to send/receive in a round. In the NCC_1, a node is allowed to send or receive at most $O(\log n)$ messages in a round, unlike the CC model, in which we don't have a bound on the number of messages. When a node receives more than $O(\log n)$ messages, it chooses to drop the excess. Note that the model immediately implies a $n/\log n$ lower bound in terms of time complexity for our version of the graph realization, as each node needs to learn $n - 1$ degrees in a clique. Our solution takes $O(nf/\log n)$ rounds in the NCC_1 model, but it is optimal in the number of messages.

The key idea is to change how each node sends its degree to every other node in the network. We leverage the idea of parallelism and cyclic permutation so that each node can in one round (i) inform $O(\log n)$ other nodes and (ii) receive the degree (or faulty IDs as the case may be) from at most $O(\log n)$ other nodes. Thus, we divide the nodes into $n/\log n$ groups $g_1, g_2 \ldots, g_{\frac{n}{\log n}}$ such that each group has no more than $O(\log n)$ nodes. This allows all nodes in a group g_i to send their degree to all nodes in the group g_j while satisfying the message constraints present in NCC_1. By taking advantage of the parallelism present in the setting (and working with different permutations in each round) we can guarantee that all nodes learn the degrees in the network in $O(n/\log n)$ round. Theorem 5 presents the main result of this section.

Theorem 5. *There exists a fault-tolerant algorithm that solves graph realization in the Node Capacitated Clique model in $O(nf/\log n)$ rounds and uses $O(n^2)$ messages.*

6   Conclusion and Future Work

In this paper, we studied the graph realization problem in the Congested Clique with faults and provided efficient algorithms for realizing overlays for a given degree sequence. Our algorithm is simultaneously optimal in both the round and the message complexity. Further, we also show how the algorithm may be adapted to a setting, in which nodes are allowed to send (and receive) a limited number of messages per round. Given the relevance of graph realization techniques in overlay construction and the presence of faulty nodes in the peer-to-peer networks, we believe there can be several interesting questions to explore in the future. Such as (1) Is it possible to remove the assumption of known IDs, that is, would it be possible to achieve optimal round and message complexity if the IDs of the clique nodes are not known? (2) This paper and the previous paper on distributed graph realization [5] consider a clique network. It would be interesting to study the problem beyond clique network. (3) Finally, it would be interesting to study the graph realization problem in the presence of Byzantine faults. Since a Byzantine node is malicious and can send wrong information, the graph realization problem needs to be defined carefully.

References

1. Abraham, I., et al.: Communication complexity of byzantine agreement, revisited. In: PODC, pp. 317–326 (2019)
2. Arikati, S.R., Maheshwari, A.: Realizing degree sequences in parallel. SIAM J. Discrete Math. **9**(2), 317–338 (1996)
3. Aspnes, J., Shah, G.: Skip graphs. Trans. Algorithms **3**(4), 37-es (2007)
4. Attiya, H., Welch, J.L.: Distributed Computing - Fundamentals, Simulations, and Advanced Topics. Wiley Series on Parallel and Distributed Computing, 2nd edn. Wiley, Hoboken (2004)
5. Augustine, J., Choudhary, K., Cohen, A., Peleg, D., Sivasubramaniam, S., Sourav, S.: Distributed graph realizations. IEEE Trans. Parallel Distrib. Syst. **33**(6), 1321–1337 (2022)
6. Augustine, J., et al.: Distributed computation in node-capacitated networks. In: The 31st ACM on Symposium on Parallelism in Algorithms and Architectures, pp. 69–79. ACM (2019)
7. Augustine, J., Molla, A.R., Pandurangan, G.: Sublinear message bounds for randomized agreement. In: PODC, pp. 315–324. ACM (2018)
8. Augustine, J., Sivasubramaniam, S.: Spartan: a framework for sparse robust addressable networks. In: 2018 IEEE International Parallel and Distributed Processing Symposium (IPDPS), pp. 1060–1069. IEEE (2018)
9. Bagchi, A., Bhargava, A., Chaudhary, A., Eppstein, D., Scheideler, C.: The effect of faults on network expansion. Theory Comput. Syst. **39**(6), 903–928 (2006)
10. Barenboim, L., Khazanov, V.: Distributed symmetry-breaking algorithms for congested cliques. arXiv preprint arXiv:1802.07209 (2018)
11. Becker, F., Montealegre, P., Rapaport, I., Todinca, I.: The impact of locality on the detection of cycles in the broadcast congested clique model. In: Bender, M.A., Farach-Colton, M., Mosteiro, M.A. (eds.) LATIN 2018. LNCS, vol. 10807, pp. 134–145. Springer, Cham (2018). https://doi.org/10.1007/978-3-319-77404-6_11
12. Behzad, M., Simpson, J.E.: Eccentric sequences and eccentric sets in graphs. Discret. Math. **16**(3), 187–193 (1976)
13. Ben-Or, M., Pavlov, E., Vaikuntanathan, V.: Byzantine agreement in the full-information model in o(log n) rounds. In: Proceedings of the 38th Annual ACM Symposium on Theory of Computing, pp. 179–186. ACM (2006)
14. Censor-Hillel, K., Dory, M., Korhonen, J.H., Leitersdorf, D.: Fast approximate shortest paths in the congested clique. Distrib. Comput. **34**(6), 463–487 (2021)
15. Chlebus, B.S., Kowalski, D.R.: Robust gossiping with an application to consensus. J. Comput. Syst. Sci. **72**, 1262–1281 (2006)
16. Chlebus, B.S., Kowalski, D.R., Olkowski, J.: Brief announcement: deterministic consensus and checkpointing with crashes: time and communication efficiency. In: PODC 2022: ACM Symposium on Principles of Distributed Computing, Salerno, Italy, 25–29 July 2022, pp. 106–108. ACM (2022)
17. Chlebus, B.S., Kowalski, D.R., Strojnowski, M.: Fast scalable deterministic consensus for crash failures. In: PODC, pp. 111–120. ACM (2009)

18. Dolev, D., Lenzen, C., Peled, S.: "Tri, Tri Again": finding triangles and small subgraphs in a distributed setting. In: Aguilera, M.K. (ed.) DISC 2012. LNCS, vol. 7611, pp. 195–209. Springer, Heidelberg (2012). https://doi.org/10.1007/978-3-642-33651-5_14
19. Dolev, D., Strong, H.R.: Requirements for agreement in a distributed system. In: Proceedings of the Second International Symposium on Distributed Data Bases, pp. 115–129 (1982)
20. Drucker, A., Kuhn, F., Oshman, R.: On the power of the congested clique model. In: Proceedings of the 2014 ACM Symposium on Principles of Distributed Computing, pp. 367–376 (2014)
21. Erdös, P., Gallai, T.: Graphs with prescribed degrees of vertices [Hungarian]. Mat. Lapok (N.S.) **11**, 264–274 (1960)
22. Feldman, P., Micali, S.: An optimal probabilistic protocol for synchronous byzantine agreement. SIAM J. Comput. **26**(4), 873–933 (1997)
23. Fiat, A., Saia, J.: Censorship resistant peer-to-peer content addressable networks. In: Proceedings of the Thirteenth Annual ACM-SIAM Symposium on Discrete Algorithms, pp. 94–103 (2002)
24. Frank, A.: Augmenting graphs to meet edge-connectivity requirements. SIAM J. Discrete Math. **5**, 25–43 (1992)
25. Frank, A.: Connectivity augmentation problems in network design. In: Mathematical Programming: State of the Art, pp. 34–63. University of Michigan (1994)
26. Frank, H., Chou, W.: Connectivity considerations in the design of survivable networks. IEEE Trans. Circuit Theory **CT-17**, 486–490 (1970)
27. Galil, Z., Mayer, A.J., Yung, M.: Resolving message complexity of byzantine agreement and beyond. In: 36th Annual Symposium on Foundations of Computer Science, pp. 724–733. IEEE Computer Society (1995)
28. Ghaffari, M., Nowicki, K.: Congested clique algorithms for the minimum cut problem. In: Proceedings of the 2018 ACM Symposium on Principles of Distributed Computing (PODC), pp. 357–366 (2018)
29. Ghaffari, M., Parter, M.: MST in log-star rounds of congested clique. In: Proceedings of 35th ACM Symposium on Principles of Distributed Computing (PODC), pp. 19–28 (2016)
30. Gilbert, S., Kowalski, D.R.: Distributed agreement with optimal communication complexity. In: SODA, pp. 965–977 (2010)
31. Gomory, R., Hu, T.: Multi-terminal network flows. J. Soc. Ind. Appl. Math. **9**, 551–570 (1961)
32. Hakimi, S.L.: On realizability of a set of integers as degrees of the vertices of a linear graph - I. SIAM J. Appl. Math. **10**, 496–506 (1962)
33. Havel, V.: A remark on the existence of finite graphs. Casopis Pest. Mat. **80**, 477–480 (1955)
34. Jurdziński, T., Nowicki, K.: Connectivity and minimum cut approximation in the broadcast congested clique. In: Lotker, Z., Patt-Shamir, B. (eds.) SIROCCO 2018. LNCS, vol. 11085, pp. 331–344. Springer, Cham (2018). https://doi.org/10.1007/978-3-030-01325-7_28
35. Jurdziński, T., Nowicki, K.: MST in $o(1)$ rounds of congested clique. In: SODA, pp. 2620–2632 (2018)
36. Kapron, B.M., Kempe, D., King, V., Saia, J., Sanwalani, V.: Fast asynchronous byzantine agreement and leader election with full information. In: SODA, pp. 1038–1047. SIAM (2008)
37. King, V., Saia, J.: Byzantine agreement in expected polynomial time. J. ACM **63**(2), 13:1–13:21 (2016)
38. Konrad, C.: MIS in the congested clique model in $\log \log \Delta$ rounds. arXiv preprint arXiv:1802.07647 (2018)
39. Korhonen, J.H., Suomela, J.: Towards a complexity theory for the congested clique. In: Proceedings of the 30th on Symposium on Parallelism in Algorithms and Architectures, SPAA 2018 (2018)

40. Kowalski, D.R., Mosteiro, M.A.: Time and communication complexity of leader election in anonymous networks. In: ICDCS 2021, pp. 449–460. IEEE (2021)
41. Kumar, M., Molla, A.R.: Brief announcement: on the message complexity of fault-tolerant computation: leader election and agreement. In: PODC 2021, pp. 259–262. ACM (2021)
42. Lesniak, L.: Eccentric sequences in graphs. Period. Math. Hung. 6(4), 287–293 (1975). https://doi.org/10.1007/BF02017925
43. Lotker, Z., Patt-Shamir, B., Pavlov, E., Peleg, D.: Minimum-weight spanning tree construction in $o(\log \log n)$ communication rounds. SIAM J. Comput. 35(1), 120–131 (2005)
44. Lua, E.K., Crowcroft, J., Pias, M., Sharma, R., Lim, S.: A survey and comparison of peer-to-peer overlay network schemes. Commun. Surv. Tutor. 7(2), 72–93 (2005)
45. Malatras, A.: State-of-the-art survey on P2P overlay networks in pervasive computing environments. J. Netw. Comput. Appl. 55, 1–23 (2015)
46. Patt-Shamir, B., Teplitsky, M.: The round complexity of distributed sorting. In: Proceedings of the 30th Annual ACM SIGACT-SIGOPS Symposium on Principles of Distributed Computing, pp. 249–256 (2011)
47. Peleg, D.: Distributed Computing: A Locality-Sensitive Approach (2000)
48. Ratnasamy, S., Francis, P., Handley, M., Karp, R.M., Shenker, S.: A scalable content-addressable network. In: SIGCOMM, pp. 161–172. ACM (2001)
49. Raynal, M.: Fault-Tolerant Message-Passing Distributed Systems - An Algorithmic Approach. Springer, Heidelberg (2018). https://doi.org/10.1007/978-3-319-94141-7
50. Scheideler, C.: Models and techniques for communication in dynamic networks. In: Alt, H., Ferreira, A. (eds.) STACS 2002. LNCS, vol. 2285, pp. 27–49. Springer, Heidelberg (2002). https://doi.org/10.1007/3-540-45841-7_2
51. Stoica, I., et al.: Chord: a scalable peer-to-peer lookup protocol for internet applications. IEEE/ACM Trans. Netw. (TON) 11(1), 17–32 (2003)
52. Upfal, E.: Tolerating linear number of faults in networks of bounded degree. In: Proceedings of the Eleventh Annual ACM Symposium on Principles of Distributed Computing, pp. 83–89. PODC 1992. ACM (1992)

The Complexity of Growing a Graph

George B. Mertzios[1], Othon Michail[2], George Skretas[2,3]($\boxtimes$),
Paul G. Spirakis[2,4], and Michail Theofilatos[2]

[1] Department of Computer Science, Durham University, Durham, UK
george.mertzios@durham.ac.uk
[2] Department of Computer Science, University of Liverpool, Liverpool, UK
{othon.michail,p.spirakis}@liverpool.ac.uk, theofilatos.michail@gmail.com
[3] Hasso Plattner Institute, University of Potsdam, Potsdam, Germany
georgios.skretas@hpi.de
[4] Computer Engineering and Informatics Department, University of Patras,
Patras, Greece

Abstract. We study a new algorithmic process of graph growth. The
process starts from a single initial vertex u_0 and operates in discrete time-
steps, called *slots*. In every slot $t \geq 1$, the process updates the current
graph instance to generate the next graph instance G_t. The process first
sets $G_t = G_{t-1}$. Then, for every $u \in V(G_{t-1})$, it adds at most one
new vertex u' to $V(G_t)$ and adds the edge uu' to $E(G_t)$ alongside any
subset of the edges $\{vu' \mid v \in V(G_{t-1})$ is at distance at most $d-1$
from u in $G_{t-1}\}$, for some integer $d \geq 1$ fixed in advance. The process
completes slot t after removing any (possibly empty) subset of edges from
$E(G_t)$. Removed edges are called *excess edges*. G_t is the graph *grown* by
the process after t slots. The goal of this paper is to investigate the
algorithmic and structural properties of this process of graph growth.

Graph Growth Problem: Given a graph family F, we are asked
to design a *centralized* algorithm that on any input *target graph* $G \in F$,
will output such a process growing G, called a *growth schedule* for G.
Additionally, the algorithm should try to minimize the total number of
slots k and of excess edges ℓ used by the process.

We show that the most interesting case is when $d = 2$ and that there
is a natural trade-off between k and ℓ. We begin by investigating growth
schedules of $\ell = 0$ excess edges. On the positive side, we provide polynomial-time algorithms that decide whether a graph has growth schedules
of $k = \log n$ or $k = n - 1$ slots. Along the way, interesting connections
to cop-win graphs are being revealed. On the negative side, we establish
strong hardness results for the problem of determining the minimum
number of slots required to grow a graph with zero excess edges. In
particular, we show that the problem (i) is NP-complete and (ii) for any
$\varepsilon > 0$, cannot be approximated within $n^{\frac{1}{3}-\varepsilon}$, unless P = NP. We then
move our focus to the other extreme of the (k, ℓ)-spectrum, to investigate
growth schedules of (poly)logarithmic slots. We show that trees can be
grown in a polylogarithmic number of slots using linearly many excess

George B. Mertzios was supported by the EPSRC grant EP/P020372/1.
Paul G. Spirakis was supported by the EPSRC grant EP/P02002X/1.

© The Author(s), under exclusive license to Springer Nature Switzerland AG 2022
T. Erlebach and M. Segal (Eds.): ALGOSENSORS 2022, LNCS 13707, pp. 123–137, 2022.
https://doi.org/10.1007/978-3-031-22050-0_9

edges, while planar graphs can be grown in a logarithmic number of slots using $O(n \log n)$ excess edges. We also give lower bounds on the number of excess edges, when the number of slots is fixed to $\log n$.

Keywords: Temporal graph · Cop-win graph · Graph process · Polynomial-time algorithm · Lower bound · NP-complete · Hardness result

1   Introduction

1.1   Motivation

Growth processes are found in a variety of networked systems. In nature, crystals grow from an initial nucleation or from a "seed" crystal and a process known as embryogenesis develops sophisticated multicellular organisms, by having the genetic code control tissue growth [11,28]. In human-made systems, sensor networks are being deployed incrementally to monitor a given geographic area [12,19], social-network groups expand by connecting with new individuals [13], DNA self-assembly automatically grows molecular shapes and patterns starting from a seed assembly [14,31,34], and high churn or mobility can cause substantial changes in the size and structure of computer networks [4,6]. Graph-growth processes are central in some theories of relativistic physics. For example, in dynamical schemes of causal set theory, causets develop from an initial emptiness via a tree-like birth process, represented by dynamic Hasse diagrams [9,30].

Though diverse in nature, all these are examples of systems sharing the notion of an underlying graph-growth process. In some, like crystal formation, tissue growth, and sensor deployment, the implicit graph representation is bounded-degree and embedded in Euclidean geometry. In others, like social-networks and causal set theory, the underlying graph might be free from strong geometric constraints but still be subject to other structural properties, as is the special structure of causal relationships between events in casual set theory.

Inspired by such systems, we study a high-level, graph-theoretic abstraction of network-growth processes. We do not impose any strong *a priori* constraints, like geometry, on the graph structure and restrict our attention to *centralized* algorithmic control of the graph dynamics. We do include, however, some weak conditions on the permissible dynamics, necessary for non-triviality of the model and in order to capture realistic abstract dynamics. One such condition is "locality", according to which a newly introduced vertex u' in the neighborhood of a vertex u, can only be connected to vertices within a reasonable distance $d - 1$ from u. At the same time, we are interested in growth processes that are "efficient", under meaningful abstract measures of efficiency. We consider two such measures, to be formally defined later, the *time* to grow a given target graph and the number of auxiliary connections, called *excess edges*, employed to assist the growth process. For example, in cellular growth, a useful notion of time is the number of times all existing cells have divided and is usually polylogarithmic in the size of the target tissue or organism. In social networks, it is quite typical that new connections can only be revealed to an individual u' through its connection to another individual u who is already a member of a group. Later, u' can drop its connection to u but still maintain some of its connections to u's group. The dropped connection uu' can be viewed as an excess edge, whose creation and removal has an associated cost, but was nevertheless necessary for the formation of the eventual neighborhood of u'.

The present study is also motivated by recent work on dynamic graph and network models [1–3,7,8,10,15–18,20,21,21,23–27,32,35].

1.2 Our Approach

We study the following centralized graph-growth process. The process, starting from a single initial vertex u_0 and applying vertex-generation and edge-modification operations, grows a given target graph G. It operates in discrete time-steps, called slots. In every slot, it generates at most one new vertex u' for each existing vertex u and connects it to u. Then, for each new vertex u', it connects u' to any (possibly empty) subset of the vertices within a "local" radius around u, described by a distance parameter d, essentially representing that radius plus 1, i.e., as measured from u'. Finally, it removes any (possibly empty) subset of edges whose removal does not disconnect the graph, before moving on to the next slot. These edge-modification operations are essentially capturing, at a high level, the local dynamics present in most of the applications discussed previously. In these applications, new entities typically join a local neighborhood or a group of other entities, which then allows them to easily connect to any of the local entities. Moreover, in most of these systems, existing connections can be easily dropped by a local decision of the two endpoints of that connection. The rest of this paper exclusively focuses on $d = 2$. It is not hard to observe that, without additional considerations, any target graph can be grown by the following straightforward process. In every slot t, the process generates a new vertex u_t which it connects to u_0 and to all neighbors of u_0. The graph grown by this process by the end of slot t, is the clique K_{t+1}, thus, any K_n is grown by it within $n - 1$ slots. As a consequence, any target graph G on n vertices can be grown by extending the above process to first grow K_n and then delete all edges in $E(K_n) \setminus E(G)$, at the end of the last slot. Such a clique growth process maximizes both complexity parameters that are to be minimized by the developed processes. One is the time to grow a target graph G, to be defined as the number of slots used by the process to grow G, and the other is the total number of deleted edges during the process, called excess edges. The above process always uses $n - 1$ slots and may delete up to $\Theta(n^2)$ edges for sparse graphs, such as a path graph or a planar graph.

There is an improvement of the clique process, which connects every new vertex u_t to u_0 and to exactly those neighbors v of u_0 for which vu_t is an edge of the target graph G. At the end, the process deletes those edges incident to u_0 that do not correspond to edges in G, in order to obtain G. If u_0 is chosen to represent the maximum degree, $\Delta(G)$, vertex of G, then it is not hard to see that this process uses $n - 1 - \Delta(G)$ excess edges, while the number of slots remains $n - 1$ as in the clique process. However, we shall show that there are (poly)logarithmic-time processes using close to linear excess edges for some of those graphs. In general, processes considered *efficient* in this work will be those using (poly)logarithmic slots and linear (or close to linear) excess edges.

The goal of this paper is to investigate the algorithmic and structural properties of such processes of graph growth, with the main focus being on studying the following problem, which we call the *Graph Growth Problem*. In this problem, a centralized algorithm is provided with a target graph G, usually from a graph family F, and non-negative integers k and ℓ as its input. The goal is for the algorithm to compute, in the form of a *growth schedule* for G, such a process growing G with at most k slots and using at most ℓ excess edges, if one exists. All algorithms we consider are polynomial-time.[1]

For an illustration of the discussion so far, consider the graph family $F_{star} = \{G \mid G \text{ is a star on } n = 2^\delta \text{ vertices}\}$ and assume that edges are activated within local distance $d = 2$. We describe a simple algorithm returning a time-optimal and linear excess-edges growth process, for any target graph $G \in F_{star}$ given as input. To keep this exposition simple, we do not give k and ℓ as input-parameters to the algorithm. The process computed by the algorithm, shall always start from $G_0 = (\{u_0\}, \emptyset)$. In every slot $t = 1, 2, \ldots, \delta$ and every vertex $u \in V(G_t)$ the process generates a new vertex u', which it connects to u. If $t > 1$ and $u \neq u_0$, it then activates the edge $u_0 u'$, which is at distance 2, and removes the edge uu'. It is easy to see that by the end of slot t, the graph grown by this process is a star on 2^t vertices centered at u_0, see Fig. 1. Thus, the process grows the target star graph G within $\delta = \log n$ slots. By observing that $2^t/2 - 1$ edges are removed in every slot t, it follows that a total of $\sum_{1 \leq t \leq \log n} 2^{t-1} - 1 < \sum_{1 \leq t \leq \log n} 2^t = O(n)$ excess edges are used by the process. Note that this algorithm can be easily designed to compute and return the above growth schedule for any $G \in F_{star}$ in time polynomial in the size $|\langle G \rangle|$ of any reasonable representation of G.

Note that there is a natural trade-off between the number of slots and the number of excess edges that are required to grow a target graph. That is, if we aim to minimize the number of slots (resp. of excess edges) then the number of excess edges (resp. slots) increases. To gain some insight into this trade-off, consider the example of a path graph G on n vertices $u_0, u_1, \ldots, u_{n-1}$, where n is even for simplicity. If we are not allowed to activate any excess edges, then the only way to grow G is to always extend the current path from its endpoints, which implies that a schedule that grows G must have at least $\frac{n}{2}$ slots. Conversely, if the growth schedule has to finish after $\log n$ slots, then G can only be grown by activating $\Omega(n)$ excess edges.

---

[1] Note that this reference to *time* is about the running time of an algorithm computing a growth schedule. But the length of the growth schedule is another representation of time: the time required by the respective growth process to grow a graph. To distinguish between the two notions of time, we will almost exclusively use the term *number of slots* to refer to the length of the growth schedule and *time* to refer to the running time of an algorithm generating the schedule.

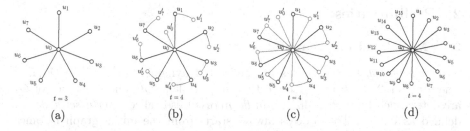

Fig. 1. The operations of the star graph process in slot $t = 4$. (a) A star of size 2^3 grown by the end of slot 3. (b) For every u_i, a vertex u'_i is generated by the process and is connected to u_i. (c) New vertices u'_i are connected to u_0. (d) Edges between peripheral-vertices are being removed to obtain the star of size 2^4 grown by the end of slot 4. Here, we also rename the vertices for clarity. Red color appears as grey in print.

In this paper, we mainly focus on this trade-off between the number of slots and the number of excess edges.

1.3 Contribution

Section 2 presents the model and problem statement and gives two basic subprocesses that are recurrent in our growth processes.

In Sect. 3, we study the *zero-excess growth schedule* problem, where the goal is to decide whether a graph G has a growth schedule of k slots and $\ell = 0$ excess edges. We define the *candidate elimination ordering* of a graph G as an ordering $v_1, v_2, \ldots, v_n$ of $V(G)$ so that for every vertex v_i, there is some v_j, where $j < i$ such that $N[v_i] \subseteq N[v_j]$ in the subgraph induced by $v_i, \ldots, v_n$, for $1 \leq i \leq n$. We show that a graph has a growth schedule of $k = n-1$ slots and $\ell = 0$ excess edges if and only if it is has a *candidate elimination ordering*. Our main positive result is a polynomial-time algorithm that computes whether a graph has a growth schedule of $k = \log n$ slots and $\ell = 0$ excess edges. If it does, the algorithm also outputs such a growth schedule. On the negative side, we give two strong hardness results. We first show that the decision version of the zero-excess growth schedule problem is NP-complete. Then, we prove that, for every $\varepsilon > 0$, there is no polynomial-time algorithm which computes a $n^{\frac{1}{3}-\varepsilon}$-approximate zero-excess growth schedule, unless P = NP.

In Sect. 4, we study growth schedules of (poly)logarithmic slots. We provide two polynomial-time algorithms. One outputs, for any tree graph, a growth schedule of $O(\log^2 n)$ slots and only $O(n)$ excess edges, and the other outputs, for any planar graph, a growth schedule of $O(\log n)$ slots and $O(n \log n)$ excess edges.

2 Preliminaries

2.1 Model and Problem Statement

A *growing graph* is modeled as an undirected dynamic graph $G_t = (V_t, E_t)$, where $t = 1, 2, \ldots, k$ is a discrete time-step, called *slot*. The dynamics of G_t are determined by a centralized *growth process* (also called *growth schedule*) σ, defined as follows. The process always starts from the initial graph instance $G_0 = (\{u_0\}, \emptyset)$, containing a single initial vertex u_0, called the *initiator*. In every slot t, the process updates the current graph instance G_{t-1} to generate the next, G_t, according to the following vertex and edge update rules. The process first sets $G_t = G_{t-1}$. Then, for every $u \in V_{t-1}$, it adds at most one new vertex u' to V_t (*vertex generation* operation) and adds to E_t the edge uu' alongside any subset of the edges $\{vu' \mid v \in V_{t-1} \text{ is at distance at most } d-1 \text{ from } u \text{ in } G_{t-1}\}$, for some integer *edge-activation distance* $d \geq 1$ fixed in advance (*edge activation* operation). Throughout the rest of the paper, $d = 2$ is always assumed. We call u' the vertex generated by the process for vertex u in slot t. We also say that u is the *parent* of u' and that u' is the *child* of u at slot t and write $u \xrightarrow{t} u'$. The process completes slot t after deleting any (possibly empty) subset of edges from E_t (*edge deletion* operation). We also denote by V_t^+, E_t^+, and E_t^- the set of vertices generated, edges activated, and edges deleted in slot t, respectively. Then, $G_t = (V_t, E_t)$ is also given by $V_t = V_{t-1} \cup V_t^+$ and $E_t = (E_{t-1} \cup E_t^+) \setminus E_t^-$. Deleted edges are called *excess edges* and we restrict attention to excess edges whose deletion does not disconnect G_t. We call G_t the graph *grown* by process σ after t slots and call the final instance, G_k, the *target graph* grown by σ. We also say that σ is a *growth schedule for* G_k that grows G_k in k slots using ℓ *excess edges*, where $\ell = \sum_{t=1}^{k} |E_t^-|$, i.e., ℓ is equal to the total number of deleted edges. This brings us to the main problem studied in this paper:

Graph Growth Problem: Given a target graph G and non-negative integers k and ℓ, compute a growth schedule for G of at most k slots and at most ℓ excess edges, if one exists.

The *target graph* G, which is part of the input, will often be drawn from a given graph family F, e.g., the family of planar graphs. Throughout, n denotes the number of vertices of the target graph G. In this paper, computation is always to be performed by a *centralized* polynomial-time algorithm.

Let w be a vertex generated in a slot t, for $1 \leq t \leq k$. The *birth path* of vertex w is the unique sequence $B_w = (u_0, u_{i_1}, \ldots, u_{i_{p-1}}, u_{i_p} = w)$ of vertices, where $i_p = t$ and $u_{i_{j-1}} \xrightarrow{i_j} u_{i_j}$, for every $j = 1, 2, \ldots, p$. That is, B_w is the sequence of vertex generations that led to the generation of vertex w. Furthermore, the *progeny* of a vertex u is the set P_u of descendants of u, i.e., P_u contains those vertices v for which $u \in B_v$ holds.

2.2   Basic Subprocesses

We start by presenting simple algorithms for two basic growth processes that are recurrent both in our positive and negative results. One is the process of growing any path graph and the other is that of growing any star graph. Both returned growth schedules use a number of slots which is logarithmic and a number of excess edges which is linear in the size of the target graph. Logarithmic being a trivial lower bound on the number of slots required to grow graphs of n vertices, both schedules are optimal w.r.t. their number of slots.

Path **Algorithm:** Let u_0 always be the "left" endpoint of the path graph being grown. For any target path graph G on n vertices, the algorithm computes a growth schedule for G as follows. For every slot $1 \leq t \leq \lceil \log n \rceil$ and every vertex $u_i \in V_{t-1}$, for $0 \leq i \leq 2^{t-1} - 1$, it generates a new vertex u_i' and connects it to u_i. Then, for all $0 \leq i \leq 2^{t-1} - 2$, it connects u_i' to u_{i+1} and deletes the edge $u_i u_{i+1}$. Finally, it renames the vertices $u_0, u_1, \ldots, u_{2^t-1}$ from left to right, before moving on to the next slot.

Lemma 1. *For any path graph G on n vertices, the* **path** *algorithm computes in polynomial time a growth schedule σ for G of $\lceil \log n \rceil$ slots and $O(n)$ excess edges.*

Star **Algorithm:** The description of the algorithm can be found in Sect. 1.2.

Lemma 2. *For any star graph G on n vertices, the* **star** *algorithm computes in polynomial time a growth schedule σ for G of $\lceil \log n \rceil$ slots and $O(n)$ excess edges.*

3   Growth Schedules of Zero Excess Edges

In this section, we study which target graphs G can be grown using $\ell = 0$ excess edges for $d = 2$. We begin by providing an algorithm that decides whether a graph G can be grown by any schedule σ. We build on to that, by providing an algorithm that computes a schedule of $k = \log n$ slots for a target graph G, if one exists. We finish with our main technical result showing that computing the smallest schedule for a graph G is NP-complete and any approximation of the shortest schedule cannot be within a factor of $n^{\frac{1}{3}-\varepsilon}$ of the optimal solution, for any $\varepsilon > 0$, unless $P = NP$. First, we check whether a graph G has a growth schedule of $\ell = 0$ excess edges. Observe that a graph G has a growth schedule if and only if it has a schedule of $k = n - 1$ slots.

Definition 1. *Let $G = (V, E)$ be any graph. A vertex $v \in V$ can be the last generated vertex in a growth schedule σ of $\ell = 0$ for G if there exists a vertex $w \in V \setminus \{v\}$ such that $N[v] \subseteq N[w]$. In this case, v is called a* candidate vertex *and w is called the* candidate parent *of v. Furthermore, the set of candidate vertices in G is denoted by $S_G = \{v \in V : N[v] \subseteq N[w] \text{ for some } w \in V \setminus \{v\}\}$.*

Definition 2. *A candidate elimination ordering of a graph G is an ordering $v_1, v_2, \ldots, v_n$ of $V(G)$ such that v_i is a candidate vertex in the subgraph induced by $v_i, \ldots, v_n$, for $1 \le i \le n$.*

Lemma 3. *A graph G has a growth schedule of $n-1$ slots and $\ell = 0$ excess edges if and only if G has a candidate elimination ordering.*

The following algorithm can decide whether a graph has a candidate elimination ordering, and therefore, whether it can be grown with a schedule of $n-1$ slots and $\ell = 0$ excess edges. The algorithm computes the slots of the schedule in reverse order.

Candidate Elimination Ordering **Algorithm:** Given the graph $G = (V, E)$, the algorithm finds all candidate vertices and deletes an arbitrary candidate vertex and its incident edges. The deleted vertex is added in the last empty slot of the schedule σ. The algorithm repeats the above process until there is only a single vertex left. If that is the case, the algorithm produces a growth schedule. If the algorithm cannot find any candidate vertex for removal, it decides that the graph cannot be grown.

Theorem 1. *The* candidate elimination ordering *algorithm is a polynomial-time algorithm that, for any graph G, decides whether G has a growth schedule of $n-1$ slots and $\ell = 0$ excess edges, and it outputs such a schedule if one exists.*

The notion of candidate elimination orderings turns out to coincide with the notion of cop-win orderings, discovered in the past in graph theory for a class of graphs, called cop-win graphs [5, 22, 29]. In particular, it is not hard to show that *a graph has a candidate elimination ordering if and only if it is a cop-win graph*. This implies that our candidate elimination ordering algorithm is probably equivalent to some folklore algorithms in the literature of cop-win graphs.

Our next goal is to decide whether a graph $G = (V, E)$ on n vertices has a growth schedule σ of $\log n$ slots and $\ell = 0$ excess edges. The *fast growth* algorithm computes the slots of the growth schedule in reverse order.

Fast Growth **Algorithm:** The algorithm finds set S_G of candidate vertices in G. It then tries to find a subset $L \subseteq S_G$ of candidates that satisfies all of the following:1. $|L| = n/2$. 2. L is an independent set. 3. There is a perfect matching between the candidate vertices in L and their candidate parents in G. Any set L that satisfies the above constraints is called *valid*. The algorithm finds such a set by creating a 2-SAT formula ϕ whose solution is a valid set L. If the algorithm finds such a set L, it adds the vertices in L to the last slot of the schedule. It then removes the vertices in L from graph G along with their incident edges. The above process is then repeated to find the next slots. If at any point, graph G has a single vertex, the algorithm terminates and outputs the schedule. If at any point, the algorithm cannot find a valid set L, it outputs "no".

Theorem 2. *For any graph G on 2^δ vertices, the* fast growth *algorithm computes in polynomial time a growth schedule σ for G of $\log n$ slots and $\ell = 0$ excess edges, if one exists.*

We will now show that the problem of computing the minimum number of slots required for a graph G to be grown is NP-complete, and that it cannot be approximated within a $n^{\frac{1}{3}-\varepsilon}$ factor for any $\varepsilon > 0$, unless P = NP.

Definition 3. *Given any graph G and a natural number κ, find a growth schedule of κ slots and $\ell = 0$ excess edges. We call this problem zero-excess growth schedule.*

Theorem 3. *The decision version of the zero-excess graph growth problem is NP-complete.*

Theorem 4. *Let $\varepsilon > 0$. If there exists a polynomial-time algorithm, which, for every graph G, computes a $n^{\frac{1}{3}-\varepsilon}$-approximate growth schedule (i.e., a growth schedule with at most $n^{\frac{1}{3}-\varepsilon}\kappa(G)$ slots), then P = NP.*

Proof. The reduction is from the minimum coloring problem. Given an arbitrary graph $G = (V, E)$ with n vertices, we construct in polynomial time a graph $G' = (V', E')$ with $N = 4n^3$ vertices, as follows: We create $2n^2$ isomorphic copies of G, which are denoted by $G_1^A, G_2^A, \ldots, G_{n^2}^A$ and $G_1^B, G_2^B, \ldots, G_{n^2}^B$, and we also add n^2 clique graphs, each of size $2n$, denoted by $C_1, C_2, \ldots, C_{n^2}$. We define $V' = V(G_1^A) \cup \ldots \cup V(G_{n^2}^A) \cup V(G_1^B) \cup \ldots \cup V(G_{n^2}^B) \cup V(C_1) \cup \ldots \cup V(C_{n^2})$. Initially we add to the set E' the edges of all graphs $G_1^A, \ldots, G_{n^2}^A, G_1^B, \ldots, G_{n^2}^B$, and $C_1, \ldots, C_{n^2}$. For every $i = 1, 2, \ldots, n^2 - 1$ we add to E' all edges between $V(G_i^A) \cup V(G_i^B)$ and $V(G_{i+1}^A) \cup V(G_{i+1}^B)$. For every $i = 1, \ldots, n^2$, we add to E' all edges between $V(C_i)$ and $V(G_i^A) \cup V(G_i^B)$. Furthermore, for every $i = 2, \ldots, n^2$, we add to E' all edges between $V(C_i)$ and $V(G_{i-1}^A) \cup V(G_{i-1}^B)$. For every $i = 1, \ldots, n^2 - 1$, we add to E' all edges between $V(C_i)$ and $V(C_{i+1})$. For every $i = 1, 2, \ldots, n^2$ and for every $u \in V(G_i^B)$, we add to E' the edge uu', where $u' \in V(G_i^A)$ is the image of u in the isomorphism mapping between G_i^A and G_i^B. To complete the construction, we pick an arbitrary vertex a_i from each C_i. We add edges among the vertices $a_1, \ldots, a_{n^2}$ such that the resulting induced graph $G'[a_1, \ldots, a_{n^2}]$ is a graph on n^2 vertices which can be grown by a **path** schedule within $\lceil \log n^2 \rceil$ slots and with zero excess edges (see Lemma 1[2]). This completes the construction of G'. Clearly, G' can be constructed in time polynomial in n.

Now we will prove that there exists a growth schedule σ' of G' of length at most $n^2\chi(G) + 4n - 2 + \lceil 2\log n \rceil$. The schedule will be described inversely, that is, we will describe the vertices generated in each slot starting from the last slot of σ' and finishing with the first slot. First note that every $u \in V(G_{n^2}^A) \cup V(G_{n^2}^B)$ is a candidate vertex in G'. Indeed, for every $w \in V(C_{n^2})$, we have that $N[u] \subseteq V(G_{n^2}^A) \cup V(G_{n^2}^B) \cup V(G_{n^2-1}^A) \cup V(G_{n^2-1}^A) \cup V(C_{n^2}) \subseteq N[w]$. To provide the desired growth schedule σ', we assume that a minimum coloring of the input graph G (with $\chi(G)$ colors) is known. In the last $\chi(G)$ slots, σ' generates all vertices in

---

[2] From Lemma 1 it follows that the path on n^2 vertices can be constructed in $\lceil \log n^2 \rceil$ slots using $O(n^2)$ excess edges. If we put all these $O(n^2)$ excess edges back to the path of n^2 vertices, we obtain a new graph on n^2 vertices with $O(n^2)$ edges. This graph is the induced subgraph $G'[a_1, \ldots, a_{n^2}]$ of G' on the vertices $a_1, \ldots, a_{n^2}$.

$V(G_{n^2}^A) \cup V(G_{n^2}^B)$, as follows. At each of these slots, one of the $\chi(G)$ color classes of the minimum coloring c_{OPT} of $G_{n^2}^A$ is generated on sufficiently many vertices among the first n vertices of the clique C_{n^2}. Simultaneously, a different color class of the minimum coloring c_{OPT} of $G_{n^2}^B$ is generated on sufficiently many vertices among the last n vertices of the clique C_{n^2}.

Similarly, for every $i = 1, \ldots, n^2 - 1$, once the vertices of $V(G_{i+1}^A) \cup \ldots \cup V(G_{n^2}^A) \cup V(G_{i+1}^B) \cup \ldots \cup V(G_{n^2}^B)$ have been added to the last $(n^2 - i)\chi(G)$ slots of σ', the vertices of $V(G_i^A) \cup V(G_i^B)$ are generated in σ' in $\chi(G)$ more slots. This is possible because every vertex $u \in V(G_i^A) \cup V(G_i^B)$ is a candidate vertex after the vertices of $V(G_{i+1}^A) \cup \ldots \cup V(G_{n^2}^A) \cup V(G_{i+1}^B) \cup \ldots \cup V(G_{n^2}^B)$ have been added to slots. Indeed, for every $w \in V(C_i)$, we have that $N[u] \subseteq V(G_i^A) \cup V(G_i^B) \cup V(G_{i-1}^A) \cup V(G_{i-1}^A) \cup V(C_i) \subseteq N[w]$. That is, in total, all vertices of $V(G_1^A) \cup \ldots \cup V(G_{n^2}^A) \cup V(G_1^B) \cup \ldots \cup V(G_{n^2}^B)$ are generated in the last $n^2 \chi(G)$ slots.

The remaining vertices of $V(C_1) \cup \ldots \cup V(C_{n^2})$ are generated in σ' in $4n - 2 + \lceil \log n^2 \rceil$ additional slots. First, for every odd index i and for $2n - 1$ consecutive slots, for vertex a_i of $V(C_i)$ exactly one other vertex of $V(C_i)$ is generated. This is possible because for every vertex $u \in V(C_i) \setminus a_i$, $N[u] \subseteq V(C_i) \cup V(C_{i-1}) \cup V(C_{i+1}) \subseteq N[a_i]$. Then, for every even index i and for $2n - 1$ further consecutive slots, for vertex a_i of $V(C_i)$ exactly one other vertex of $V(C_i)$ is generated. That is, after $4n - 2$ slots only the induced subgraph of G' on the vertices $a_1, \ldots, a_{n^2}$ remains. The final $\lceil \log n^2 \rceil$ slots of σ' are the ones obtained by Lemma 1. To sum up, G' is grown by the growth schedule σ' in $k = n^2 \chi(G) + 4n - 2 + \lceil \log n^2 \rceil$ slots, and thus $\kappa(G') \leq n^2 \chi(G) + 4n - 2 + \lceil 2 \log n \rceil$ (1).

Suppose that there exists a polynomial-time algorithm A which computes an $N^{\frac{1}{3} - \varepsilon}$-approximate growth schedule σ'' for graph G' (which has N vertices), i.e., a growth schedule of $k \leq N^{\frac{1}{3} - \varepsilon} \kappa(G')$ slots. Note that, for every slot of σ'', all different vertices of $V(G_i^A)$ (resp. $V(G_i^B)$) which are generated in this slot are independent. For every $i = 1, \ldots, n^2$, denote by χ_i^A (resp. χ_i^B) the number of different slots of σ'' in which at least one vertex of $V(G_i^A)$ (resp. $V(G_i^B)$) appears. Let $\chi^* = \min\{\chi_i^A, \chi_i^B : 1 \leq i \leq n^2\}$. Then, there exists a coloring of G with at most χ^* colors (i.e., a partition of G into at most χ^* independent sets).

Now we show that $k \geq \frac{1}{2} n^2 \chi^*$. Let $i \in \{2, \ldots, n^2 - 1\}$ and let $u \in V(G_i^A) \cup V(G_i^B)$. Assume that u is generated at slot t in σ''. Then, either all vertices of $V(G_{i-1}^A) \cup V(G_{i-1}^B)$ or all vertices of $V(G_{i+1}^A) \cup V(G_{i+1}^B)$ are generated at a later slot $t' \geq t + 1$ in σ''. Indeed, it can be easily checked that, if otherwise both a vertex $x \in V(G_{i-1}^A) \cup V(G_{i-1}^B)$ and a vertex $y \in V(G_{i+1}^A) \cup V(G_{i+1}^B)$ are generated at a slot $t'' \leq t$ in σ'', then u cannot be a candidate vertex at slot t, which is a contradiction to our assumption. That is, in order for a vertex $u \in V(G_i^A) \cup V(G_i^B)$ to be generated at some slot t of σ'', we must have that i is either the currently smallest or largest index for which some vertices of $V(G_i^A) \cup V(G_i^B)$ have been generated until slot t. On the other hand, by definition of χ^*, the growth schedule σ'' needs at least χ^* different slots to generate all vertices of the set $V(G_i^A) \cup V(G_i^B)$, for $1 \leq i \leq n^2$. Therefore, since at every slot, σ'' can potentially generate vertices of at most two indices i (the smallest and the largest respectively), it needs to use at least $\frac{1}{2}n^2\chi^*$ slots to grow the whole graph G'. Therefore $k \geq \frac{1}{2}n^2\chi^*$ (2).

Recall that $N = 4n^3$. It follows that

$$\frac{1}{2}n^2\chi^* \leq k \leq N^{\frac{1}{3}-\varepsilon}\kappa(G')$$
$$\leq N^{\frac{1}{3}-\varepsilon}(n^2\chi(G) + 4n - 2 + \lceil 2\log n \rceil)$$
$$\leq 4n^{1-3\varepsilon}(n^2\chi(G) + 6n)$$

and thus $\chi^* \leq 8n^{1-3\varepsilon}\chi(G) + 48n^{-3\varepsilon}$. Note that, for sufficiently large n, we have that $8n^{1-3\varepsilon}\chi(G) + 48n^{-3\varepsilon} \leq n^{1-\varepsilon}\chi(G)$. That is, given the $N^{\frac{1}{3}-\varepsilon}$-approximate growth schedule produced by the polynomial-time algorithm A, we can compute in polynomial time a coloring of G with χ^* colors such that $\chi^* \leq n^{1-\varepsilon}\chi(G)$. This is a contradiction since for every $\varepsilon > 0$, there is no polynomial-time $n^{1-\varepsilon}$-approximation for minimum coloring, unless P = NP [36]. $\qquad\square$

4   Growth Schedules of (Poly)logarithmic Slots

In this section, we study graphs that have growth schedules of (poly)logarithmic slots, for $d = 2$. As we have proven in the previous section, an integral factor in computing a growth schedule for any graph G, is computing a k-coloring for G. Since we consider polynomial-time algorithms, we have to restrict ourselves to graphs where the k-coloring problem can be solved in polynomial time and, additionally, we want small values of k since we want to produce fast growth schedules. Therefore, we investigate tree, planar and k-degenerate graph families since there are polynomial-time algorithms that solve the k-coloring problem for graphs drawn from these families.

4.1   Trees

We now provide an algorithm that computes growth schedules for tree graphs. Let G be the target tree graph. The algorithm applies a decomposition strategy on G, where vertices and edges are removed in phases, until a single vertex is left. We can then grow the target graph G by reversing its decomposition phases, using the **path** and **star** schedules as subroutines.

Tree Algorithm: Starting from a tree graph G, the algorithm keeps alternating between two phases, a *path-cut* and a *leaf-cut* phase. Let G_{2i}, G_{2i+1}, for $i \geq 0$, be the graphs obtained after the execution of the first i pairs of phases and an additional path-cut phase, respectively.

Path-cut Phase: For each path subgraph $P = (u_1, u_2, \ldots, u_\nu)$, for $2 < \nu \leq n$, of the current graph G_{2i}, where $u_2, u_3, ..., u_{\nu-1}$ have degree 2 and u_1, u_ν have degree $\neq 2$ in G_{2i}, edge $u_1 u_\nu$ between the endpoints of P is activated and vertices $u_2, u_3, ...u_{\nu-1}$ are removed along with their incident edges. If a single vertex is left, the algorithm terminates; otherwise, it proceeds to the leaf-cut phase.

Leaf-cut Phase: Every leaf vertex of the current graph G_{2i+1} is removed along with its incident edge. If a single vertex is left, the algorithm terminates; otherwise, it proceeds to the path-cut phase.

Finally, the algorithm reverses the phases (by decreasing i) to output a growth schedule for the tree G as follows. For each path-cut phase $2i$, all path subgraphs that were decomposed in phase i are regrown by using the *path* schedule as a subprocess. These can be executed in parallel in $O(\log n)$ slots. The same holds true for leaf-cut phases $2i + 1$, where each can be reversed to regrow the removed leaves by using *star* schedules in parallel in $O(\log n)$ slots. In the last slot, the schedule deletes every excess edge. By proving that a total of $O(\log n)$ phases are sufficient to decompose any tree G and that at most one excess edge per vertex of G is activated, the next theorem follows.

Theorem 5. *For any tree graph G on n vertices, the* **tree** *algorithm computes in polynomial time a growth schedule σ for G of $O(\log^2 n)$ slots and $O(n)$ excess edges.*

4.2   Planar Graphs

In this section, we provide an algorithm that computes a growth schedule for any target planar graph $G = (V, E)$. The algorithm first computes a 5-coloring of G and partitions the vertices into color-sets V_i, $1 \le i \le 5$. The color-sets are used to compute the growth schedule for G. The schedule contains five sub-schedules, each sub-schedule i generating all vertices in color-set V_i. In every sub-schedule i, we use a modified version of the *star* schedule to generate set V_i.

Pre-processing: By using the algorithm of [33], the pre-processing step computes a 5-coloring of the target planar graph G. This creates color-sets $V_i \subseteq V$, where $1 \le i \le 5$, every color-set V_i containing all vertices of color i. W.l.o.g., we can assume that $|V_1| \ge |V_2| \ge |V_3| \ge |V_4| \ge |V_5|$. Note that every color-set V_i is an independent set of G.

Planar **Algorithm:** The algorithm picks an arbitrary vertex from V_1 and makes it the initiator u_0 of all sub-schedules. Let $V_i = \{u_1, u_2, \ldots, u_{|V_i|}\}$. For every sub-schedule i, $1 \le i \le 5$, it uses the *star* schedule with u_0 as the initiator, to grow the vertices in V_i in an arbitrary sequence, with some additional edge activations. In particular, upon generating vertex $u_x \in V_i$, for all $1 \le x \le |V_i|$:

1. Edge vu_x is activated if $v \in \bigcup_{j<i} V_j$ and $u_y v \in E$, for some $u_y \in V_i \cap P_{u_x}$, both hold (recall that P_{u_x} contains the descendants of u_x).
2. Edge wu_x is activated if $w \in \bigcup_{j<i} V_j$ and $wu_x \in E$ both hold.

Once all vertices of V_i have been generated, the schedule moves on to generate V_{i+1}. Once all vertices have been generated, the schedule deletes every edge $uv \notin E$. Note that every edge activated in the growth schedule is an excess edge with the exception of edges satisfying (2). For an edge wu_x from (2) to satisfy the edge-activation distance constraint it must hold that every vertex in the birth path of u_x has an edge with w. This holds true for the edges added in (2), due to the edges added in (1).

The edges of the *star* schedule are used to quickly generate the vertices, while the edges of (1) are used to enable the activation of the edges of (2). By proving that the *star* schedule activate $O(n)$ edges, (1) activates $O(n \log n)$ edges, and by observing that the schedule contains *star* sub-schedules that have $5 \times O(\log n)$ slots in total, the next theorem follows.

Theorem 6. *For any planar graph G on n vertices, the* planar *algorithm computes in polynomial time a growth schedule for G of $O(\log n)$ slots and $O(n \log n)$ excess edges.*

Definition 4. *A k-degenerate graph G is an undirected graph in which every subgraph has a vertex of degree at most k.*

Corollary 1. *The* planar *algorithm can be extended to compute, for any graph G on n vertices and in polynomial time, a growth schedule of $O((k_1 + 1) \log n)$ slots, $O(k_2 n \log n)$ and excess edges, where (i) $k_1 = k_2$ is the degeneracy of graph G, or (ii) $k_1 = \Delta$ is the maximum degree of graph G and $k_2 = |E|/n$.*

References

1. Akrida, E.C., Mertzios, G.B., Spirakis, P.G., Zamaraev, V.: Temporal vertex cover with a sliding time window. J. Comput. Syst. Sci. **107**, 108–123 (2020)
2. Angluin, D., Aspnes, J., Chen, J., Wu, Y., Yin, Y.: Fast construction of overlay networks. In: Proceedings of the 17th ACM Symposium on Parallelism in Algorithms and Architectures (SPAA), pp. 145–154 (2005)
3. Aspnes, J., Shah, G.: Skip graphs. ACM Transactions on Algorithms **3**(4), 37:1-37:25 (2007)
4. Augustine, J., Pandurangan, G., Robinson, P., Upfal, E.: Towards robust and efficient computation in dynamic peer-to-peer networks. In: Proceedings of the 23rd Annual ACM-SIAM Symposium on Discrete Algorithms (SODA), pp. 551–569 (2012)
5. Bandelt, H.-J., Prisner, E.: Clique graphs and helly graphs. J. Comb. Theory Series B **51**(1), 34–45 (1991)
6. Becchetti, L., Clementi, A., Pasquale, F., Trevisan, L., Ziccardi, I.: Expansion and flooding in dynamic random networks with node churn. In: Proceedings of the 41st IEEE International Conference on Distributed Computing Systems (ICDCS), pp. 976–986 (2021)
7. Berman, K.A.: Vulnerability of scheduled networks and a generalization of Menger's theorem. Netw.: Int. J. **28**(3), 125–134 (1996)
8. Bollobás, B.: Random Graphs. Number 73 in Cambridge Studies in Advanced Mathematics, 2nd edn. Cambridge University Press, Cambridge (2001)
9. Bombelli, L., Lee, J., Meyer, D., Sorkin, R.D.: Space-time as a causal set. Phys. Rev. Lett. **59**(5), 521 (1987)
10. Casteigts, A., Flocchini, P., Quattrociocchi, W., Santoro, N.: Time-varying graphs and dynamic networks. Int. J. Parallel Emergent Distrib. Syst. **27**(5), 387–408 (2012)

11. Chan, M.M., et al.: Molecular recording of mammalian embryogenesis. Nature **570**(7759), 77–82 (2019)
12. Chatzigiannakis, I., Kinalis, A., Nikoletseas, S.: Adaptive energy management for incremental deployment of heterogeneous wireless sensors. Theory Comput. Syst. **42**, 42–72 (2008). https://doi.org/10.1007/s00224-007-9011-z
13. Cordeiro, M., Sarmento, R.P., Brazdil, P., Gama, J.: Evolving networks and social network analysis methods and techniques, Chapter 7. In: Social Media and Journalism (2018)
14. Doty, D.: Theory of algorithmic self-assembly. Commun. ACM **55**(12), 78–88 (2012)
15. Enright, J., Meeks, K., Mertzios, G.B., Zamaraev, V.: Deleting edges to restrict the size of an epidemic in temporal networks. J. Comput. Syst. Sci. **119**, 60–77 (2021)
16. Gilbert, S., Pandurangan, G., Robinson, P., Trehan, A.: Dconstructor: efficient and robust network construction with polylogarithmic overhead. In: Proceedings of the 39th ACM Symposium on Principles of Distributed Computing (PODC) (2020)
17. Götte, T., Hinnenthal, K., Scheideler, C.: Faster construction of overlay networks. In: Censor-Hillel, K., Flammini, M. (eds.) SIROCCO 2019. LNCS, vol. 11639, pp. 262–276. Springer, Cham (2019). https://doi.org/10.1007/978-3-030-24922-9_18
18. Götte, T., Hinnenthal, K., Scheideler, C., Werthmann, J.: Time-optimal construction of overlay networks. In: Proceedings of the 40th ACM Symposium on Principles of Distributed Computing (PODC), pp. 457–468 (2021)
19. Howard, A., Matarić, M.J., Sukhatme, G.S.: An incremental self-deployment algorithm for mobile sensor networks. Auton. Robots **13**, 113–126 (2002). https://doi.org/10.1023/A:1019625207705
20. Kempe, D., Kleinberg, J., Kumar, A.: Connectivity and inference problems for temporal networks. J. Comput. Syst. Sci. **64**(4), 820–842 (2002)
21. Kleinberg, J.M., Kumar, R., Raghavan, P., Rajagopalan, S., Tomkins, A.S.: The web as a graph: measurements, models, and methods. In: Asano, T., Imai, H., Lee, D.T., Nakano, S., Tokuyama, T. (eds.) COCOON 1999. LNCS, vol. 1627, pp. 1–17. Springer, Heidelberg (1999). https://doi.org/10.1007/3-540-48686-0_1
22. Lin, M.C., Soulignac, F.J., Szwarcfiter, J.L.: Arboricity, h-index, and dynamic algorithms. Theoret. Comput. Sci. **426**, 75–90 (2012)
23. Mertzios, G.B., Michail, O., Spirakis, P.G.: Temporal network optimization subject to connectivity constraints. Algorithmica **81**(4), 1416–1449 (2019)
24. Michail, O.: An introduction to temporal graphs: an algorithmic perspective. Internet Math. **12**(4), 239–280 (2016)
25. Michail, O., Skretas, G., Spirakis, P.G.: On the transformation capability of feasible mechanisms for programmable matter. J. Comput. Syst. Sci. **102**, 18–39 (2019)
26. Michail, O., Skretas, G., Spirakis, P.G.: Distributed computation and reconfiguration in actively dynamic networks. In: Proceedings of the 39th ACM Symposium on Principles of Distributed Computing (PODC), pp. 448–457 (2020)
27. Michail, O., Spirakis, P.G.: Elements of the theory of dynamic networks. Commun. ACM **61**(2), 72 (2018)
28. Méndez-Hernández, H.A., et al.: Signaling overview of plant somatic embryogenesis. Front. Plant Sci. **10**, 77 (2019)
29. Poston, T.: Fuzzy geometry. Ph.D. thesis, University of Warwick (1971)
30. Rideout, D.P., Sorkin, R.D.: Classical sequential growth dynamics for causal sets. Phys. Rev. D **61**(2), 024002 (1999)
31. Rothemund, P.W.K.: Folding DNA to create nanoscale shapes and patterns. Nature **440**(7082), 297–302 (2006)

32. Scheideler, C., Setzer, A.: On the complexity of local graph transformations. In: Proceedings of the 46th International Colloquium on Automata, Languages, and Programming (ICALP). Schloss Dagstuhl-Leibniz-Zentrum fuer Informatik (2019)
33. Williams, H.: A linear algorithm for colouring planar graphs with five colours. Comput. J. **28**, 78–81 (1985)
34. Woods, D., Chen, H.L., Goodfriend, S., Dabby, N., Winfree, E., Yin, P.: Active self-assembly of algorithmic shapes and patterns in polylogarithmic time. In: Proceedings of the 4th Conference on Innovations in Theoretical Computer Science (ITCS), pp. 353–354 (2013)
35. Zschoche, P., Fluschnik, T., Molter, H., Niedermeier, R.: The complexity of finding small separators in temporal graphs. J. Comput. Syst. Sci. **107**, 72–92 (2020)
36. Zuckerman, D.: Linear degree extractors and the inapproximability of max clique and chromatic number. Theory Comput. **3**, 103–128 (2007)

Dispersing Facilities on Planar Segment and Circle Amidst Repulsion

Vishwanath R. Singireddy[ID] and Manjanna Basappa[✉][ID]

CSIS Department, BITS Pilani, Hyderabad Campus, Hyderabad, India
{p20190420,manjanna}@hyderabad.bits-pilani.ac.in

Abstract. In this paper we consider the problem of locating k obnoxious facilities (congruent disks of maximum radius) amidst n demand points (existing repulsive facility sites) ordered from left to right in the plane so that none of the existing facility sites are affected (no demand point falls in the interior of the disks). We study this problem in two restricted settings: (i) the obnoxious facilities are constrained to be centered on a predetermined horizontal line segment $\overline{pq}$, and (ii) the obnoxious facilities are constrained to lie on the boundary arc of a predetermined disk $\mathcal{C}$. An $(1 - \epsilon)$-approximation algorithm was given recently to solve the constrained problem in (i) in time $O((n + k) \log \frac{||pq||}{2(k-1)\epsilon})$, where $\epsilon > 0$ [14]. Here, for the problem in (i), we first propose an exact algorithm based on an exhaustive search where all candidate radii will be computed explicitly. This algorithm runs in $O((nk)^2)$ time. We then show that using the parametric search technique of Megiddo [11]; we can solve the problem exactly in $O((n + k)^2)$ time, which is faster than the former. Continuing further, using the improved parametric technique we give an $O(n \log n)$-time algorithm for $k = 2$. We finally show that the above $(1 - \epsilon)$-approximation algorithm of [14] can be easily adapted to solve the circular constrained problem of (ii) with an extra multiplicative factor of n in the running time.

Keywords: Obnoxious facility location · Parametric search · Continuous location

1 Introduction

The obnoxious facility location is a well-known topic in the operations research community. This paper addresses a variant of the problem, namely, the continuous obnoxious facility location on a line segment (COFL) problem, motivated by the following application. We wish to find locations for establishing k obnoxious or undesirable facilities (such as garbage dump yards, industries generating pollution, etc.) along a straight highway road such that the pairwise distance between these new facilities and the distance between each of the new facilities and other existing non-obnoxious facilities (such as hospitals, schools, etc.) are maximized. The following scenario in establishing sensor network used for security purpose can also be modeled as a COFL problem. Suppose we are given a

© The Author(s), under exclusive license to Springer Nature Switzerland AG 2022
T. Erlebach and M. Segal (Eds.): ALGOSENSORS 2022, LNCS 13707, pp. 138–151, 2022.
https://doi.org/10.1007/978-3-031-22050-0_10

line segment $\overline{pq}$ representing a continuous set of potential locations to place a fixed number of sensors. These sensors have to monitor suspicious users originating from the continuous region around $\overline{pq}$. However, there are also fair users (point set P) around $\overline{pq}$. Now we need to place these sensors on $\overline{pq}$ with their range maximized and no interference, but none of the fair users falling within the range. The formal definition of the problem is below:

The COFL problem: Given a horizontal line segment $\overline{pq}$ and an ordered set P of n points lying above a line through $\overline{pq}$ in the Euclidean plane, we aim to locate points on $\overline{pq}$ for centering k non-overlapping congruent disks of maximum radius r_{max} such that none of the points in P lie interior to any of these disks.

Recently, it has been shown in [14] that we can solve the decision version of this problem (in which we are also given a radius L as input along with $\overline{pq}$ and the set P of n points) in time $O(n+k)$ if the points in P are given in order. Then, using this decision algorithm as a subroutine, an $(1-\epsilon)$-approximation algorithm (FPTAS) has been given to solve the COFL problem in time $O((n+k)\log\frac{\|pq\|}{2(k-1)\epsilon})$, where $\epsilon > 0$ and $\|pq\|$ is the length of the segment $\overline{pq}$ [14].

In this work, we show that it is, in fact, possible to solve the COFL problem exactly in polynomial time for a fixed k. Using the linear-time decision algorithm of [14] again as a subroutine, we present two polynomial-time exact algorithms based on two different approaches: (i) the algorithm is based on doing an exhaustive search by computing all candidate radii L explicitly and runs in $O((nk)^2)$ time, and (ii) the algorithm is based on Megiddo's parametric search [11], and runs in $O((n+k)^2)$ time. We then discuss an $O(n\log n)$-time algorithm to solve the COFL problem for $k = 2$, which is faster than the previous two algorithms. Finally, we show how to solve the circular COFL problem using the algorithm of [14].

2   Related Work

Several variants of obnoxious facility location problems have been investigated by the operations research and computational geometry communities. A recent review of many variants of obnoxious facility location problems and specialized heuristics to solve them may be found in [4]. Katz et al. [10] studied two variants of k-obnoxious facility location problems (i) max-min k-facility location, in which the distance between any two facilities is at least some fixed value and the minimum distance between a facility and a demand point is to be maximized, and (ii) min-sum one-facility location problem in which the sum of weights of demand points lying within a given distance to the facility is to be minimized. In the rectilinear metric, they solved the first problem in $O(n\log^2 n)$ time for $k = 2$ or 3, and for any $k \geq 4$ they gave an algorithm in $O(n^{(k-2)}\log^2 n)$ time. In the same paper, Katz et al. [10] solved (i) in Euclidean metric for $k = 2$ in $O(n\log n)$ time. For the second problem, their algorithm runs in $O(n\log n)$ time (rectilinear case) and $O(n^2)$ time (Euclidean case). Qin et al. [12] studied a variant of k-obnoxious facility location problem in which the facilities are restricted to lie within a given convex polygonal domain. They proposed a 2-factor approximation algorithm based on a Voronoi diagram for this problem, and its running time is $O(kN \log N)$, where $N = n + m + k$, n denotes the number of demand points, m denotes the number of vertices of the polygonal domain and k is the number of obnoxious facilities to be placed. Díaz-Báñez et al. [7] modelled obnoxious facility as empty circular annulus whose width is maximum. This refers to a max-min facility location problem such that the facility is a circular ring of maximum width, where the width is the absolute difference between the radii of the two concentric circles. They solved the problem in $O(n^3 \log n)$ time, and if the inner circle contains a fixed number of points then the problem can be solved in $O(n \log n)$ time. Maximum width empty annulus problems for axis parallel square and rectangles can be solved in $O(n^3)$ and $O(n^2 \log n)$ time respectively [3]. Abravaya and Segal [1] studied the problem of locating maximum cardinality set of obnoxious facilities within a bounded rectangle in the plane such that their pairwise rectilinear distance and rectilinear distance to a set of demand points is at least a given threshold. They proposed a 2-approximation algorithm and also a PTAS based on shifting strategy [9]. Agarwal et al. [2] showed the application of Megiddo's parametric search [11] method to solve several geometric optimization problems in the Euclidean plane such as the big stick problem, the minimum width annulus problem, and the problem of finding largest mutual visible spheres.

3   Polynomial Time Exact Algorithms

Given a horizontal segment $\overline{pq}$, without loss of generality, we can assume that all the points in P lie in the upper half-plane defined by a line through $\overline{pq}$. After fixing the segment $\overline{pq}$, we define the following decision version of the COFL problem as follows:

DCOFL(P, k, L): Given an ordered set P of n points lying above a line through $\overline{pq}$, a real number L and an integer k, can we pack k non-overlapping disks of radius L centered on $\overline{pq}$ such that none of these disks contains a point of P in their interior?

Let $I = \{[x_{i,1}, x_{i,2}] | p_i \in P\}$ be the set of maximal intervals on $\overline{pq}$ ordered from p to q (ordered by the x-coordinates $x(p_i)$ of $p_i \in P$), where every point in each interval $[x_{i,1}, x_{i,2}]$ is at distance at most L from $p_i \in P$ (see Fig. 1). The decision algorithm returns YES if we can place k pairwise interior-disjoint disks of radius L, centered on $\overline{pq}$ such that none of the disk centers lie in the interior of the intervals in I. Otherwise the algorithm returns NO. Let $I^c = \{[x_{i,2}, x_{j,1}] | p_i, p_j \in P, i < j\} \cup \{[x_{0,2}, x_{1,1}], [x_{n,2}, x_{n+1,1}]\}$ be the set of complemented intervals of I, where every point in each interval $[x_{i,2}, x_{j,1}] \in I^c$ is at distance at least L from every point in P and $x_{0,2} = x(p)$, $x_{n+1,1} = x(q)$. Note that for every interval $[x_{i,2}, x_{j,1}] \in I^c$, no other interval of I lie entirely or partially between $x_{i,2}$ and $x_{j,1}$. We use the algorithm of [14] for solving the decision version of the problem. For completeness and for the purpose of describing exact algorithms here, we have reproduced that decision algorithm again here. Note that there is a minor bug in (line 9) the decision algorithm of [14]. We have now fixed it and presented the correct algorithm here (see Algorithm 1 in Appendix A). Let $\mathcal{R}$ be the Minkowski sum of $\overline{pq}$ and a disk of radius L, i.e., the union of $\overline{pq}$ and the region swept by a disk of radius L when its center moves along $\overline{pq}$.

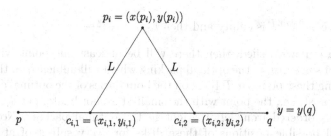

Fig. 1. A point p_i is having two center points of $\overline{pq}$ which are at unknown distance L

3.1 Algorithm Based on Exhaustive Search

The approach here is that we first compute the set $\mathcal{L}$ of all candidate radii L, based on some observations of possible positions of all k disks in an optimal packing. We then repeatedly call the selection algorithm (e.g., see [6]) for finding the median of $\mathcal{L}$. Then, we invoke the decision algorithm (Algorithm 1) each time we peek the median element by setting L to this element as the candidate radius. We continue this search until we find the radius L^* (maximum radius) by removing half of the elements of $\mathcal{L}$ until there is only one element, based on the result returned by the decision algorithm. Hence, $L^* = r_{max}$.

Consider an instance of the COFL problem, i.e., a line segment $\overline{pq}$, an ordered set P of n points, and an integer k. As already assumed, without loss of generality, let all the points of P be lying above the line through the segment $\overline{pq}$. Now, we need to place k non-overlapping congruent disks of maximum radius with centers lying on $\overline{pq}$ without violating the constraint that no point of P lies inside any of these disks. The maximum radius of the disks depends on some "*influencing points*" in P for the given position of the fixed horizontal line segment $\overline{pq}$.

Definition 1. *The influencing points $P^{inf} \subseteq P$ are those points which satisfy the following criteria: given a point $p_i \in P^{inf}$ (or a pair of points $p_i, p_{i'} \in P^{inf}$), we can place k pairwise disjoint congruent disks centered on $\overline{pq}$ such that (i) p_i lies on the boundary of one of these disks (or p_i and $p_{i'}$ lie on the boundary of the same disk or on the boundaries of two different disks), and (ii) if p_i (or $p_{i'}$ or both) is removed from P, then the radius of these disks may be increased while their centers are perturbed on $\overline{pq}$ to keep their pairwise disjointness intact, and (iii) none of the other points of P lie in the interior of any of these disks before and after the radius increases.*

Lemma 1. *Given that the position of $\overline{pq}$ is fixed, for any optimal solution to the COFL problem in ℓ_2 metric, there are at most two points in $P^{inf} \subseteq P$ that will determine the optimal radius r_{max} of the disks in the corresponding packing, and also $|\mathcal{L}| = O(n^2 k^2)$.*

Proof. The proof is based on case analysis. First, let $r_{\text{CAN}} \in \mathcal{L}$ be a candidate radius.

Case 1. The set P^{inf} is empty and then $r_{\text{CAN}} = \frac{\|pq\|}{2(k-1)}$.

If this case is not satisfied, then there will be at least one point lying on the boundary of some disk in the optimal packing which will influence on the value of r_{max}. Among these points in P lying on the boundaries of the optimal disks, let p_i be the left most, i.e., the point with the smallest x-coordinate. Let $d_1, d_2, \ldots, d_k$ be the disks ordered from left to right in the optimal packing. Now we will examine all possible positions of these disks for every subset of at most two influencing points in P^{inf}. We will also show how to compute the corresponding candidate radii $r_{\text{CAN}} \in \mathcal{L}$. To this end, consider a disk d centered on $\overline{pq}$. Divide the part of the boundary arc ∂d of d lying above $\overline{pq}$ into left and right arc segments by a vertical line through the center of d (see Fig. 2). We then show that at most two points $p_i, p_{i'} \in P^{inf} \subseteq P$ determine the radius r_{max} of the disks in an optimal packing. Let d_j and $d_{j'}$ (possibly $j = j'$) be the two disks, on whose boundary arc segments L_{arc}^j or R_{arc}^j, and $L_{arc}^{j'}$ or $R_{arc}^{j'}$ the two points p_i and $p_{i'}$ lie. Based on all possible positions of d_j and $d_{j'}$ for any pair p_i and $p_{i'}$, we have the following cases.

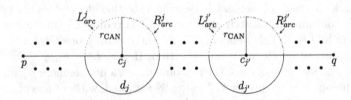

Fig. 2. Left arc segment and right arc segment of disks d_j and $d_{j'}$

Case 2. Assume that p_i lies on R_{arc}^j of d_j such that its position determines the radius of the disk (there is no point $p_{i'}$ that influences the radius) (see Fig. 3). For any $j = 1, 2, \ldots, k$ in the optimal packing, p_i can lie on R_{arc}^j of d_j. For each such point $p_i \in P^{inf}$ the candidate radius r_{CAN} can be calculated and stored in $\mathcal{L}$. Hence the number of candidate radii in this case is $O(nk)$. The candidate radius r_{CAN} with respect to every point can be calculated using the below equation:

$$2(j-1)r_{\text{CAN}} = x(p_i) - \sqrt{r_{\text{CAN}}^2 - (y(p_i) - y(q))^2} - x(p)$$

The candidate radius $r_{\text{CAN}} \in \mathcal{L}_{\ell_2}$ is calculated from the above equation as we know the value of every term of the equation except r_{CAN}. The mirror case of this where the point $p_{i'}$ is the right most point and lies on $L_{arc}^{j'}$ of $d_{j'}$ can be handled similarly. In this case, r_{CAN} can be calculated using the below equation.

$$(2(k-j')+1)r_{\mathrm{CAN}} = ||pq|| - x(p_{i'}) + x(p) + r_{\mathrm{CAN}} - \sqrt{r_{\mathrm{CAN}}^2 - (y(p_{i'}) - y(q))^2}$$

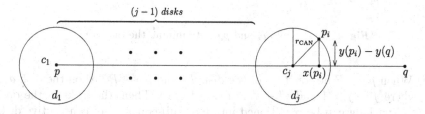

Fig. 3. Illustration of case 2

Case 3. Let both the points $p_i, p_{i'} \in P$ be determining the radius of the disks in the optimal packing. Then the point p_i can lie on L_{arc}^j or R_{arc}^j of d_j, where $j = 1, 2, \ldots, k$ (see Fig. 4). Similarly, the point $p_{i'}$ can also lie on $L_{arc}^{j'}$ or $R_{arc}^{j'}$ of $d_{j'}$, where $j' = j, j+1, j+2, \ldots, k$. Here, the disks centered between p_i and $p_{i'}$ are compactly packed and determining the optimal radius along with the positions of p_i and $p_{i'}$. It is easy to observe that there are a constant number c of possible positions for the two disks d_j and $d_{j'}$ in an optimal solution such that the two points $p_i, p_{i'}$ lie on their boundaries and does not let their radius r_{CAN} to increase by repositioning all the k disks. Therefore, the number of all candidate radii r_{CAN} is $\binom{n}{2} \sum_{j=1}^{k} \sum_{j'=j}^{k} c = k^2 c \binom{n}{2} = O(cn^2 k^2)$. The candidate radii values $r_{\mathrm{CAN}} \in \mathcal{L}$ can be computed from the following equation:

$$x(p_{i'}) - x(p_i) = 2(j'-j)r_{\mathrm{CAN}} \pm_{(1)} \sqrt{r_{\mathrm{CAN}}^2 - (y(p_i) - y(q))^2}$$
$$\pm_{(2)} \sqrt{r_{\mathrm{CAN}}^2 - (y(p_{i'}) - y(q))^2}$$

where in $\pm_{(1)}$, $+$ indicate p_i lies on L_{arc}^j of d_j and $-$ indicate p_i lies on R_{arc}^j of d_j, similarly, in $\pm_{(2)}$, $+$ indicate $p_{i'}$ lies on $R_{arc}^{j'}$ of $d_{j'}$ and $-$ indicate $p_{i'}$ lies on $L_{arc}^{j'}$ of $d_{j'}$.

Case 4. Assume the point $p_i \in P$ lies on R_{arc}^j of some disk d_j and there are also other (optional) points $p_{i'}, p_{i''} \in P$ lying on boundary arcs of the disks on the right of d_j. Based on all possible positions of p_i, $p_{i'}$ and $p_{i''}$ we can observe that at most two of these points will determine r_{CAN} and each of these cases corresponds to one of the above cases.

(i) When $p_{i'} \in P$ lies on L_{arc}^{j+1} of the disk d_{j+1} and there is empty space between d_j and d_{j+1} (see Fig. 5). This corresponds to *Case 2* above as either $j - 1$ disks on the left of p_i or $k - j - 1$ disks on the right of $p_{i'}$ are compactly packed with their radius increased to the maximum possible value.

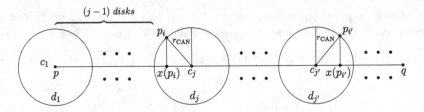

Fig. 4. Two points p_i and $p_{i'}$ determining the radius r_{CAN}

(ii) When $p_{i'} \in P$ lies on $L_{arc}^{j'}$ of the disk $d_{j'}$ and $p_{i''} \in P$ lies on the disk $d_{j''}$, where $j' - j > 1$ and $j'' - j' > 1$ (see Fig. 6). Then, the disks in the optimal packing can be partitioned into four subsequences of consecutive disks $d_1, d_2, \ldots, d_j, d_j, d_{j+1}, \ldots, d_{j'}, d_{j'}, d_{j'+1}, \ldots, d_{j''}$, and $d_{j''}, d_{j''+1}, \ldots, d_k$. In at least one of these, the disks must be compactly packed with their radius increased to the maximum possible value, otherwise it would contradict that we have the optimal packing. Hence, one of the above cases applies and at most two points among $p_i, p_{i'}, p_{i''}$ determine the value of r_{CAN}.

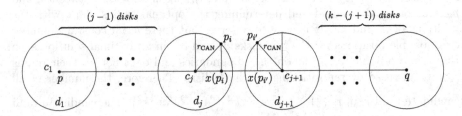

Fig. 5. Illustration of case 4(i)

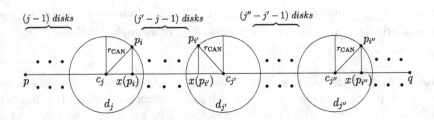

Fig. 6. Illustration of case 4(ii)

The constant $c = 10$ because of the following: (i) no point lies on the boundary of any disk in optimal packing, (ii) p_i lies on L_{arc}^j or R_{arc}^j, (iii) both $p_i, p_{i'}$ lie on L_{arc}^j or R_{arc}^j, (iv) p_i lies on L_{arc}^j and $p_{i'}$ lies on R_{arc}^j, (v) p_i lies on R_{arc}^j and

$p_{i'}$ lies on $R^{j'}_{arc}$ or p_i lies on R^j_{arc} and $p_{i'}$ lies on $L^{j'}_{arc}$ or p_i lies on L^j_{arc} and $p_{i'}$ lies on $R^{j'}_{arc}$ or p_i lies on L^j_{arc} and $p_{i'}$ lies on $L^{j'}_{arc}$. Observe that (i) corresponds to *Case 1* and contributes 1, (ii) corresponds to *Case 2* and contributes 2, (iii) contributes 2, (iv) contributes 1, (v) contributes 4, hence $c = 1+2+2+1+4 = 10$. Therefore, $|\mathcal{L}| = O((nk)^2)$. Thus the lemma follows. $\square$

Theorem 1. *For a given line segment $\overline{pq}$ and an ordered set P of n points in the Euclidean plane, we can solve the COFL problem optimally in $O((nk)^2)$ time.*

Proof. From Lemma 1 we know that the cardinality of the set $\mathcal{L}$ of all candidate radii is finite and is $O((nk)^2)$. Hence, we find $r_{max} \in \mathcal{L}$ by repeatedly applying the selection algorithm for finding the median of $\mathcal{L}$ and removing half of the elements in $\mathcal{L}$ based on the output of the decision algorithm each time. This will take $O((nk)^2)$ time and then invoking the decision algorithm $O(\log(nk))$ times results in overall time of $O((nk)^2 + (n + k) \log (nk)) = O((nk)^2)$. $\square$

3.2 Algorithm Based on Parametric Search

The FPTAS given in [14] for the COFL problem is weakly polynomial because the number of calls to the decision algorithm is proportional to the number of bits of precision of accuracy for the desired approximation. Here, we discuss an algorithm based on (slower version of) Megiddo's parametric search [11] so that its running time is independent of any numerical precision parameter ($\frac{1}{\epsilon}$). As we know, in a solution based on parametric search, there is a test algorithm, and a decision algorithm wherein the test algorithm is typically a step-by-step simulation of the decision algorithm. We now will describe how to simulate the steps of Algorithm 1 at the unknown maximum $L^*(= r_{max})$.

Consider a point $p_i \in P$ which is having two center points $c_{i,1}$ and $c_{i,2}$ on the segment $\overline{pq}$ (see Fig. 1). Let the coordinates of these points be $p_i = (x(p_i), y(p_i))$, $c_{i,1} = (x_{i,1}, y_{i,1})$ and $c_{i,2} = (x_{i,2}, y_{i,2})$. Clearly, these points and L satisfy the equations:

$$L^2 = (x(p_i) - x_{i,1})^2 + (y(p_i) - y(q))^2 \tag{1}$$

$$L^2 = (x(p_i) - x_{i,2})^2 + (y(p_i) - y(q))^2 \tag{2}$$

where $y_{i,1} = y_{i,2} = y(p) = y(q)$ as both the points $c_{i,1}$ and $c_{i,2}$ are located on $\overline{pq}$. Since we know the coordinate values $y(q)$, $x(p_i)$ and $y(p_i)$, the values of $x_{i,1}$, $x_{i,2}$ are given as follows:

$$x_{i,1} = x(p_i) - (L^2 - (y(p_i) - y(q))^2)^{\frac{1}{2}} \text{ and}$$
$$x_{i,2} = x(p_i) - (L^2 - (y(p_i) - y(q))^2)^{\frac{1}{2}}$$

respectively, if

$$y(p_i) \leq y(q) + L \tag{3}$$

Now, consider the end points of the ith complemented interval as $[r_{i-1}l_i]$ (at line 5 of Algorithm 1). Let the coordinates $r_{i-1} = (x_{i-1,2}, y_{i-1,2})$, and $l_i = (x_{i,1}, y_{i,1})$, then

$$\gamma = (\|r_{i-1}l_i\|)/2L = ((x_{i,1} - x_{i-1,2}))/2L,$$
$$\gamma = (x(p_i) - (L^2 - (y(p_i) - y(q))^2)^{\frac{1}{2}} -$$
$$(x(p_{i-1}) - (L^2 - (y(p_{i-1}) - y(q))^2)^{\frac{1}{2}}))/2L.$$

In the *for*-loop, at line 4 of Algorithm 1, we know the values of j and k. With these values known we need to perform the comparison $j + \gamma + 1 - k \leq 0$. Note that this is a branching point depending on a comparison which involves a polynomial in L, $poly(L)$.

$$j + (x(p_i) - (L^2 - (y(p_i) - y(q))^2)^{\frac{1}{2}} - (x(p_{i-1}) -$$
$$(L^2 - (y(p_{i-1}) - y(q))^2)^{\frac{1}{2}}))/2L + 1 - k \leq 0,$$

$$2(j + 1 - k)L + (x(p_i) - x(p_{i-1})) \leq$$
$$(L^2 - (y(p_i) - y(q))^2)^{\frac{1}{2}} - (L^2 - (y(p_{i-1}) - y(q))^2)^{\frac{1}{2}}.$$

On simplification the above inequality becomes

$$2((j + 1 - k)^2 - 1)L^2 + 4(j + 1 - k)(x(p_i) - x(p_{i-1}))L + (x(p_i) - x(p_{i-1}))^2$$
$$+ 2\{(L^2 - (y(p_i) - y(q))^2)(L^2 - (y(p_{i-1}) - y(q))^2)\}^{\frac{1}{2}} \leq 0.$$

that involves a degree-two polynomial, $poly(L)$: $AL^2 + BL + C + 2((L^2 - D)(L^2 - E))^{\frac{1}{2}} = 0$, where the coefficients A, B, C, D and E depend on the values known at the point of execution of the corresponding comparison step. To simulate comparison steps in the *for* loop at line 6, we compute all the roots of the associated polynomial $poly(L)$ and invoke Algorithm 1 with the value of L equal to each of these roots. This yields an interval between two roots or a root and 0 or $\|pq\|/(2(k-1))$ that contains L^*. This enables us to determine the sign of $poly(L^*)$ and proceed with the generic execution of the next step of the algorithm. Essentially, each time Algorithm 1 returns YES for the guessed value of L, the region $\mathcal{R}$ (which depends on the right end of interval containing L^*) is shrinking, and hence the number of complemented intervals in I^c on which we have to run Algorithm 1 is reducing, until the shrunken $\mathcal{R}$ corresponds to L^*. Finally, after completing the simulation of the *for* loop, if $j = k$, then we return L^*. To construct the set $D = \{d_1, d_2, \ldots, d_k\}$, we run Algorithm 1 with the computed L^* one more time. Therefore, we have the following theorem.

Theorem 2. *We have an algorithm to solve the* COFL *problem in* $O((n + k)^2)$ *using parametric search technique.*

Proof. From [14] we know that Algorithm 1 runs in $O(n + k)$ time. In the worst case, for each step of Algorithm 1 we obtain two different values of L and invoke Algorithm 1 on each of them as the candidate radius. Let $L_1, L_2, \ldots, L_t$ be those different values of L across the entire simulation, where $t = O(n + k)$. Then, initially $r_{max} \in [0, \frac{\|pq\|}{2(k-1)}]$. After the entire simulation is completed, clearly

$r_{max} = L^* = \max\{L_u \mid \text{DCOFL}(P, k, L_u) = \text{YES}, \ u = 1, 2, \ldots, t\}$. Since degree of the polynomial $poly(L)$ is at most 2 and the decision algorithm $\text{DCOFL}(P, k, L_u)$ is monotone for any $L_u \in \mathbb{R}^+ \cup \{0\}$, the entire setup fits in the framework of parametric search. Hence, the correctness of the algorithm follows and the overall time for the simulation is $O((n + k)^2)$. □

Improved Algorithm for $k = 2$. Here, we show that the decision problem $\text{DCOFL}(P, 2, L)$ can be solved in $O(\log n)$ parallel time using n processors. Let $Q(L, P)$ be the complement of the union of n open disk of radius L centered at the demand points in P. Let $S(\overline{pq}, L)$ be the intersection of $Q(L, P)$ and $\overline{pq}$, which is the collection I^c of $O(n)$ disjoint feasible intervals $[r_{i-1} l_i] \subset \overline{pq}$, $i = 1, 2, \ldots, m$, where the coordinates $r_{i-1} = (x_{i-1,2}, y_{i-1,2})$, and $l_i = (x_{i,1}, y_{i,1})$ and $m = O(n)$. Let an infeasible interval $[x_{i,1}, x_{i,2}]$ be an interval on $\overline{pq}$, which is not feasible for centering a facility in that (excluding its endpoints). When we have the infeasible intervals computed, implicitly we also have computed the feasible intervals in I^c. A parallel algorithm for computing these intervals and to order them left to right is as follows: (1) We assign one demand point from P to each of the n processors. (2) Let each processor compute the corresponding infeasible interval $[x_{i,1}, x_{i,2}] = d_i \cap \overline{pq}$, where d_i is the open disk of radius L centered at $p_i \in P$ for $i = 1, 2, \ldots, n$. (3) Then, the merging of consecutive overlapping infeasible intervals into one bigger infeasible interval is performed by processors as follows: If an interval is not overlapping with its adjacent intervals then this interval is maintained on the same processor and for each pair of consecutive overlapping intervals, the processor of the first interval merges them into one and the second processor sits idle. In this way, for a sequence of consecutive overlapping intervals, alternating processors will perform the merging. This process will be repeated until there are only isolated intervals. Since in every step we merge a pair of consecutive overlapping intervals there will be at most $\log n + 1$ steps in total and each step will take $O(1)$ parallel time. Also, the serial time to construct $S(\overline{pq}, L)$ is only $O(n)$.

Now choosing two farthest points on the intervals in $S(\overline{pq}, L)$ is easy, just pick the left end point of the left most interval and right end point of the right most interval in I^c, in $O(1)$ parallel time, and place the two facilities centered at these points.

Therefore, overall time of the parametric algorithm to solve COFL for $k = 2$ is $O(n \cdot T_p + T_p \cdot T_s \cdot \log n) = O(n \cdot \log n + \log n \cdot n \cdot \log n) = O(n \log^2 n)$ time, where T_p denotes a parallel time and T_s denotes a serial time for solving $\text{DCOFL}(P, 2, L)$ with n processors. In essence, the problem solved by the parallel algorithm is the ordering of the end points of the intervals of $S(\overline{pq}, L)$ from left to right so that a pair of endpoints apart by at least $2L$ distance, if existing, can be found in $O(1)$ parallel time. Since the problem essentially involves sorting without knowing the optimal radius, using Cole's parametric search technique [5] (which trims a factor of $O(\log n)$) results in improvement in the running time for $k = 2$, that is $O(n \cdot T_p + T_s(T_p + \log n)) = O(n \cdot \log n + n(\log n + \log n)) = O(n \log n)$.

Remark 1. The COFL under the Euclidean norm for $k = 2$ can be solved in $O(n \log n)$ time using the Cole's parametric search [5].

This is an improvement over the earlier FPTAS [14] as well as the two proposed exact algorithms here for $k = 2$.

4   Circular COFL Problem

In this section, we define a variant of the COFL problem in which the centers of the disks are restricted to lie on the boundary arc of a predetermined circle.

The *circular constrained obnoxious facility location problem* (CCOFL) problem is defined as follows: Given a set $P = \{p_1, p_2, p_3, \ldots, p_n\}$ of n demand points and a predetermined circle C with radius r_c in the plane and a positive integer k, the problem is to locate k facility sites centered on the boundary of C such that each demand point in P is farthest from its closest facility site (i.e., in terms of their Euclidean distance), and the facility sites are placed farthest from each other along the boundary of C (i.e., in terms of arc length). Observe here that two disks representing two consecutive facility sites centered on the boundary of C may overlap strictly inside C.

The decision version of this problem $\mathrm{DCCOFL}(P, k, L)$ can be solved by using a similar method that was used to solve the $\mathrm{DCOFL}(P, k, L)$ problem under the assumption that $r_c \gg L$. When $r_c < L$, it is trivial that only one disk with radius L will be packed on ∂C as the center of C will lie inside that packed disk. Now, to solve the decision version of CCOFL problem, we consider two circles C_1 and C_2 which are concentric with C and whose radii are $r_c - L$ and $r_c + L$, where L is a real number (see Fig. 7). We can observe that the points lying inside C_1 and outside of C_2 will not influence the packing of the disks. Similar to that of $\mathrm{DCOFL}(P, k, L)$ problem here, we can obtain at least one center point and at most two center points on the boundary of C which are at a distance of L from each point lying outside of C_1 and inside of C_2 (see p_i, p_j and p_k in Fig. 7).

Let $c_{i,1}$ and $c_{i,2}$ be the center-points corresponding to p_i, then none of the k disks in an optimal solution to $\mathrm{DCOFL}(P, k, L)$ will have their center points lying on the open arc interval $(c_{i,1}, c_{i,2})$ of the boundary of C.

Now, let $(c_{j,1}, c_{j,2})$ and $(c_{k,1}, c_{k,2})$ be the center points corresponding to p_j and p_k respectively. In Fig. 7, we can observe that the intervals $[c_{i,1}, c_{i,2}]$, $[c_{j,1}, c_{j,2}]$ and $[c_{k,1}, c_{k,2}]$ formed by $\overwidehat{c_{i,1}c_{i,2}}$, $\overwidehat{c_{j,1}c_{j,2}}$ and $\overwidehat{c_{k,1}c_{k,2}}$ are overlapping. Hence, none of the k disks in the optimal solution will have their centers lying on the interval $([c_{i,1}, c_{i,2}] \cup [c_{j,1}, c_{j,2}] \cup [c_{k,1}, c_{k,2}]) \setminus \{c_{i,1}, c_{k,2}\}$, excluding the end-points of the union of the two intervals.

Without loss of generality, let $\{p_1, p_2, \ldots, p_m\}$ be the points of P lying strictly outside of C_1 and inside of C_2, ordered along the boundary of C in clockwise angular fashion, where $m \leq n$. We know that for every point p_i lying strictly outside of C_1 and inside of C_2 there will be two center-points on the boundary of C which are at distance L, i.e., there is an interval $[l_i, r_i]$ for every point p_i, where $l_i = c_{i,1}$ and $r_i = c_{i,2}$. Merge all the overlapping intervals and then update the end-points

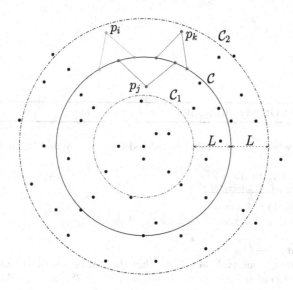

Fig. 7. C_1 and C_2 which are at distance L from C

of the new intervals on boundary of C. Let $I = \{[l_1, r_1], [l_2, r_2], \ldots, [l_{m'}, r_{m'}]\}$ be the set of resulting pairwise disjoint intervals ordered clockwise, where $m' \leq m$. Consider the complement of I with respect to the boundary of C, denoted as $I^c = \{[r_1, l_2], \ldots, [r_{m'}, l_1]\}$.

The arc length of the complemented intervals in I^c can be calculated using the law of cosines formula as follows: The angle (θ) subtended by arc at the center of C is $\theta = \arccos\left(1 - \frac{d^2}{2r_c^2}\right)$ where d is the Euclidean distance between the end-points of the arc segment. Then, the length of the arc interval $[r_i l_{i+1}]$ is $\|\widehat{r_i l_{i+1}}\| = r_c \theta$, where $\theta = \arccos\left(1 - \frac{d^2}{2r_c^2}\right)$ for $i = 1, 2, \ldots, m'$.

Observation 1. *Without loss of generality, we can assume that the first disk d_1 is centered at one of the end-points of arc segment in I^c.*

Since we don't know, the position of the disks for given L in the optimal packing, we greedily pack disks by placing centers on ∂C with the first disk d_1 at every endpoint of the arc segments in I^c. As there are $O(n)$ end-points in I^c, we have the following theorem.

Lemma 2. *Given the set I^c of complemented intervals and an integer $k > 0$, Algorithm 1 solves the DCCOFL(P, k, L) problem in $O(n(n + k))$ time.*

Proof. Follows from Observation 1.   □

Theorem 3. *We can get an $(1 - \epsilon)$-factor approximation algorithm with $\epsilon > 0$ (FPTAS) for the CCOFL problem, that runs in $O(n(n + k) \log(\frac{\|pq\|}{2(k-1)\epsilon}))$ time, by employing doubling search and bisection methods.*

Appendix

A.

Algorithm 1: Greedy_LPacking(P, k, L)

---

1 Compute I
2 Compute I^c where the intervals are ordered from p to q, and let $m = |I^c|$
3 $j \leftarrow 0$
4 **for** *each* $i \leftarrow 1$ *to* m **do**
5 $\quad \gamma \leftarrow \left\lfloor \frac{\text{length of } i\text{th interval of } I^c}{2L} \right\rfloor$
6 $\quad$ **if** $(j + \gamma + 1) \le k$ **then**
7 $\quad\quad$ On the ith interval of I^c, pack the disks $d_{j+1}, d_{j+2}, \ldots, d_{j+\gamma+1}$ of radius L.
8 $\quad\quad$ update $j \leftarrow (j + \gamma + 1)$
9 $\quad\quad$ update the intervals in I^c such that the distance between the left end point r_i of the left most interval $[r_i, l_{i+1}]$ in I^c and the right most point of ∂d_j on $\overline{pq}$ is at least L.
10 $\quad\quad$ **if** $j = k$ **then**
11 $\quad\quad\quad$ **break**
12 $\quad\quad$ **end**
13 $\quad$ **end**
14 $\quad$ **else**
15 $\quad\quad$ On the ith interval of I^c, pack the disks $d_{j+1}, d_{j+2}, \ldots, d_k$ of radius L.
16 $\quad\quad$ update $j \leftarrow k$
17 $\quad\quad$ **break**
18 $\quad$ **end**
19 **end**
20 **if** $j = k$ **then**
21 $\quad$ **return** *(*YES, $\{d_1, d_2, \ldots, d_k\}$*)*
22 **end**
23 **else**
24 $\quad$ **return** *(*NO, $\emptyset$*)*
25 **end**

References

1. Abravaya, S., Segal, M.: Maximizing the number of obnoxious facilities to locate within a bounded region. Comput. Oper. Res. **37**(1), 163–171 (2010)
2. Agarwal, P.K., Sharir, M., Toledo, S.: Applications of parametric searching in geometric optimization. J. Algorithms **17**(3), 292–318 (1994)
3. Bae, S.W., Baral, A., Mahapatra, P.R.S.: Maximum-width empty square and rectangular annulus. Comput. Geom. **96**, 101747 (2021)
4. Church, R.L., Drezner, Z.: Review of obnoxious facilities location problems. Comput. Oper. Res. **138**, 105468 (2022)

5. Cole, R.: Slowing down sorting networks to obtain faster sorting algorithms. J. ACM (JACM) **34**(1), 200–208 (1987)
6. Cormen, T.H., Leiserson, C.E., Rivest, R.L., Stein, C.: Introduction to Algorithms, 3rd edn. MIT Press, Cambridge (2009)
7. Díaz-Báñez, J.M., Hurtado, F., Meijer, H., Rappaport, D., Sellarès, J.A.: The largest empty annulus problem. Int. J. Comput. Geom. Appl. **13**(04), 317–325 (2003)
8. Frederickson, G., Johnson, D.: Generalized selection and ranking: sorted matrices. SIAM J. Comput. **13**, 14–30 (1984)
9. Hochbaum, D.S., Maass, W.: Approximation schemes for covering and packing problems in image processing and VLSI. J. ACM (JACM) **32**(1), 130–136 (1985)
10. Katz, M.J., Kedem, K., Segal, M.: Improved algorithms for placing undesirable facilities. Comput. Oper. Res. **29**(13), 1859–1872 (2002)
11. Megiddo, N.: Applying parallel computation algorithms in the design of serial algorithms. J. ACM (JACM) **30**(4), 852–865 (1983)
12. Qin, Z., Xu, Y., Zhu, B.: On some optimization problems in obnoxious facility location. In: Du, D.-Z.-Z., Eades, P., Estivill-Castro, V., Lin, X., Sharma, A. (eds.) COCOON 2000. LNCS, vol. 1858, pp. 320–329. Springer, Heidelberg (2000). https://doi.org/10.1007/3-540-44968-X_32
13. Shamos, M.I., Hoey, D.: Closest-point problems. In: 16th Annual Symposium on Foundations of Computer Science (SFCS 1975), pp. 151–162 (1975)
14. Singireddy, V.R., Basappa, M.: Constrained obnoxious facility location on a line segment. In: Proceedings of the 33rd Canadian Conference on Computational Geometry, Halifax, pp. 362–367 (2021)

Author Index

Almalki, Nada   1

Basappa, Manjanna   138
Betti Sorbelli, Francesco   18
Bilò, Davide   31

Cicerone, Serafino   45
Connor, Matthew   60

D'Angelo, Gianlorenzo   31
Di Fonso, Alessia   45
Di Stefano, Gabriele   45

Georgiou, Konstantinos   77
Gualà, Luciano   31

Jang, Woojin   77

Karakostas, George   91
Kolliopoulos, Stavros G.   91
Kumar, Manish   108

Leucci, Stefano   31

Mertzios, George B.   123
Michail, Othon   1, 60, 123
Molla, Anisur Rahaman   108

Navarra, Alfredo   18, 45

Palazzetti, Lorenzo   18
Pinotti, Cristina M.   18
Prencipe, Giuseppe   18

Rossi, Mirko   31

Singireddy, Vishwanath R.   138
Sivasubramaniam, Sumathi   108
Skretas, George   123
Spirakis, Paul G.   123

Theofilatos, Michail   123

Printed in the United States
by Baker & Taylor Publisher Services

Printed in the United States
by Baker & Taylor Publisher Services